Chronicle of a Downfall

Leopold Schwarzschild (1891–1950) was a German Jewish journalist and co-editor of the influential liberal political magazine *Das Tage-Buch*, published in Berlin from 1920 to 1933. Following Hitler's ascent to power, Schwarzschild fled to Paris in 1933, where, with the help of the Dutch lawyer Johan C.S. Warendorf, he resumed publication of *Das Neue Tage-Buch*. The NTB became one of the most influential and most widely-read émigré weeklies during the 1930s. Schwarzschild emigrated to the USA in 1940. His books include *World in Trance: From Versailles to Pearl Harbour*; *Primer of the Coming World* and *The Red Prussian: The Life and Legend of Karl Marx*. This volume collects some of his most important articles in the *Tage-Buch* and the *Neue Tage-Buch*.

Andreas Wesemann was educated at Cambridge University and the London School of Economics and now works as a merchant banker in London. He was born in Vienna and is the great-grandson of Stefan Grossmann, the founder of *Das Tage-Buch*.

Michael Mitchell is an award-winning translator whose translations include works by Goethe, Meyrink, Adolf Loos, and Oskar Kokoschka. He was short-listed for the 2008 Oxford-Weidenfeld Prize for his translation of Georges Rodenbach's *The Bells of Bruges* and, in 1998 won the Schlegel-Tieck Prize for his translation of Herbert Rosendorfer's *Letters Back to Ancient China*.

'A recovery of an important voice ... a poignant source.' – *Fritz Stern, University Professor Emeritus, Columbia University*

'I highly recommend this edition of selected articles by Leopold Schwarzschild, one of the strongest democratic voices against Hitler's rise to power in Germany, who continued his anti-Nazi publications in exile both in France and later in the US.' – *Oliver Rathkolb, Professor of Contemporary History, University of Vienna*

'Leopold Schwarzschild's clear vision of Adolf Hitler's criminal ambition to achieve unlimited power and to destroy freedom all over Europe was outstanding and remains impressive even in hindsight.' – *Hans Mommsen, Emeritus Professor of Modern History, The Ruhr University, Bochum*

CHRONICLE

— OF A —

DOWNFALL

Germany 1929-1939

Leopold Schwarzschild

Edited by
Andreas Wesemann

Translated by
Michael Mitchell

BLOOMSBURY ACADEMIC
LONDON · NEW YORK · OXFORD · NEW DELHI · SYDNEY

BLOOMSBURY ACADEMIC
Bloomsbury Publishing Plc
50 Bedford Square, London, WC1B 3DP, UK
1385 Broadway, New York, NY 10018, USA

BLOOMSBURY, BLOOMSBURY ACADEMIC and the Diana
logo are trademarks of Bloomsbury Publishing Plc

First published in Great Britain by I.B. Tauris 2010
Paperback edition first published by Bloomsbury Academic 2020

A catalogue record for this book is available from the British Library.

A catalog record for this book is available from the Library of Congress.

ISBN: HB: 978-1-8488-5289-1
PB: 978-1-3501-6941-8
ePDF: 978-0-8577-1822-8
ePub: 978-0-8577-3085-5

Designed and Typeset by 4word Ltd, Bristol

To find out more about our authors and books visit
www.bloomsbury.com and sign up for our newsletters.

Contents

v

Publisher's Note

Historical context provided by the editor, Andreas Wesemann, appears as italicized text. The translations of Leopold Schwarzschild's articles are non-italicized.

Introduction

In January 1920 the Viennese journalist Stefan Grossmann founded a liberal weekly magazine in Berlin called *Das Tage-Buch* (*The Diary*). Alongside the more left-leaning *Die Weltbühne*, published initially by Siegfried Jacobsohn, the *Tage-Buch* was to become one of most influential voices in support of the Weimar Republic. Within a year of the first issue, the then 30-year old Leopold Schwarzschild joined Grossmann at the *Tage-Buch* to take over responsibility for the economic and financial sections of the magazine. In January 1922 he formally became co-editor. Schwarzschild came from an orthodox Jewish family in Frankfurt which had been established there since the sixteenth century. While studying politics, history and economics at a university in Frankfurt, he started writing occasional theatre and film reviews for the *Frankfurter Zeitung*, but as he was called up following the outbreak of the First World War in August 1914, Schwarzschild did not return there until October 1918. After short stints at the Ministry of Finance and the *General-Anzeiger der Stadt Frankfurt*, a small local newspaper, Schwarzschild joined forces with Grossmann. They also established in 1923 the weekly *Montag Morgen* (Monday Morning) and the *Tage-Buch* publishing house, replacing Ernst Rowohlt as the publisher of the magazine. For a time Schwarzschild remained involved with other publishing enterprises, but it was the *Tage-Buch* that became the cornerstone of his activities and the foundation for his rising reputation as one of the most brilliant observers of the Weimar Republic's struggle for survival, more so when he became sole proprietor and editor in 1928, following Grossmann's retirement due to illness.

By the time he took over as managing editor, the *Tage-Buch* had acquired a stellar reputation. Published every Thursday in distinctive light green quarto format (in contrast to the *Weltbühne*'s red), with a circulation of about 16,000, it featured most of the leading German writers of the time, covering a very eclectic range of subjects – among them Walter Benjamin, Bertolt Brecht, Egon Friedell, Hugo von Hofmannsthal, Thomas Mann, Walter Mehring, Walter Rathenau, Joseph Roth, Hans Sahl and Ernst Polgar. They were free to represent very different points of view, as long as they were consistent with the basic republican position of the *Tage-Buch*. Schwarzschild ruled with an iron hand – his staff were at liberty to deal with the 'daily chores' (*Tageskram*), but the big opinion pieces and analyses were very much his own affair. He worked tirelessly, writing one or two articles every week in addition to the many editorials in which he set out his views on the key issues of the day. While he initially focused primarily on financial and economic affairs, after about 1927 he spent more and more time on the increasingly fraught political developments in Germany and Europe. 'Politics is fate' is how he entitled one of his articles in the middle of the financial crisis of 1932, in recognition of the primacy of politics over economics, choosing to side with Napoleon (who had coined the phrase originally) over Keynes whose view, expressed in *The Economic Consequences of the Peace*, that the most serious problems 'were not political or territorial but financial and economic, and that the perils of the future lay not in frontiers and sovereignties, but in food, coal and transport' was to prove so tragically influential and so terribly wrong. There can be no doubt that Schwarzschild was one of the most significant German journalists between the wars. Carl von Ossietzky, who worked for the *Tage-Buch* in 1924–26, and Kurt Tucholsky may be better known today, but their analyses of the last years before Hitler and the dark years thereafter appear at times almost pedestrian compared with the clairvoyant brilliance of Schwarzschild's essays. He combined relentless logic with a political understanding that, in the words of Golo Mann, 'was almost without parallel in the history of German publishing'. His essays were widely discussed in the French and British press and read widely in political institutions, including the French foreign ministry and the Russian embassy in Berlin. Churchill, a frequent contributor to *Das Neue Tage-Buch*, the *Tage-Buch*'s successor publication in Paris, where Schwarzschild had moved to in the spring of 1933, praised his 'invaluable contribution to the enlightenment of those who care to be enlightened.'

This collection brings together some articles that Schwarzschild wrote between 1929 and 1939. It focuses on a number of topics that dominated that decade more than any other: the political and economic developments in Germany leading up to Hitler's assumption of power in January 1933, German preparation for war, and the Western powers' response to it between 1933 and 1939. These issues shaped the history of the world, as well as Schwarzschild's fate. Schwarzschild wrote persuasively and perceptively about many other topics of the day, such as the Spanish Civil War, Stalin's Soviet Union and Italy under Mussolini. In particular the Moscow show trials and the increasingly assertive activities of the Comintern in places like Paris, where many German exiles had fled to after 1933, had a strong and lasting influence on Schwarzschild. They hastened his departure from some left-of-centre positions that he had occupied in his early years, and affirmed his conviction that communism was a moral and political evil that had to be opposed aggressively. This was not a position that endeared him to many of his fellow émigrés in Paris, a large number of whom looked to Stalin to lead a global fight against fascism. While Schwarzschild supported a tactical alliance between the West and the Soviet Union, he remained a vocal opponent of Stalin's regime and had no illusions about its reliability as a partner. Indeed in April 1937 he speculated about the possibilities of a German-Russian partnership – one that was formed with terrible consequences two years later. He was 'a lone wolf', as one commentator described him – a supremely bright, fiercely independent proponent of liberal ideas, more at home in an Anglo-Saxon liberalism than the political extremism prevailing on the continent, where not belonging to a political party in those years could attract as much condemnation as belonging to the wrong one. However, the power of Schwarzschild's writings is not only based on his ideas, impressive as they were – he was, and wrote as, a representative of an extraordinarily rich culture that found a violent death between 1933 and 1945: the assimilated, educated Jewish bourgeoisie of Central Europe. Its demise has been a tragic loss to the countries in the region, some of which – Austria above all – never recovered from it.

The collection of articles commences in August 1929. The Weimar Republic was ten years old, and Schwarzschild's resumée reveals the exhaustion of a country that has been convulsed in the most violent upheavals. The years of the Dawes Plan appeared to have been a great success economically and, it seemed, politically – the Locarno pact in 1925 had been hailed as 'the most important and significant development of the European order since 1919', 'a turning point in history', as British Foreign Secretary Sir Austen Chamberlain put it, and Germany's entry into the League of Nations a year later suggested to some that a new era of trust and cooperation had commenced. Schwarzschild had always been sceptical about the value of these international initiatives – what additional security was obtained by reconfirming, rather than adding to the core principles of the Treaty of Versailles with respect to Germany's Western (*nota bene*, not her Eastern) borders, the demilitarisation of the Rhineland, and its peaceful intentions vis-à-vis France or Belgium? What security indeed, if Chancellor Luther, on the eve of signing the Locarno pact, warned the Allied Powers that Germany could only abide by the principles of the pact if the Allies also satisfied her other, new demands, especially concerning rearmament? And so on – every agreement was followed by new, 'final' demands in the spirit of 'equality' for the new German partner. For Schwarzschild 'Locarno marked the beginning of the age of complacency in the democratic Western world. The years of self-destruction began. After them would come years of paralysis. But first there were several years of euphoria.'

This period of euphoria came to a spectacular end in 1929, and many of Schwarzschild's subsequent articles deal with the causes and consequences of the crisis that unfolded. His particular bête noire was Hjalmar Schacht, the megalomaniac, power-hungry, volatile and turncoat President of the Reichsbank. While he was famous for having stabilised the currency in 1923 (albeit with the intellectual help of the more competent, if even more right-wing Karl Helfferich), he became notorious for pursuing and defending an at times incoherent economic policy in support of his political objectives, primarily to end German reparation payments, and ultimately to strengthen his own standing among the nationalist right of Messrs Hugenberg, Hindenburg and Hitler. Schacht's departure from the Reichsbank – usually labelled a 'resignation' (Schacht's preferred term), although in fact, as the notes of Max Warburg, the German banker and a board member of the Reichsbank, make clear, he was fired – coincided with the arrival of Heinrich Brüning as Chancellor in the spring of 1930. Brüning's 'cabinet of front fighters', as it styled itself, continued the relentless assault on the main provisions of the Versailles settlement – economically, territorially and militarily – and became the target of some of Schwarzschild's fiercest attacks. His 'An Imaginary Speech by Brüning', published six days after the dramatic elections of 14 September 1930 in which the NSDAP won 18.3 per cent of the votes to become the second-largest party in the Reichstag, initiates his criticism of Brüning's deflationary economic policies which, in the course of the next 18 months, he refined into detailed policy proposals. In these articles Schwarzschild developed an economic programme that relied on additional public spending, funded by credit creation, as the means to end the deflationary spiral caused by insufficient aggregate demand. Here, as in many other points of detail, his analyses and proposals are similar to those developed by Keynes in his speeches in the US in the summer of 1931, later developed in full in his *General Theory*, although Schwarzschild worked independently. The 'Imaginary Speech' article also shows how agnostic Schwarzschild was about the means by which the stabilisation of the Republic could be achieved – even if it meant supporting the temporary use of the emergency powers granted under Article 48 of the constitution to implement legislation by presidential decree. This does not mean that he supported

Hindenburg's or Brüning's persistent reliance on these powers, which went far beyond what the constitution actually permitted and set a disastrous precedent gratefully adopted by the Nazis. It merely reflected his conviction that the right leader occasionally would have to resort to extreme, unusual measures to stabilise the Republic at a time when it was in the process of being torn apart by the deepening depression and growing political radicalism. However, there were no leaders of any calibre available – one of Schwarzschild's great regrets. His early hopes in Brüning were soon dashed, and he had never had any hope in the 'mediocre, ignorant, unintellectual Party secretaries' of the Social Democrats, 'awful second-generation nonentities'. This absence of true leadership, of individuals capable of grasping the nettle and crushing those who wanted to crush the Republic was, in his view, what ultimately brought about the end of Germany's experiment with democracy. This assessment must surely be right, even if Schwarzschild was probably a bit harsh on the Social Democrats, who operated in an environment that was in all respects – culturally, politically and economically – extremely hostile.

In the immediate aftermath of the watershed elections of September 1930, Schwarzschild believed that it would be a mistake to permit government by the National Socialists – once you made them 'socially acceptable' they could establish themselves as a permanent force, and if that were to happen, 'the curse and contempt of our children and our children's children will be upon the generation that murdered their future'. He later revised this point of view when he argued, in February 1933, that:

> [t]he country is paying dearly for the fact that Herr Brüning was allowed to continue in office after the elections of 1930, breaking the rules of the democratic game, instead of letting those who voted National Socialist have the trial with their chosen one they so clearly wanted.

In his article six months earlier, 'Let him have a go', in April 1932, Schwarzschild had argued that Hitler was most likely to be neutralised if he could be made in part responsible for the economic crisis in Germany – a recommendation that struck the young Eric Hobsbawm as suicidal. However, a pre-condition for Schwarzschild's recommendation in his article was that the democratic apparatus of Germany was still functioning, and that it therefore could control Hitler. He also must have assumed that Brüning, who had displayed some dexterity in handling both Hindenburg and Hitler in the past, would continue to lead the government. However, when von Papen crushed the legitimate government in Prussia a couple of months later, that apparatus fell apart and Hindenburg's dismissal of Brüning in May also showed that the latter's position was less secure than Schwarzschild may have thought. He therefore withdrew his recommendation before the year was out.

It is tempting to speculate about what would have happened had Brüning brought Hitler into his government one or two years earlier. After all, many of Brüning's policies were similar to those propounded by the Nazis. What is certainly clear is that the NSDAP was seriously weakened towards the end of 1932 as a result of its defeat in the November elections, its precarious financial position and Schleicher's attempts to break off with the left wing – especially as there were the first signs of an economic recovery at that time. When Hitler nonetheless became Chancellor two months later, Schwarzschild could write with complete justification that 'Herr Hitler was already a defeated man when victory was gifted to him. ... It wasn't a march on Berlin that brought the German Mussolini to power, but a piece of chicanery by the camarilla of Prussian *Junkers* and Westphalian industrialists.'

After moving the magazine's offices to Munich following the Prussian coup in the summer of 1932, to evade possible retaliations by the von Papen government, the last issue of the *Tage-Buch* was published on 9 March 1933. Immediately thereafter the magazine was shut down by the SS. Schwarzschild escaped to Vienna (the SS had planned for him to be sent to Dachau), where he was introduced by Maurits Kann, an occasional contributor to the *Tage-Buch*, to Johan C.S. Warendorf, a Dutch lawyer who agreed to provide the initial capital for the *Tage-Buch* to be re-launched as *Das Neue Tage-Buch* in Paris. Warendorf not only shared Schwarzschild's conviction that the Nazis had to be fought with determination, he also arranged for the distribution of the magazine from Amsterdam, until the German occupation of Holland. Schwarzschild, his nephew Rudi Aron (who wrote under the alias Joachim Haniel) and Joseph Bornstein (a.k.a. Erich Andermann) moved into small offices opposite the British Embassy on the Rue du Faubourg St Honoré. From there this small team, supported by regular contributors from across Europe, including Winston Churchill, produced a weekly magazine with a circulation of around 15,000. The first issue was dated 1 July 1933 and very quickly the *Neue Tage-Buch* established itself as the leading émigré newspaper and source of information about developments in Germany. It lasted longer than any of the more than 400 exile publications – from July 1933 to May 1940 – and, rare among them, represented a liberal-centre point of view, rather than the more usual left-leaning orientation of German émigrés.

In the first edition of the *Neue Tage-Buch* Schwarzschild set out unequivocally the *sine qua non* of Hitler's plans:

> Whatever happens, one thing is already beyond question today: part of the innate and immutable characteristics of the new era is an unremitting psychological and physical descent into some kind of military conflagration. The field of war is the only area in which National Socialist theory and practice are completely clear and in harmony, the only area in which from day one a consistent line has been pursued.

A central purpose of the *Neue Tage-Buch* was therefore to educate the Western world about the nature of National Socialism, and its very distinct, entirely aggressive and utterly inhuman designs on European domination. From the very beginning Schwarzschild and his team wrote about the early measures against Jews in Germany (starting in March 1933), and other Nazi actions against political opponents and the Churches, and the establishment of concentration camps such as Dachau and Oranienburg. Above all they sought to dissect the statistics coming out of Schacht's Economy Ministry to quantify, and draw attention to, the huge rearmament programme that was initiated immediately after Hitler came to power. Like many others, they were often misled by Schacht's ingenious financing structures, especially the invisible Mefo bills with which a large part of the armament programme was funded, but Schwarzschild knew nonetheless what was going on and therefore was able to issue a stark warning as early as 1934:

> A few last months still remain in which to make good the mistakes of fourteen years. During these few months it is a task of overwhelming importance to the whole world to throttle at all costs the continuation of German rearmament. In this task is crystallised the rescue of civilisation ... By force and yet without war Europe's rush towards a war of annihilation can yet be arrested. But only by force. And only for a few months more. War need not come immediately after the elapse of those few months; it might be postponed for a considerable time longer, perhaps even for years. But after the lapse of those few months there will be nothing more to prevent.

When in March 1935 Hitler announced the reintroduction of conscription and the existence of a significant air force, illegal under the Versailles Treaty, it happened at exactly that point in time that Schwarzschild had identified as the Rubicon which, once crossed, would inevitably mean war. It is not possible to speak of any clear military superiority of Germany at that time; but in relative terms, her military power had increased so much that only war could now crush it. In 1931 Schwarzschild had predicted that the only way French military superiority over Germany would come to an end was 'by means of a war that France loses'. The events that he thus foresaw were to prove him right.

The central recommendation of the *Neue Tage-Buch* was the creation of a 'cordon sanitaire' around Germany, a system similar to the 'Triple Entente' that would bring together all European powers, including the Soviet Union, fascist Italy and clerico-fascist Austria. The period of Louis Barthou's position as French Foreign Minister in 1934 and the Franco-Russian alliance of May 1935 briefly led the normally gloomy Schwarzschild to feel somewhat optimistic about the future. Alas, without Britain's cooperation, this strategy of 'encirclement' – the encirclement that, in German – and apparently British – eyes had preceded and therefore caused the First World War – was stillborn; and Britain had no interest in, and was adamantly opposed to undertaking anything that would upset the 'balance of power in Europe', as she perceived it, and disturb her attempts to reach some amicable settlement with Germany. 'A clear and determined concentration of power against the approaching offensive of the new German military power will never come about if one looks to Britain to take the initiative, hoping to jump on the bandwagon', was Schwarzschild's assessment in March 1935.

Schwarzschild's political position was that of a classic liberal in the tradition of the Scottish enlightenment. He had enormous respect for the sophisticated political process that had developed in England over many centuries, and admired a culture which nurtured the civilised tolerance of people with very diverse points of view. That made it particularly painful to witness her prevarications in the face of the growing threat to peace in Europe. Britain completely misunderstood the military and political ambitions of the German establishment. The effect of the terrible slaughter of 1914–18 had been to instill a longing for peace in Britain – whereas in Germany it reinforced a cultural desire for war and instilled a longing for revenge. Only in Germany could people like Ernst Jünger glorify a soldier's life as a mystical experience; it was Franz von Papen who in May 1933, when he was still Vice Chancellor, gave a speech in which he ridiculed the idea of a peaceful death and proclaimed 'that war was as natural a destiny for man as giving birth to children was the natural destiny of woman.' Stanley Baldwin's view, by contrast, was that war risked 'every piece of all the life we and our fathers have made in this land.' For that reason, one must assume, it was impossible for him and others to comprehend that Hitler really meant what he said, and had been proclaiming loudly and clearly ever since publishing *Mein Kampf*. Furthermore, there were powerful pro-German sentiments in Britain that exerted a huge influence on public opinion – probably none more so than those of John Maynard Keynes, whose *Economic Consequences of the Peace* is a long plea, utterly wrong-headed in this writer's opinion, to spare Germany the consequences of her terrible belligerence between 1914 and 1918. Without the loss of faith in their powers, without this feeling of guilt over having 'strangled' Germany at Versailles, Britain and her allies might well have acted earlier and more decisively against Hitler – thereby responding to the premonitions expressed by one of her own diplomats, Sir Robert Morier, six decades earlier in a letter to the Crown Prince Frederick III, Queen Victoria's son-in-law and, in contrast to his son Wilhelm II, a very capable and humane man: 'The malady under which Europe at present is suffering, is caused by German chauvinism, a new and far more formidable type of the disease, than the French, for instead of being spasmodical and undisciplined, it is methodical, calculating, cold-blooded and self-contained.'

Despite ongoing German rearmament Schwarzschild showed some signs of optimism between late 1936 and 1937 that Hitler's war aims might encounter serious obstacles. Politically, the Allies had forged stronger links to assist each other in the face of a German attack. Economically, Germany was 'already gasping for breath', in the absence of reliable raw material supplies. In foreign policy matters, 1937 was a year of relative quiet. Yet, as the Hossbach Protocol from November 1937 demonstrates, Hitler used this period of calm to concentrate the preparation for the next phase of his plans, the territorial aggressions that started with the annexation of Austria in March 1938.

Over the next 18 months, Schwarzschild wrote furiously about the impending danger, culminating in his vitriolic denunciation of the passivity of the Western powers in his article 'The Ides of March', which he wrote immediately following the annexation of the remainder of Czechoslovakia by the Germans in March 1939:

We've finally got there. After six years we've finally got there … For six long years we tried to make people understand. For six long years most did not understand, or they resisted the realisation that was gradually dawning on them. We told them when the Moloch was still weak or when it was just gathering its strength. 'Watch out before it's too late!' we said. 'Night and day it is scheming and plotting how to crush you, all of you without exception, and enslave you.' …

There was no mirage that wasn't used to cover up the increasingly apparent truth that the sole aim of these people was power and control over all, a pan-European, a pan-global despotism. 'It won't come to that!' and 'It's not aimed at us!' were the words of reassurance, of self-reassurance, employed to the limits of human error and well beyond. That is over now.

Against the background of the impending war, Schwarzschild dedicated two articles in the summer of 1939 to the future of Germany. More was at stake than merely the liberation of some territory, or the victory of one ideology over another. At the heart of the conflict was a battle over basic individual rights and freedoms. The objective of the war had to be the preservation of a liberal world order, in which states serve the needs and protect the rights of their citizens. This world order, this system of liberal government had to be saved: 'A free world – our spiritual fatherland – can exist alongside an unliberated Germany. A liberated Germany is completely unthinkable alongside a world which has lost its freedom' wrote Schwarzschild in 'The Priority' in July 1939. In setting this goal for victory, Schwarzschild gave full expression to a cultural heritage that was to die in the process but which had formerly had a small place in Germany: the cosmopolitan liberalism that was typical of the assimilated German Jewish bourgeoisie that contributed so much to her cultural, scientific and economic progress in the Wilhelmine age. A logical consequence of his position was his recommendation (in the article 'The day after', two weeks later – the last in this volume) that the Allies occupy and directly control Germany after the war. He had no confidence that any of the political forces that would be active in Germany at that time would have the capacity, vision or reputation to lead Germany out of her darkest hour into a European family of nations where she would live peacefully alongside her neighbours. It was a remarkably far-sighted and perceptive recommendation. It comes as no surprise, however, that he encountered stiff resistance to his ideas among many of the German émigrés in Paris, who dismissed them as utopian dreams – although the response of the French press was much more positive. Nonetheless, for Schwarzschild it was self-evident that after the catastrophe of the war and the painful memories of the wreckage of the Weimar Republic, the German people would have no reputable leaders, untarnished by the events of the past, capable of rebuilding Germany as a civilised country in Europe. This assessment was to prove correct initially, even if the Allies ultimately found a more capable leader in Konrad Adenauer than they might have expected, difficult and often contradictory as he may have been.

With this look into the future, Schwarzschild's life in Europe came to an end. On 9 May 1940, one day before the German attack on France, the last issue of the *Neue Tage-Buch* was published. After a brief internment as an enemy alien, Schwarzschild volunteered for a French army unit which, after the fall of France on 22 June 1940, made its way to Marseille in the unoccupied zone. In the summer Schwarzschild and his wife Valerie managed with the help of various American rescue organisations to obtain an emergency visa and left via Lisbon for New York. There he worked for the *New York Times*, *Voice of America* and *The Nation*, for whom, from 1942 to 1945, under the alias 'Argus' he wrote a regular column entitled 'Behind the Enemy Line'. His first attempt as a book author was, however, unsuccessful. A completed manuscript about National Socialism and Communism (*Gog and Magog. The Nazi-Bolshevik Twins*) was withdrawn from publication by Oxford University Press after the German attack on the Soviet Union in June 1941. However, in 1942 he successfully published a very idiosyncratic and quite excellent history of the inter-war period, *World in Trance. From Versailles to Pearl Harbor*, and two years later he wrote *Primer of the Coming World*, a cool, clear-headed analysis of the system of international relations at the end of the war which was well received and much valued by Winston Churchill. His central recommendation, to achieve 'freedom of fear from Germany', was the complete de-militarisation of Germany and Allied occupation for 50 years, as he also put it in an article in the *New York Times Magazine*. Subsequent events confirmed several of the main tenets of the book, such as his optimism about the speed and extent of European economic recovery after the war and his pessimistic assessment of the future relationship between the USA and the Soviet Union. His last book was a biography of Karl Marx (*The Red Prussian. The Life and Legend of Karl Marx*), whom he thought to be an unscrupulous, power-hungry fraud, a view he had not always held, but which he defended vociferously in his later years.

Despite the occasional success, life in America was a disappointment. Schwarzschild had lost his platform and hence his mission, and his relationship with his fellow émigrés was not the best, partly due to rather poor behaviour on his part to old friends like Klaus Mann in the late 1930s. After a failed suicide attempt in 1949, he died on vacation in Santa Margherita in Italy in September 1950.

Twelve years earlier he wrote to Klaus Mann:

There is definitely a division of labour in this world; and while I can concede that the army of daily-news agitators has a right to exist – I do not want to argue about that – a writer has decidedly a different role to fulfil. He must search for what has the prospect of being true for ever. If he does not do that he abandons his claim to being a writer.

Schwarzschild's life was dedicated to the pursuit of a truth that could last for ever – based on facts, not propaganda, and on a sound moral framework, not just expedience. When he failed in his endeavour, it was often because people like Schacht and Goebbels were particularly adept at covering their tracks. On 14 March 1945, six weeks before his suicide, Goebbels wrote in his diary:

> The Jews are re-emerging. Their spokesman is the well-known notorious Leopold Schwarzschild … Anyone in a position to do so should kill these Jews off like rats. In Germany, thank God, we have already done a fairly complete job.

Schwarzschild survived, but many more like him died, and with them an extraordinarily rich civilisation. It is worth re-reading him, and to remember and marvel at his visionary power.

Das Tage-Buch 1929–33

The Weimar constitution 10 years on   10 August 1929

Ten years after the adoption of the Weimar constitution Germany had a coalition government made up of five parties: the Social Democratic Party (SPD), the Centre Party, the Bavarian People's Party (BVP), the German People's Party (DVP) and the Democrats. The Social Democrat Hermann Müller was chancellor, Gustav Stresemann foreign minister and Rudolf Hilferding (SPD) finance minister – for the second time after 1923. This 'grand coalition' appeared to have a secure majority in the Reichstag (334 out of 491 seats), but in fact it had been created simply as a cabinet of experts because the parliamentary parties had not been able to agree on a joint programme. The coalition had an inauspicious start. Stresemann, the figurehead who had reached an agreement with Müller in the course of a telephone discussion on 23 June and who was supposed to keep the right wing in check, died eight weeks later, on 3 October. Passions were inflamed by the negotiations on the Young Plan taking place in The Hague, and Stresemann's achievement in getting agreement on the final evacuation of the Rhineland was not enough to satisfy Hugenberg's 'nationalist opposition'. Only after the referendum to reject the Young Plan was defeated in December 1929 did the mood in foreign policy calm down. There was, however, hardly any agreement between the coalition parties on questions of domestic policy. Whilst the number of unemployed rose from 1.7 million in the summer of 1928 to 3 million in the winter of 1928/29, the right and left wings of the coalition – the SPD and the DVP (which after Stresemann's death openly supported the interests of industry) – could not agree on a programme to reform the unemployment insurance scheme that had been introduced in 1927. As a consequence the government collapsed on 27 March 1930. The immediate reason was disagreement on a key question of social policy, but the breakdown of the coalition can be put down not least (and not for the first time) to the tactical incompetence and political shortsightedness of the SPD: behind their rigorous refusal to compromise there was no strategy for effective opposition. It seemed more important to keep the unions sweet and to cultivate their self-image as a bulwark against everything on the right. But by eliminating itself from consideration it made it easier for their political opponents to form the right-wing government which President Hindenburg and his cronies (above all General Schleicher) had been desperate to form for some time, with or without the agreement of parliament. With the resignation of the Müller cabinet the time had come for the transition to authoritarian government by presidential decree.

The Weimar Constitution 10 years on   10 August 1929

On the last day of July, 1919, a fifth of the seats in the Weimar theatre were unoccupied; 85 of the 423 members of parliament were missing. Was the constitution that was to be adopted that day a matter of indifference to them? It certainly wasn't to its opponents. After all, of the 85 members of the German National Party, the People's Party and the Independent Socialists 75 were there and voted No. But why had only 262 of the 331 members of the ruling coalition bothered to turn up? Why did 67 Social Democratic, Democratic and Centre Party members have to go home early? – It's all settled, that's why! The will of the people expressed itself in no uncertain terms six months ago: 80 per cent in favour of democracy and the Republic, and the remaining 20 per cent tearing each other apart, idiot Soviets and idiot Imperialists. Never was a house built on such solid foundations. We've got Noske[1] to deal with any little red flames that might flicker up here or there, he's put out much more dangerous fires. And black-white-and-red[2] ghosts rising from their graves to haunt us are just a laughing stock now that the people have discarded their superstition. There won't be any more surprises, either in parliament or outside. This isn't the France of Gambetta[3] and Thiers.[4] There the Republicans, who opposed the third Napoleon's war and, after Sedan and the revolution, spent five bitter months leading an unsuccessful mass uprising, could only win a third of the seats in the national elections of 1871. Daily there was a threat of the restoration of the monarchy and it was only after the swing in the elections of 1875 that they could even think of a new constitution. True, we didn't oppose our Emperor's war, we voted for it, but at least a kindly fate stepped in at the last moment to prevent us from lumbering ourselves with responsibility for the madness of a mass uprising (have you seen any masses around lately?), even though *Vorwärts*[5] and then Rathenau[6] recommended it. Thus, when the floodgates suddenly opened, we were instantly transformed into men of peace once more. Fifty days of opposition had wiped four times 50 weeks of collaboration from public memory. The cry of 'Republic!' from the Reichstag window had reached more corners of the land than days of conspiring behind those very same windows to see how the dynasty might still be saved. What do the people want? The people want peace. Who do they think will bring peace? Us! What are we for them? Republicans. The Republic rests on this system of equations as on basalt columns, a glorious, towering, noble structure. All that remains are the formalities, we might as well go home, brother.

Ten years on only one of the three parties opposing the constitution is actually left. Stresemann, who at the time it was debated was black-red-and-white down to his underpants and always had a loyal telegram to Amerongen[7] ready in his pocket, has come to terms with Weimar and happily occupies his seat in Hermann Müller's cabinet[8] – that Hermann Müller of whom he scornfully said in 1919 that attending a few international congresses did not qualify him to be a minister. The Independents[9] have completely disappeared; Hilferding[10] is no longer a pioneer of 'freedom' but a pillar of 'society'; his Mercedes does not fly the red flag, he calmly sails round our lovely, weary world on naval cruisers. Two of the three anti-Weimar parties have ended up safe in the haven of democracy. But does that mean the Republic is secure? Hasn't the Hydra of its enemies, having lost two heads, grown other, more powerful ones: the right-wing nationalists on the one side, the Communists on the other, with 35 per cent of the vote between them instead of the 20 per cent of 1919? And that's not counting those who might change their mind. And if we don't just count the votes, but weigh them, do we not find almost all the socially important forces among the 35 per cent: property owners, intellectuals, the military; it is a more threatening distribution than in France after the war with Prussia where the Republicans, though quantitatively in the minority, were transformed into a qualitative majority by a phalanx of eminent personalities.

Let us be clear about our terms. What is meant by 'republic'? There are all kinds of republics and there is only one thing they have in common: the absence of a monarchy. That is how they start: by driving out the monarch. And that tends to determine their initial struggles which are to prevent his return. From the day the archives opened their doors and the memoirs flooded the market, the cult of the Kaiser in this country was no more than a matter of politeness or imbecility. Never has a monarch been more finished than Wilhelm the Charlatan, finished for all social classes, apart from a few old women. No one, whether in palaces, factories or the mines, has any desire for a repeat of his buffoonery; it didn't just put people off the man himself, it also turned them away from an institution which placed the fate of the state and the nation in the hands of such chance products of a chance copulation, with no way of exercising control. The worm-eaten family still possessed curiosity value, remaining an object of historical simulation in upper-middle-class houses and of hysterical stimulation at coffee mornings for bigoted old women. None of that has any connection with reality; the reality is that a monarchist – a Hohenzollern-monarchist – movement does not, and never did exist. There have never been even the faintest signs of a desire for restoration. Even the Kapp[11] and Hitler putsches flew the nationalist colours alone and carefully avoided the monarchist flag. And none of Hindenburg's official acts was ever directed towards what was MacMahon's[12] sole aim. Do you define a republic as an absence of monarchy? That is achieved throughout the country.

Where is the Republic heading? It doesn't know. It doesn't even know whether it is democratic or not. For no one could be so superficial as to assume that this is democracy: the *demos* elects its representatives every four years, only to be ignored by them as soon as the elections are over. A question: Do you feel your member of parliament represents you? I don't! The one I elected represents lots of things – which seldom include his promises. It doesn't have to be like that, it's a perversion of the system. But even if things were different, where do we think we should be heading? After all, a republic and a democracy are only instruments and as such arouse neither enthusiasm nor revulsion, it all depends on the use that is made of them. Is the ideal we are looking for the minimal state or the 'big-brother' state? An individualistic or collective economy? With a patriotic or an international outlook? Rearing standard citizens or cultivating variety? It's all surprisingly confused. We take a step in one direction one day, one in another the next. After ten years we ought to be a bit farther on than that. Perhaps this is not the time of great decisions, just as it isn't the time of great men. Nations are not minerals with fixed characteristics, which react in a specific way to a specific chemical, day in, day out, nations are organisms with changing dispositions. At about the same time as Wilhelm II received the crown, Jules Ferry[13] said, in his big election speech against Boulanger,[14] 'Every nation alternates between a need for calm and a need for progress. It is the mark of a true statesman to be able to recognise which side a nation is leaning towards at any given time.' Words of wisdom for those simple minds who have the same patent remedy for

4

everything and take no account of the state of mind or the state of nerves of the people with whom they want to put it into practice. Sometimes decisions cannot be put off, they are forced on us by developments and events. But there are others for which we can determine the right time and a statesman with a doctor's eye can say, 'The patient needs to convalesce, he needs peace and quiet.' There is much to suggest that we are going through such a period at present. But if we are, then it is because for the last 15 years we have been subjected to such a ferocious bombardment with questions regarding the state and the nation as has seldom happened to a single generation before. For 15 years these issues have been tearing part of our normal private life to shreds. With their overriding demands, their destruction and torments they rode roughshod over our little bit of life, that bit of life we have and can't put off until times are better. Do we not have a right, at last, to rest and recuperation?

We do. And if this is an argument used to justify many omissions, it doesn't excuse everything but as a general principle there's much to be said for it. On its tenth birthday the German Republic has much in the way of mistakes, thoughtlessness and crimes to look back on. But there are welcome signs that the position of the individual is being strengthened, and more than elsewhere. We have fewer regulations, fewer prohibitions, but also greater guarantees of personal liberty than almost any other country on this ravaged continent. If the Republic's intention is to develop this freedom of the individual, even if only for therapeutic reasons, it would be a good birthday resolution. The state, every state is a necessary evil and the fact that it is necessary doesn't change matters. Other necessities are repulsive too. We ought to distance ourselves from the mindless idolisation of the state as quickly as other nations, unfortunately, are falling prey to it. Even the state we approve of will only become dear to us once we see and hear as little of it as possible. Processions are being prepared, bands are tuning up their instruments, flags are being hoisted. All very nice, who would deride public holidays? But weekdays work on the opposite principle. During those invisibility is the state's best advert.

Dr Schacht makes his mark   **14, 21 & 28 December 1929**
No marks for Dr Schacht   **18 January 1930**
The liberation of the Reichsbank   **15 March 1930**

On 31 August 1929 the Young Plan was signed by the Western powers in The Hague and came into force. The negotiations that preceded it had been turbulent and once more the most controversial participant had been the ambitious president of the Reichsbank, Hjalmar Schacht. Schacht led the German delegation to the experts' conference in Paris; another leading member of the delegation was the managing director of the Vereinigte Stahlwerke, Dr Albert Vögler. On 17 April 1929 Schacht submitted a memorandum to the Allies which almost brought about the collapse of the conference. First of all Schacht proposed that Germany should pay an annual sum of 1.65 billion Reichsmarks over 37 years, but he then made this offer conditional on Germany obtaining access to raw materials from overseas and being compensated for the loss of agricultural areas in the east. The Allies understood this to mean that Germany was demanding the return of its colonies and the Polish Corridor. In doing this, Schacht was well aware that he was ignoring the instructions from the government, which did not want these questions discussed at a reparations conference. As a result Lord Revelstoke, the English chairman of a specially convened committee, recommended the conference be discontinued. Rumours about the events in Paris caused serious turbulence on the financial markets and within only a few days the Reichsbank lost over a billion Reichsmarks in foreign currency, which forced it on 25 April 1929 to raise the discount rate by 1 per cent. Before it came to the suspension of the conference, however, Revelstoke died, which meant the conference could be saved. Schacht accepted the annual payments suggested by the chairman, but immediately tried to escape the responsibility for accepting them. Despite all his efforts, however, as the leader of the German delegation he could not avoid signing the experts' report (the Young Plan) on 7 June 1929.

At a conference in The Hague (6–31 August 1929) the Young Plan was then adopted by the Allies and Germany. The nominal value of the total reparation liabilities was fixed at 114 billion Reichsmarks and the annual payment under the Dawes Plan of 2.5 billion Reichsmarks was reduced to an average of 2.1 billion during the 58 years to 1988. The reduction was particular significant in the early years – for instance, in 1929/30 only 743 million Reichsmarks were due, 70 per cent less than under Dawes. Of the annual payments, 660 million Reichsmarks were 'protected', that is they were payable under all circumstances. However, Germany could request to postpone (by up to two years) payment of the remainder in times of current or expected economic hardship, subject to the approval of a special committee of the Bank for International Settlements (BIS) which was established to oversee implementation of the Young Plan. Germany made use of that provision almost immediately. All other controls of the Dawes Plan were eliminated, including the position of the reparation agent. In particular, the

Allies agreed to vacate the Rhineland on 30 June 1930, five years earlier than envisaged in the Versailles Treaty. This constituted a very significant political concession.

Despite the diplomatic success of the evacuation of the Rhineland, the Young Plan became the object of a virulent nationalist campaign in Germany. Agitators such as Hugenberg, the chairman of the DNVP, could point out that the annual payments, even if they were now significantly less than under Dawes, would have to be made until 1988; or that the total sum was still much too high, even if the present value of all payments (ca. 37 billion Reichsmarks) was now two-thirds less than the last time a total value for Germany's reparation liabilities was fixed at the London Conference in April 1921. In July 1929 Hugenberg and Hitler, together with Franz Seldte of the Stahlhelm and Heinrich Class of the Alldeutscher Verband (Pan-German Association), set up the 'Reichsausschuss für ein Volksbegehren gegen den Young-Plan' (National Committee for a Referendum against the Young Plan). Article 73 of the Weimar Constitution gave voters the opportunity to influence parliament directly through referendums. A successful campaign in October collected enough signatures to enforce a referendum on a 'Freedom Law' prepared by the Reichsausschuss which called for a revision not only of reparations but of all Germany's obligations under the Treaty of Versailles and proposed prison sentences for the signatories of the Young Plan for treason. The referendum was set for 22 December 1929. Just two weeks before that, on 6 December, Schacht handed the government a memorandum in which he expressed his opposition to the referendum, but also to the Young Plan. In addition he attacked the financial policy of Hilferding, the Social Democratic finance minister. Without waiting for a response from the government, he published his pamphlet in which everyone in Germany could read that, 'For my own part I quite categorically reject the suggestion that I was responsible for the coming into force of the Young Plan …' Schacht wanted to keep in with the nationalist right wing without endangering his position as president of the Reichsbank. The result of the referendum was a resounding defeat for the initiators, despite their propaganda campaign. Instead of the required 50 per cent, only 13.8 per cent of all those entitled to vote were in favour of the proposed law.

When, on 31 December 1929, Schacht sent out a letter in which he set conditions for the Reichsbank's membership of the BIS, his position, although legally inviolable, had become politically untenable. On 7 March 1930 he was therefore forced to resign – this is made clear by Max Warburg, the *eminent German banker who was a member of the Reichsbank Generalrat, and contradicts subsequent claims by Schacht that he resigned in protest against the final protocol of the Hague conference (20 January 1930) in which the terms of the transition from the Dawes Plan to the Young Plan were laid down. He was no longer an official expert there, but he had still gone public with views which were contrary to those of the government. At that point he had at least forced the resignation of Hilferding, the finance minister, and his powerful permanent secretary Johannes Popitz. Schacht was succeeded by the former chancellor, Hans Luther. After this Schacht quickly made contact with the radical right wing in the faint hope that he might succeed Hindenburg as president. In November 1932 he made his support for Hitler public, after he had already introduced him to powerful industrial and financial circles. In March 1933 Hitler then reinstalled him as head of the Reichsbank.*

Dr Schacht Makes his Mark   14, 21 & 28 December 1929

I

Horace Greely Hjalmar Schacht – it is not by chance that his Anglo-Saxon Christian names are now hidden behind his Nordic one – is the broom from Goethe's poem 'The Sorcerer's Apprentice'. For decades he stood in the corner, more or less ignored; first of all he was the archivist, later deputy director of the Dresdner Bank, one of the umpteen hundred deputy directors who have to deal with the minutiae of high finance. Then came the war and swept him into prominence as head of the German money factory in Belgium;[15] for a while the radiance emanating from this governmental office made him look like a star, so much so that the Nationalbank für Deutschland thought him the right man to arrest the decline of its modest business. Wrong! Soon they found themselves obliged to subordinate their disappointing acquisition to a new man who, though technically his equal, acted as his boss – Jacob Goldschmidt[16] with his dazzling reputation for shrewdness and effectiveness. Immediately Hjalmar Schacht was back in the obscurity of the second eleven. The bank prospered, merged with the Darmstädter Bank and at times its prestige took on almost mythical proportions – but no one bothered with Dr Schacht, twiddling his thumbs in his corner. That was until 1923, when some sorcerer's apprentices chanted the magic words:

8

Get up, old broom, come over here,
Put on these rags I hand you.
You've been a slave for many a year
Today I will command you.
Two legs so you can stand,
A head so you can look.
Now hurry up, go quickly and
Fill the pail at the brook.

The apprentices were Hilferding, Bernhard,[17] Feiler,[18] Pinner[19] – and the writer of these lines added his own modest voice to the chorus. They were not guided by any strong conviction of quality – no one had ever heard Schacht express particularly profound insights or particularly striking discoveries. It was not without difficulty that certain basic aspects of monetary theory were explained to him at Borchardt breakfasts. It took substantial assistance to produce the mediocre article in the *Berliner Tageblatt* which came to be known – rather presumptuously – as the 'Schacht Currency Project' and was blown up for public consumption into a significant event. But there was a terrible threat, which went under the name of Helfferich.[20] Helfferich, the Ruhr warrior, Helfferich, the hater of the Republic, Helfferich, the rye-currency man. Helfferich, who had the support of the the entire banking sector, industry and the Reichsbank.[21] Any candidate who opposed him would have, in those times of economic psychosis, at least to be invested with the divine halo of 'banker'; would have, in those weeks of the Hitler putsch, at least to be blond of hair and name; would have, in those weeks when the Ruhr was abandoned, at least to make up for a willingness to accept the Treaty of Versailles by being middle-class, capitalist and antisocialist. Among all those who were capable of distinguishing between debit and credit, who didn't confuse discount with descant, there was only one who satisfied all these requirements: Hjalmar Schacht. A report, that was accepted unanimously by the board of the Reichsbank, rejected him in blunt terms as 'completely unsuitable'. With just three votes against, the central committee – the world of high finance – endorsed the report. But the government – both Marx's[22] socialist-free cabinet and Stresemann's cabinet with its leavening of socialists –, desperate to put the Ruhr fiasco behind them and quivering like jellies at the threat of Helfferich, were beside themselves with joy at the substitute the sorcerer's apprentices had created for them. The bells rang out over Germany: the Stabiliser is arisen, the Reich Currency Commissar, the new president of the

9

Reichsbank. Having brought him from nowhere into the glare of public attention, his creators looked on fondly to see how well he acquitted himself.

II

It wasn't easy. Stabilising the currency was less difficult than all those believed, or affected to believe, who persisted until the very last day in denying that the devaluation of the German banknotes had anything at all to do with the mass production of those same notes. As soon as the orders with the dozens of printing presses working day and night were abruptly cancelled, the currency stabilised itself, so to speak; the only person facing any difficulty was the minister of finance, Luther,[23] who had to resort to the brutal pressure of taxation to extract the money with which until then the printing presses had happily supplied him.

But the president of the Reichsbank had other problems. During the previous few months anyone who was energetic or quick-witted enough had established their own private bank. Two hundred kinds of emergency currency, issued by local councils, companies, chambers of commerce, were floating around in the country and their elimination was opposed by all those who had made – and hoped to continue to make – money out of them. Even more difficult was persuading those patriotic captains of industry, Hugo Stinnes[24] and Louis Hagen[25], to abandon their proposal to set up their Rheinisch-Westfälische Notenbank, which would issue its own money. As late as January 1924, two months after the stabilisation, they issued an ultimatum demanding permission to set it up (by which Hagen evidently demonstrated his suitability for his present position on the supervisory board of the Reichsbank). And when that was turned down, King Hugo even went so far as to notify the government, in the name of the industry of the Ruhr Valley, that henceforth he refused to have any further dealings with Dr Schacht. The latter, however, having swallowed the sorcerer's apprentices' watchword: 'honesty is the best monetary policy', defied the plutocratic tempter and also obeyed the pacifist command of his creators. He appeared in Paris before the great men around Dawes, desperate for their good opinion, keenness and willingness personified. He explained the situation, put his case, described his project for a new central bank[26] and brought home from London not only a new hoard of gold, a secure foundation for the new currency, but also permission to continue with the old Reichsbank, even though it had completely discredited itself and even though the danger of a new central bank based entirely on private capital, entirely free of state control, had been close. A triumph for the sorcerer's apprentices' triple principle: *sound money, sound politics, sound administration.*

Something was not quite right, however, even though it didn't attract much attention at the time: a certain arrangement concerning the Reichsbank shares. As today, they were quoted on the stock market. But since the fortunes of the Reichsbank were tied to the fortunes of the mark, in September 1923 the 1000-mark shares could be bought for three dollars. Where, then, did all the interest in them come from, which drove the price up to 40 dollars within two months? Who were the buyers? Banks and bankers. What did they expect to get out of holdings in an institution whose liabilities ran into trillions? That became evident in the middle of 1924. By then Schacht had drawn up the Bank Law and the Reichstag passed it with a two-thirds majority. The law had been meticulously drafted, but there was just one loophole – it said nothing precise about the old Reichsbank shares. They were to be converted into new ones, but the exchange ratio 'was to be decided by the management board of the Reichsbank' – that is, by the management board that was dependent on the president who, for his part, was dependent on the supervisory board or, to be more precise, on the six bankers on the supervisory board. And at what level did the management board set the conversion rate? Five-hundred-mark new shares for the 1000-mark old ones. What a nice present for those unsuspecting souls who only recently had bought up shares for between 12 and 120 marks which now had a par value of 500 marks and were even occasionally being traded at 750! What a marvellous turnaround even for those who had paid the full face value in the dim and distant past. Definitely the most splendid in the whole of Germany. Even the Berliner Handelsgesellschaft, which throughout the inflation period had refused to dilute its capital with bad money, could now only convert at 5:1. Deutsche Bank and AEG went down to 10:1 and other well-known firms even as low as 100:1. But the Reichsbank, which owed its new funds not to its own efforts, but to a loan from the state, and which paid not a single new *Rentenbank* pfennig for an old 1000-mark note – that is for a piece of paper that ranks ahead of its own share capital – , the Reichsbank converted at 2:1, handed out 80 million of its new capital to its shareholders, who couldn't have complained if they had received a tenth of that, thus reducing the annual levy to be paid to the government, which, as is well known, ranks behind dividends payable to shareholders.

Small presents maintain friendship, larger ones can create it. The banks and bankers on the supervisory board and central committee, to whom alone the president is answerable (in no other country in the world is the head of the central bank answerable to no one but the very people to whom he can grant or refuse credit), these banks and bankers would have been quite right in thinking that Schacht had been very nice to them. Certainly he could not have done anything better calculated to allay distrust and create harmony. A sacrifice to the god of the clique. But was not the opposite the intention when the novice was first ordained?

III

Still, at that point no suspicion was aroused. Perhaps it was another idol before which he was bowing down, the idol of property rights. Over the previous ten years they had been so thoroughly torn apart by confiscators, liquidators and conquistadors from all over the world that a capitalist Draco would not have been unwelcome, a merciless lawgiver, impervious to all pleas: 'A deed is a deed! Once a property owner, always a property owner.'

But is Schacht cast in the same fanatical mould? The old lady who appealed to him not long afterwards had a quite different story to tell. In 1912, when he was still deputy bank director, she had given him a mortgage on his house in Zehlendorf, 50,000 shiny new gold marks, which in 1922 she was compelled to take back from him, very reluctantly, in the same number of crumpled banknotes. When the revaluation laws came into force, she read about the 'cut-off date' in June 1922[27] and saw that the matter of a few weeks had deprived her of a revaluation of 25 per cent. So she asked the 2:1 converter if he could see his way to increasing her payment at least to 4:1. She outlined her situation: her husband an officer killed in the war, she herself as an aristocrat not used to work, her wealth whittled away, her children still at school – did her former mortgagor not feel honour-bound to make this payment? He had salted away a fortune as a member of the Danat Bank, been given a golden handshake when he left and was paid a quarter of a million a year as president of the Reichsbank. Now he was being asked to pay a few hundred marks in additional interest of his own free will. The way a true gentleman behaves in such a situation was demonstrated at about the same time by another president, Dr Simons,[28] the president of the Supreme Court. Since the Supreme Court – what an insulting omission! – had still not been converted into an independent joint stock company with Louis Hagen on the supervisory board, Simon did not enjoy one tenth of Schacht's income, nor did he have a private fortune any more. And yet he revalued a mortgagee's extinguished claim against him[29] by 100 per cent. A fine, honourable gesture. By contrast, the filthy rich Schacht had a letter typed, six cold, curt lines:

12

'... that there is no reason, either legal or moral, for me to consider this ....' End of discussion.

What Herr Schacht considers moral remains an open question and is of topical interest. The difference between his attitude and what is the norm in civilised society was so great in this matter that the explanation that automatically occurred to people in other cases was, 'He just has a special notion of morality.' However, as far as his fanatical belief in property rights is concerned, it was – at least in this case when it was a matter of the interests of a poor woman with no influential connections – entirely absent. Perhaps the sacred flame will only light up when fuelled by the interests of rich and influential gentlemen. The financial demands of the princes, for example. By God, even Schacht must surely have been aware of how the wealth of ruling families was created: that one day the sovereign arbitrarily divided up the property of the state and the property of the prince, which were completely identical, into two piles and declared: 'This belongs to me now, and that to the country'; and that nothing stands on a shakier legal foundation. Schacht must surely have recalled now and then that the monarchs not only had their private fortunes, but also legally binding contracts, appointments for life, and even beyond, sealed by inviolable laws. There is no logic at all in idolising one point of law and denying another. But the sacred flame blazed up in Schacht. He, who had helped create the law that expropriated the widow, deemed a law to expropriate the princes intolerable. The simple fact that the German Democratic Party[30] allowed a free vote was enough for him to resign from it with a big bang. Another day, another way. The grass is greener on the other side. And on the other side is everything – apart from votes – that has power in this country. There, he felt, he would have more chance of getting somewhere than with the sorcerer's apprentices.

He is a man who has seen the inner workings of power, who knows that one good turn deserves another, that the area of public policy where our so-called democracy still has the decisive voice, has become narrower and narrower. Important areas have already been fenced off, are run by the clique of mutual backscratchers, or by simple-minded camp followers. Is it your ballot paper that governs the army? Is it your ballot paper the judiciary obeys? Are the state railways, which have the country by the throat and are the most important source of orders for our factories, the least bit dependent on the electorate? Is the Reichsbank, the heart regulating the circulation of money and credit, in any way reliant on the goodwill of the people? Nothing can be achieved with those who have nothing to show but so many million voters and who continue to act out the shadow play known as the democratic process on that basis. The delights of true power can only be found in the closed circle of those who let the shadow actors strut their stuff, while quietly removing whatever they can from their grasp. 'So what have we got safely tucked away already, my friends? Where are we free from interference by that young urchin democracy? And what shall we help ourselves to next?' 'Calm down, my dear Herr Schacht. You're so nervous, you're letting yourself get carried away, these things require a delicate touch.' A delicate touch? With those itchy fingers?

IV

A brief digression: What form does the role of the head of a central bank take? Opinions on that have changed somewhat in recent times. In the past it was regarded as a purely technical post: not to allow the exchange rate to get too high or too low, the money in circulation to get much more or less than the gold reserves allow, to manipulate the monetary system as the economy demanded. That, according to the old school, is the humble task of the head of a central bank.

In recent times a new school has emerged. Its view is that it is not the flow of money that needs to be adapted to the state of the economy but that the state of the economy should adapt to the flow of money. They no longer want the money supply to be manipulated according to the dictates of the economy, instead the money supply is to be used as a means of manipulating the economy. Is an excessive boom that is bound to be followed by a slump not brought under control by raising interest rates before it can get out of hand? Will excessive stagnation not give way to new enterprise if lower interest rates encourage risk-taking? They don't yet believe in complete control; they don't yet want a single person to be able to command the economy of a whole country, as Joshuah in Gibeon commanded, 'Sun stand thou still,' or as Peter commanded the lame man, 'Rise up and walk.' But already the heads of central banks everywhere are trying to avoid extreme peaks and troughs by restricting credit when growth is too luxuriant and making it cheaper when things are too slack. That means that the head of the central bank has acquired an economic role alongside the old, technical one. But how far does it go? When asked, Montagu Norman at the Bank of England said, 'I am only justified in influencing the economy to the extent that the instrument, which has been entrusted to me, allows. What has been entrusted to me is the job of conjuring up money, through the authority of the state, from a paper void. As I have to watch over its fate by increasing or reducing the supply, by making it cheaper or more expensive, I can try to influence the economy by the same means. Anything that can be done by increasing or reducing the supply of this money created by the state, by making it cheaper or more expensive, comes within my area of responsibility. But the hundreds of other facts, apart from the money issued by my state bank, that affect the economy, are nothing to do with me. Not private individuals, what they produce and consume, export and import, borrow or lend; nor the state, its laws and treaties, its revenue and expenditure, its assets and debts. That is all part of the economy, that all affects it. But if I cannot influence it with the money issued by my state bank, then I should neither seek to acquire influence, nor acquire means of gaining influence.'

V

Has Hjalmar Schacht stayed within these boundaries? He has not. From the very beginning, whenever he got whiff of an opportunity, he immediately went after the kinds of power and influence over the economy which were well outside his role.

What made him allow that provisional creation of 1924, the Golddiskontbank[31], to continue to operate? In those pre-Dawes times a body that had received from abroad pledges of up to 15 million pounds of loans for German businesses was very welcome. But shortly afterwards the Reichsbank was restructured, bought up all the shares in the Golddiskontbank and was supposed, according to the preamble to the legislation, to 'take over its entire business'. Why, then, was the merger not carried out? Why did the Reichsbank need an illicit relationship? Those who were familiar with its statutes knew why. In practice the Reichsbank can only use the money it issues to purchase three-month bills of exchange and to make ninety days' loans against good collateral. But the Golddiskontbank can do as it likes and its continued existence under the ownership of the Reichsbank gave Schacht the freedom to do all the things he was not actually allowed to do. And he did. He meddled in agricultural policy as he saw fit, financed mortgages for agricultural businesses with funds which, ultimately, came from the Reichsbank. Yet despite all this deviousness, this circumvention of the statutes, he never managed to develop the power he dreamt of, though at least he lived in hope for a few months.

And another operation, launched with a blare of publicity, petered out as its pointlessness became apparent. In those days after the stabilisation of the currency when the money flowed, all sorts of organisations built up large amounts of cash between the main payment dates – the railways, the post office, *Länder* and city councils, public utilities. They did what anyone with surplus money does: they made loans, either directly or through affiliated banks. Some made the same mistakes that occurred all over the place after the turmoil of inflation, some did it correctly, without incurring losses. But by exaggerating and generalising these mistakes, Schacht started to agitate for all these funds to be deposited with the Reichsbank. Once there they cannot, according to the statutes, earn any interest, which meant the owners would lose several millions whilst the Reichsbank could lend them out at interest, thus earning for itself what the others lost. And the financial dominance of Schacht's institution would certainly not be weakened if he could siphon off a few hundred millions of other organisations' money into his own reservoir. But the more evident these motives became, the gaudier the scientific rags in which the charlatan economist dressed them up. It provides the model for all later debates with him, his arguments are all as difficult to grasp as a jellyfish. When asked: 'Why with the Reichsbank?' he replies: 'Because it has always been like that.' When it is shown that it has never been like that, he declares that now it has to be like that. Currency, interest rate and discount window policies, provision of capital, the threat of nationalisation, resentment among officials – he attacked one topic after another in a chaotic jumble, but the public were mightily impressed. Until the moment, that is, when the situation the cynics had foreseen quietly crept up on us: when public sector bodies were no longer worrying about where their surpluses were being siphoned off to, but about how they were going to cover their shortfall. Sir Hjalmar was still spurring his charger on across the field of battle, but the booty had vanished unnoticed. It was a long time before he realised, at which point he rode off home, not without the self-esteem of the almost-victor in his heart.

This was not the origin of that self-esteem. The one who was most dazzled by the sham miracle of the completely unmiraculous stabilisation was the man who had carried it through. And the central significance of monetary policy had so put him at the centre of everything that mattered that every fibre in his body resisted a return to the sidelines as the normal head of a central bank. As yet, his craving for recognition had no specific focus. He went for anything and everything that could increase his status, no matter whose toes he trod on: one day an attempt to break into the banking domain, the next an attempt to break into the public domain. But don't worry, he'll soon find his focus. Germany is not a place for loners, here even dictatorships are organised as a club. Wanted: a coalition for Dr Schacht. As soon as he gets one, he will make more systematic headway.

VI

What is the strongest power in Germany? In 1927 it was industry. There was no doubt about it. Only the unions were as well organised from top to bottom, were led with such draconian, military strictness. But they were poor, not blessed with intellectuals – we don't like them, we keep them at arm's length – no instinctive tie bound them to the senior civil service and, moreover, since the fall from grace in 1914[32] they lacked serious international backing. They might, when conditions were particularly favourable, enjoy a short-lived success, but basically and in the long term they were the losers and with them, on the political level, the Social Democrats, who seldom had any choice but to be raped – when in opposition – or to lie back and think of Germany when in government. That was not the case with industry, under the autocratic leadership of Rhineland-Westphalia. It had experience in the business of politics, experience in backroom pressure; it had money, training, nepotism, an old-boy network; it lubricated all the machinery of state, it had connections across all countries and continents. There were lots of things it didn't like in Germany: capital was scarce, the burden of reparations heavy, the restrictions on business through the expansion of publicly owned enterprises were outrageous. They had breathed on the early Schacht, these Rheingold-Fafners, with their poisonous breath, they had slashed at him with their claws. But would it not be more profitable for both parties to forget the past, to let bygones be bygones, to bury their differences for the common good, as an editorial might put it? Some small gestures have already been made. Schacht has already made things awkward for the cities – the owners of those unwelcome gas and electricity works – by making access to foreign credit more difficult. He has also renewed his patriotic credentials by publicly dreaming, in these times of colonial emancipation, the most obsolete and therefore most genteel of patriotic dreams, the dream of acquiring colonies. But just as in days of yore there was no true reconciliation until the erstwhile opponents smelt the sweet aroma of the sacrificial lamb, so in this case the grand ceremony remained to be performed.

On Black Friday the stock market was offered up for sacrifice and great was the rejoicing in all mines. They had never had much affection for the stock market. It is, of course, just a marketplace for receipts – receipts for money which made the mines possible. But IOUs are never valued as highly as the payment to which they bear witness. And Schacht's show had a special effect. He said: the banks grant too much credit for stock market speculation, thus reducing the amount of credit available to industry; but industry needs our help, so let's put an end to that speculative credit. Was ever fair maid more delicately wooed? Was ever a more magnificent tourney held in a lady's honour? Nowadays no one would dare maintain that there was even a modicum of sense in this sacrificial overkill, this compulsive, frenzied intervention. Credit which is granted to the purchaser of a share goes to a seller of a share; and there must always be a final seller who does not invest the proceeds in shares but employs them elsewhere – in the economy. Thus the clear, direct consequence of this assault was not an increase but a diminution of the funds available for investment. But the indirect consequence was even worse: it set off that devastation of the equity markets which for years has made it impossible for a German enterprise to raise start-up or growth capital within Germany. It was over, it still is over and it will remain over for a long time. The fleeced small investor, cast down, trampled all over and driven away, refused to act as bait to be set out by a an economic chamaeleon. Only politicians will tolerate that kind of thing, not private individuals who are staking their own money. In Düsseldorf and Essen, however, where they were all for the build-up of the fleet and for standing by our Austrian allies through thick and thin, where they greeted the World War with cheers, forced through the U-boat war, annexed Briey, deported Belgians, gobbled up Courland, rejected universal suffrage, financed Kapp, Hitler, Ludendorff[33] and Hugenberg[34] – in those circles where a glittering superstructure of technical intelligence rises up from the foundation of a truly desperate barrenness of imagination – in those circles Hjalmar Schacht had arrived.

VII

The alliance put down firm roots and developed, it will not easily be torn apart. There were six German bankers on the supervisory board of the Reichsbank and they brought in reinforcements through co-option. No outsider can ever join the big six, but these six votes decide whether the President is to be dismissed or given a further term. Would they ever turn against him as long as he could bask in the glory of being the Champion of the Ruhr? He reached the same heights as Louis Hagen, who would not have got there by baptism[35] alone, by being a henchman of the industrial concerns on whose supervisory boards he now sat. And sitting beside him everywhere was the Deutsche Bank, whose Oscar Wassermann[36] was also with him on the supervisory board of the Reichsbank; conversely all the industrial concerns dispatched their representatives to the Deutsche Bank, on whose boards

Hagen served in turn. An inextricable network of powerful interests. An inextricable network of cause and effect as well: those who were in control of industry, were firmly established in the banks, those who were in control of the banks, were firmly established in the Reichsbank, and those who were firmly established in the Reichsbank, had control of the banks, and those who were firmly established in the banks had control of industry. It was in this soviet, well away from the limelight, not ventilated by any democratic breeze, that the Norns[37] spun the thread of fate.

It was only an abstract thread, almost invisible, but anyone who got it round their throat would be gasping for breath. The beginnings of the thread, that was now called upon to play an important role, were already there in Schacht's sewing box. He had earlier come up with the theory that foreign loans and bonds were damaging, though at that time without making any distinction between foreign bonds issued by firms and those by public-sector bodies. He was now more accommodating towards firms. The dollars they borrowed in America did nothing to ease the burden of reparations; but the dollars that the municipalities and *Länder* borrowed gave the illusion of plenty where there was poverty, financed the Dawes Plan and had to be kept outside the country. That was the beginning of the slimming diet which was to turn into an abortion. Throughout the world companies as well as governments and local councils work on the sound principle that current expenses are paid for out of current income, but long-term projects are paid for by raising capital. Annual salaries have to be paid out in full by the end of the year and therefore have to be covered by that year's revenue. A new factory or a new town hall, however, will still be in use ten, 20, 30 years hence. It does not need to be, can usually not be financed out of the income received during the year it is constructed; it is therefore perfectly reasonable to take up loans for it which will be gradually paid off by all those who will use the facility that has been built. If a firm's access to credit is blocked, then it will either have to raise its prices so much that the consumers will have to pay in one single year what could have been spread over 20; or it has to sit there, twiddling its thumbs, abandoning all innovations and accepting that it will decline or be left behind. It is no different with *Länder* and municipalities. If their access to credit is cut off, they will be forced either to increase their taxes and prices or abandon any reforms, any new roads, railway lines, hospitals or bridges. And if there are no domestic sources of credit available to fund investment, then to talk of blocking access to foreign loans and bonds has the same effect.

It is foreign loans and bonds Schacht was talking about, all the time and with less and less restraint. Once more a trial of strength was decked out in academic trappings, once more we had the confused spectacle of Schacht splashing about from one puddle of arguments to another. Hardly had you dried up one than he was spattering you from another. 'Far too simple-minded ideas,' is what Professor Ohlin[38] from Sweden called the arguments presented by the president of the Reichsbank. And a German professor, Adolf Weber,[39] counts him as one of those dangerous types 'who consider a refusal to listen to reason a virtue.' They assume he does at least believe his own nonsense. That is not always easy to accept. When someone says, 'Foreign loans and bonds ease the burden of reparations,' at the same time indicating his agreement with Parker Gilbert,[40] who, however, maintains the exact opposite, then it takes some effort to believe it is a simple misunderstanding. Another of his proofs came to an even more inglorious end. Do we need foreign loans for imports? Schacht asked. Not at all, the statistics show the opposite is true. He drew a diagram in his book and explained that one could see that imports had not risen, it was only loans that had risen. 'That shows that not all foreign loans have been used to pay for imports.' A conclusive argument? I will take the liberty of demonstrating that this deduction is based on the schoolboy error of giving imports in separate monthly figures but foreign loans and bonds as cumulative figures, from 1924 on, which means they can do nothing other than rise. If he had given cumulative figures for imports they would have demonstrated that as early as 1926 imports had already risen 20 times more than loans; that means – in a grotesque contradiction of Schacht's claim – not that an increasingly large proportion of the loans were used for other purposes than to pay for imports, but that an increasingly small proportion of imports needed foreign loans to finance them. Just look at the morass, the infantile muddle in the brain of the man who sees it as his mission to teach Germany. He mixes everything up: he talks of the danger to the money market from the influx of foreign loans and, when put on the spot, gets out of it by launching into jeremiads about the danger to the economy from the repayment of the loans; he talks of loans to private enterprises encouraging productivity in contrast to loans to public bodies which encourage consumption; and he invents, when the entrepreneurial role assumed by many public bodies is pointed out to him, the newfangled but absurd concept of 'foreign-exchange productive value'. But what is the point of going on? Why spend any more time in the pose of an academic economist, in which this would-be know-all, as he himself realises, cuts an ever sorrier figure, every new incident taking more wind out of his sails? Schacht doesn't mean the foreign loans and bonds he is talking about. He means a particular category of bond-issuers. In Bochum –

where? Talking to industrialists, of course – he abandoned his mortar board and openly put on the steel helmet of his soviet. Let's get the cities! Luxury! A waste of money! Parks, swimming pools, theatres – outrageous! Why do they need public utilities? They should sell them off. And the assembled company, the least of which, strangely enough, feel it is in their interest for the great ones to grab a few scraps from the cities – the assembled company rejoiced at such strong words. What they didn't hear were the stronger words their champion had to swallow. They didn't hear, they didn't read the response of Dr Mulert, the chairman of the Association of German Cities, who spoke of Schacht making assertions 'against his better knowledge'. They didn't learn that of the 5,500 million in foreign loans and bonds, 550 million were taken up by the cities and of that only 104 million used to finance Schacht's 'luxuries'. They didn't hear that over the same period Germans spent several times that sum on champagne, that over the same period, and with Schacht's involvement, 7,000 million, a good part of it foreign money, was channelled haphazardly and ineffectively into agriculture. Details, mere details. Schacht will know what he's doing. Just as Ludendorff did. And Tirpitz.[41] Follow my leader, that was always the German way. Was it also the German way for a custodian of our finances – and one striving to join the nation's leaders – to stand before a committee of inquiry and proclaim to the world through the open window the ruinous tidings: 'It is out of the question that we will ever be able to pay the interest on our loans.'

It was in those days that the advisory service[42] was closed down; it had been set up by Schacht to stop loan applications, though it never stopped loans to Bavaria or to the Church, even though they too required approval. It was in those days that the American government put an embargo on a Prussian bond that had already been approved by the banks. It was in those days that the iron industry on the Ruhr was preparing for the great lockout. It was in those days that a mayor, describing to the president of the Reichsbank the terrible consequences of strangling the cities – delays in payment, unrest among the unemployed – received a reply that echoed of the worst of the deposed Kaiser: 'Blood must flow, sooner or later.'

VIII

There were no Germans on Mr Dawes' committee of experts. Once he had submitted his report, German ministers negotiated with ministers of other countries about raising his report to the status of an international agreement. Mr Young's committee of experts four years later was to have two representatives of the debtor nation, with equal rights and equal votes. Whom would the German government nominate?

It was not just a matter of reducing the annual reparation payments, it was not just a matter of determining the total liability. In those things all Germans had the same goal. But there were other important questions to be decided. The Dawes Plan not only determined the required payments but also created instruments to secure payment. The statutes of the Reichsbank were a product of Dawes, the statutes that allowed neither the government nor the people the least influence over an institution whose whole existence derived from an act of sovereignty: the assignment of a note-issuing monopoly. Would the restoration of German sovereignty, which was now to take place, be achieved simply by the withdrawal of the few foreign watchdogs? Or would the demand for true sovereignty also require that the soviet for the mutual exchange of favours of the president and supervisory-boarding bankers should have some kind of ventilation built in to draw a breath of public-spirited air, of the will of the people, into the stuffy atmosphere? Another Dawes instrument was the *Bank für deutsche Industrie-Obligationen*.[43] Its task was to collect 300 million marks per year from German industrial firms as a contribution to reparations: the interest from the mortgages the companies had been forced to grant to the Bank. If in future one single debtor, Germany as a whole, was to be liable, and if the intention was to restore its sovereignty undiminished, what, then, was to become of this bank and the burden on industry? And, finally, the cardinal question: what was to become of the Reichsbahn, German Railways? It too had had a special liability for reparations since Dawes, had to pay 660 million a year. In order to make sure it did this, it had been denationalised and set up as an independent instrument of payment.[44] But the way it developed was even worse than the way the Reichsbank had developed. Just as it was the captains of industry on the supervisory board who ruled the roost at the Reichsbank, it was the captains of industry on the supervisory board who ruled the roost at the railways. But that developed into an unprecedented, outrageous situation. Remember how during the inflation years industry had rapaciously sought to get its hands on the most gigantic industrial operator in the world, the most lavish contributor to the order books of German industry? Remember also the barefaced lies, the web of intrigue, the shrill demagoguery that was brought to bear under Stinnes the Great. The conspiracy was repulsed, even though the conspirators had offered to pay handsomely for their prize. But then the Dawes Plan surpassed even their wildest dreams. It gave the failed privateers the control they had been seeking, gave it to them in everything that mattered, and saved them having to pay a penny for it. On the contrary, it even granted them annual dividends as well!

Since then it has been Herr Carl Friedrich von Siemens[45] who has wielded his mighty sceptre over German rails and rolling stock, and it is to be hoped that his firm could supply the Reichsbahn on terms that were no worse than those obtained by others. But it was not only his own sector – electricity – that he represented; since his association with Stinnes he has popped up on the supervisory boards of the most important coal mines and iron works, with whom I am sure the railways placed the odd order. And to make this liaison between suppliers and their customer even clearer, we can find even more unequivocal names in the holy of holies of the Reichsbahn: Paul Silverberg[46], for example, or Peter Klöckner.[47] The firms all these men are associated with are not only interested in supplying the Reichsbahn, they are also the largest users of its freight services and consequently obvious candidates for the special cheap rates the Reichsbahn often grants but which, as a private company with a strict belief in commercial confidentiality, it does not divulge to anyone. Do we have to add that some of these powerful men also had seats on the central committee of the Reichsbank, while members of the Reichsbank's supervisory board sat on their supervisory boards, just as they, conversely, sat on theirs? Indeed, on closer inspection there seems to be hardly any difference between the Reichsbank board and the Reichsbahn board. Those who had a foot in the one had a foot in the other as well. The logic of the situation made the amalgamation of the Schacht clique and the Siemens clique to create a single huge octopus inevitable. Did the end of the Dawes Plan, to which alone this octopus owed its existence, mean its booty would be torn from its tentacles? That – as well as the amount of reparations and related payments – was what was at stake in Paris.[48]

Whom would the German government nominate?

IX

The government nominated the octopus: Schacht and Vögler.[49] Are there no other experts in Germany? No one would imagine that Hilferding, one of the co-nominators, considered himself less of an expert. And if he, being a member of the government, was disqualified and if, as seems likely, there was no one among the intellectually hopeless Social Democrats who would be a match for the Allies' seasoned negotiators, there were other groups where half a dozen well qualified and fairly impartial representatives could have been found. But the truly remarkable fact emerged that things which are allowed to become all-powerful, suddenly turn out to be all-powerful. The government lacked the confidence to let anyone else make the pact that would decide Germany's fate apart from the men of the Reichsbank/Reichsbahn/industry clique. Whatever they wanted, was done, for no one could get things done that they didn't want. The only choice we were left with was to leave the arrangements to the octopus or to watch whatever someone else arranged being strangled at birth by the octopus. Schacht's negotiations on reparations, on the reduction of the annual Dawes payments, were widely reported in Germany. But no one knows what negotiations took place on the other matter, on the dismantling of the Dawes Plan; no one was there. All that is known is the result. The Bank für deutsche Industrie-Obligationen is to be wound up, the separate burden on industry will lapse. The Reichsbank, on the other hand, will stay as it is, impervious to the influence of the state and the people; the foreign watchdogs will leave it, that is all. And the Reichsbahn will become even more cliquified. There, too, the foreign overseers will go. And a few more of the government's minimal rights, which had survived until now, will be amputated – they only get in the way.

There was, unfortunately, nothing more that could be done. But why could nothing more be done? It is a question of intense public interest. Fortunately for us, the president of the Reichsbank lifted the veil of secrecy in a speech in Munich: 'certain members of the press' were to blame! They stabbed him in the back during the negotiations, they undermined his authority vis-à-vis the other nations. It's an old tradition in Germany, it's never the ones in charge who are responsible for poor results, but someone stabbing them in the back. Ludendorff would have brought us victory by 1920 at the latest, had not some scoundrels stopped him by shamelessly starving to death in 1918. It is not the last time Herr Schacht was to use the technique of blaming others for his own actions. He employed it again in December 1929 when he accused the government of watering down his triumph at the Young talks with new concessions, when it was none other than Schacht himself who had left those points in the Young Plan open – specifically in order to be able to make concessions later.

What, then, had happened during the talks? At a critical point in the conference, when his opponents refused to lower their demands any more, Schacht had handed over the notorious memorandum in which he mumbled something wishy-washy about colonies. It was not a condition his opponents could accept or reject. Later on Schacht himself often denied that a condition had been set and the wording, in its weak and watery way, confirms this. So what was the point of his ruminations? It was to Germany, and Germany alone, that they were addressed. It was Germany that was likely to notice this 'bold advocacy of our interests', it was Germany that was to take it seriously, it was Germany that was to cheer the would-be German Cecil Rhodes. What neater trick is there for a man who, for want of more genuine laurels, would at least like to harvest domestic renown, than to perform a pirouette which other countries would probably ignore as childish but his home audience extol as demonstrating virility. There was never the slightest likelihood of Young's chosen few looking into Germany's trauma at the loss of her colonies, and certainly not in connection with reparations. For these moneymen it is an elementary truth that colonies, at least in the initial decades, do not bring in money, but cost money. Unlike the good German burgher, who has been led up the garden path in a quite disgraceful way, they cannot be persuaded of the contrary, not even for a minute. They were certainly not going to offer any colonies to a man who declared he could not pay what they were demanding; it would only mean he could pay even less. It was not at Young, Morgan and Revelstoke that this godforsaken piece of brainlessness was aimed, but at the Lehmanns, Schmidts and Meyers.

Unfortunately the conference did prick up its collective ears; unfortunately it did not ignore the childish posturing, unfortunately it did lose patience. They were tired of having to put up with this kind of theatrical gesture aimed at the German electorate, they wanted nothing more to do with such a negotiator. As they packed their bags, Schacht was in despair; he scurried round, a pariah, stunned that his memorandum could be taken so seriously, after all, it was only words. If old Revelstoke had not suffered a stroke at that point, Schacht would have had to return home empty-handed, though even then he would certainly still have struck a pose as the saviour of the nation. But the incident provided a few days' respite – during which 'certain members of the press' could make it clear to the angry negotiators that the German representative did not represent German opinion but had his own agenda. That was what saved him, that alone. Germany's expert was allowed back in, even though he was still Hjalmar Schacht. They accepted him because they wanted to come to an agreement with the country. Germany had disowned him and that was sufficient. But Schacht the Unsteady, who was steadied by the press – by its dissent! —, this demagogue who distorted everything he brought back, both the results he wanted and those he didn't want, for propaganda purposes, had the gall to start a smear campaign against those who had saved him from political bankruptcy: They are the guilty ones, crucify them!

X

Three thousand pairs of industrialists' hands, impelled by feelings worthy of teenage girls rather than grown men, greeted the crucifier's name with frenetic applause, as they have applauded any drivel for the past 30 years, when he was announced at their Scala meeting. He had demanded tax-cuts from the government and at the same time – equally unauthorised – messed up one of their bond issues, just to teach them a lesson. 'For he's a jolly good fellow!' rang round the hall. What his fervent admirers did not yet know was that a few days later he would demand 500 million more in taxes and promise, in accepting this increased burden, not to put any more obstacles in the way of the second burden, the bond issue. But even if they had known, they wouldn't have seen the contradiction. And even if they had seen it, they would have remained convinced that it was part of a most sublime strategy, perceptible only to the most superhuman brain. A strategy to their advantage, of course, that is the cause of their uncritical rapture. Where you assume unconditional partisanship, you don't bother to check the details.

It will be a long time before these worshippers wake. They didn't wake when Paul Silverberg, the most prominent member of Schacht's expropriation soviet, came to the lectern and related his sultriest nighttime dreams: that all state-owned concerns, that conglomerate of productive enterprises worth many hundreds of millions, should be brought together in a national trust company. Dominated by? The 3,000 industrialists? No, by the president of the Reichsbank together with the 'leading financial experts in the country'. But that is precisely the clique where the voice of the textile manufacturer from Chemnitz, of the jewellery manufacturer from Pforzheim carries even less weight than one single vote! And there's more. They want this committee – the president of the Reichsbank plus the leading financial experts – to become a 'special department' within the ministry of finance in order to 'analyse and supervise the whole financial administration and activities of all government ministries as well as of the *Länder* and municipalities, with the right to set up guidelines for public finances by decree.' How do you feel about that, citizen? Can you see what's going on? This octopus – 20 filthy-rich plutocrats, accountable to no one – already has the Reichsbahn, the Reichsbank, the major banks and industries in its tentacles. Should it now get them round the rest of the state-owned enterprises? The Reich Credit Company (Reichskreditgesellschaft), say, electricity works, the United Aluminium Works (Vereinigte Aluminiumwerke), the Central German Nitrogen Works (Mitteldeutsche Stickstoffwerke), the Bavarian Power Works (Bayerische

Kraftwerke), the Deutsche Industrie-Werke as well as dozens of other state-owned enterprises? And not only that. Should it be incorporated, high above the scum of lower beings, as a central soviet in the government of the country, with the right to monitor decisions, to issue decrees even? What has this campaign to do with you, fellow citizen, friend, honest businessman? What do you say to this operation, which will hand out, free, gratis and for nothing, a million times what you had to work and pay for by the sweat of your brow, to 'colleagues', who are no more colleagues of yours than you are of the owner of the ice-cart in your street? What do you think you will get out of a reform which will not only give these same people control over all the fattest milk-cows in the economy but will even allow them to get their hands as legislators on the main control panel regulating the government's economic policy machine as well? Is that really in *your* interest, manufacturer from Chemnitz, manufacturer from Pforzheim, businessman from Hamburg? Do you think it will ease your difficulties?

Your problems are insufficient access to capital and the crushing burden of taxation. The shortage of capital comes from Schacht who, in the days when there was plenty on offer from abroad, closed the door to foreign capital markets for the best German issuers, thus letting a reservoir dry up that could have helped you indirectly, while for their part the very largest firms, your future masters, did not need to worry: they – and they alone, apart from the state, the *Länder* and municipalities – could raise long-term loans directly from abroad. And the burden of taxation? Do you really believe it should be eased by clipping off a few more marks from the miserable sums paid out to the most hard-pressed of all, the unemployed, the sick, the disabled – the core of any future revolution? Is not the useless German civil service, the grotesque permanent status for public officials, which positively encourages them to think up the most ingenious ways of doing the minimum, a greater bane? And have you ever heard that the belligerent clique said even a single word against the 'principle' of lifelong provision for civil servants? The clique that is so tireless in inveighing against the principle of provision for the needy, but treats the civil service as a sacred cow because it is to support and implement its coming rule. Are these the right teachers to deliver the important message about economising? One thing is true: Germany is living beyond its means. They're all, not just the cities, doing a little too much for their prestige and comfort. They're all living more lavishly than before the war, whereas in truth they ought to be living rather more frugally. That only aggravates the shortage of capital and makes the burden of taxation heavier. It is the highest echelons of the upper classes that lead the way with the worst possible example. The spartan Hjalmar Schacht gets up in his pulpit to tell the women of Germany that henceforth they must make do with one hat a year; but he himself is not content with the venerable building his predecessor as president of the Reichsbank was perfectly happy with. A million must be spent on building him a new one, half a million on furnishing it. In these difficult times Herr von Siemens, no less active in lecturing Germany, feels the need to erect, beside his villa, the largest and most exquisite private concert hall on earth; not for any cultural purpose – there are 20 good concerts on in Berlin every evening – nor even for any finer social occasions, but simply for ostentation, for a monthly display of wealth to 800 bored guests, who only come for the spread and then for their part feel compelled to put on a show themselves. In every issue of every magazine the clerk, the typist, the worker can see them, saviours of the nation all, sitting around in their evening dress, in their top hats, beaming, self-assured, here a party, there a party, everywhere a party. And they get talked about everywhere, by waiters, cooks and delivery boys, by maids, chauffeurs and porters. And film, the great medium of education, confirms the image. It is precisely the most patriotic films that only show respectable society in sumptuous apartments, idle, living it up, throwing money around, super-chic. Does it surprise you, then, that the lower classes feel the same desires, that among them, too, excessive consumption has gradually come to be seen as a sign of respectability?

Bring back the monarchy! At least it would be better than the miasma spread over Germany by these rulers. It had its fatal flaws, but at least it recognised more than just material values. The privy councillor with his 800 marks a month, the poor officer, the minister with shiny elbows on his jacket – they were not less, they were more than millionaires. But the clique of businessmen that has assumed imperial airs – businessmen, that and not 'captains of industry' is their profession – is based on money and nothing else; all it can claim for itself is wealth and if they want to show who they are, all they can do is show their wealth.

XI

There are two routes open to the expropriating soviet. Everywhere there are public works, everywhere the government, the municipalities and *Länder* are undertaking long-term social projects which they are under contract to complete. If, while these works are still in progress, their access to credit is cut off and if, at the same time, they are forced to lower taxes, they will get into serious difficulties and will only be able to find sufficient funds by selling off other valuable assets – at firesale prices! That is one route to their goal.

The other is more complicated, but less conspicuous. It is the precise opposite. Give them the money they need. But only give it to them on condition they commit themselves to recover from present taxpayers what future generations were to repay. And right away, in the very next year. If you make an effort to find liabilities which have to be paid off immediately, you're sure to find hundreds, each running into millions. At once you demand new taxes to the same amount. And if you manage to arrange things so that the burden – perhaps also including some old debts that have to be restructured – falls on those whose votes have so far supported the regime that is hostile to you, within a very short time they will be so outraged by the increased taxes that they will believe any propaganda about financial mismanagement and will call for the saviour who is standing ready. Then he will state his conditions. That is the second route to their goal.

It reflects Schacht's crude style that he chose the first, bullying route. He issued a memorandum: taxes to be lowered immediately. A government bond issue? There won't be one! A Berlin bond issue? There definitely won't be one! Suspend your payments for all I care. It reflects Silverberg's more subtle mind that he preferred the second route. And it reflects their relative influence that Schacht immediately changed his tune. Lower taxes? Sorry, I made a mistake, I meant raise taxes, of course. A Berlin bond? Sorry I made a mistake. I wouldn't want to harm anyone. You'll just have to raise the tariffs on gas, water and electricity, the trams, buses and underground. A government bond? Sorry, I made a mistake. I'm not a monster, I understand when necessity calls. You'll just have to ... We know the programme: increase the poll tax, the duty on tobacco and beer, the tariffs on dozens of imported consumer goods, to put an extra burden on those who can least afford it and for whom, all coming together, it will be like being hit by a thunderbolt. In Berlin, where it will coincide with raised tariffs on public services, it will mean an increase in expenditure – or a decrease in the standard of living – of 50 marks a month for the average working-class family. A terrible fact and an even more terrible shock. And if they manage to keep the safety valve of wage increases shut – that will be the battle of the next few months – their psychological calculation will work out, even if the pragmatic *Vorwärts* is much less interested in the fate of millions of workers than in the fate of Hermann Müller's government. Nothing will stop the Social Democrats from shedding votes like trees shedding their leaves in autumn. And serves them right. No German government has ever managed to achieve the opposite of its own programme as perfectly as the cabinet with the gentle Hilferding as finance minister. Everything it has done, with no exceptions or omissions, has run counter to the mandate the voters gave it. It has not one single success to show. But is that a reason to welcome Schacht's soviet? Is there no other choice than the one between the foaming hysteria of the would-be big shots and these weary little shots?

There wouldn't be too much to all this, neither benefit nor danger, if Schacht were what he is supposed to be: independent. Contrary to the stories he is only too happy to see spread around, he is not a man who is trusted the world over; apart from a few Americans, perhaps, people treat him with caution and keep him at a distance. The English idea of a gentleman is completely foreign to him, in France he is looked upon as a Hugenberg in disguise. He is of no interest to any influential world statesmen or organisation. Without his office he would be completely discredited in Germany in no time at all, or at least banished to his little nook in the Reichsbank. People who deal with him regularly are already wondering whether he needs medical attention. A volatile maniac, excitable, reacting excessively and not in control of himself at critical moments has once before been a disaster for Germany. It is not only his inability to tolerate dissent that recalls Wilhelm II; not only his uncontrollable urge to have a finger in every pie; not only his tendency to get carried away with his ideas which, based on inadequate knowledge and poor logic, spring from impulse rather than reason. Comments such as 'Blood must flow, sooner or later' contain more concrete similarities. Incidents such as the interview he gave an English newspaper at the end of 1927 which, when it appeared in the Viennese *Neue Freie Presse* a few days later, had already become so absurd and grotesque that even he had to declare its publication 'completely unwelcome and not appropriate to the times' – such incidents are a compelling reminder of those dark days when the whole of Germany rose in a fury of despair against the interview given to the *Daily Telegraph* by their divinely appointed lord and master.[50] Manic conditions are difficult to recognise in the early stages. Many symptoms can be interpreted as harmless. But it is not entirely unthinkable that his unexpectedly meteoric rise has caused some kind of psychological damage. That would explain much. But even without a psychopathic diagnosis this man could not shine for long if he had to rely on his own resources. No one likes him, no one trusts him, no one views him as irreplaceable; he would long since have gone the way of all mediocrity were he not the public face of certain powers. The broom that was woken from its sleep by the sorcerer's apprentices is now fetching and carrying water for more powerful sorcerers. That is his role – for the time being, as long as 'Back into the broom cupboard!' has not rung out.

There will come a point when it will ring out. People love a murder, but not a murderer. Some dealings require people who become unusable once the matter in hand has been accomplished. Schacht's hunger, fiercely snapping at every morsel, his aggressiveness, not sicklied o'er with the pale cast of the least noble thought, his self-importance, strained and straining at the leash, make him ideal for tasks requiring a provocative tongue, sleight of hand or a heart of stone. But the qualities required for slaughtering an ox are different from those required for transforming it into tasty pies. On the day when the clique celebrates its victory, the good soldier Schacht, whom they lured out of his dull office into the sunlight of the political arena, will be politely but firmly ushered back to the place he came from.

Will we have to put up with him until then? Will the Reichsbank cabinet remain the focus of the stultification of the nation, the corruption of public opinion, the disruption of business, conspiracy and agitation, just as von Tirpitz's Navy Department was the focus of the infection that spread across the whole of Germany? The better the country gets to know this phenomenon, the more difficult its machinations will become, the less use it will be as a public face. Anyone who has sensed that this man represents the most terrifying danger for Germany, the new Wilhelm, the new Tirpitz, the new Ludendorff, the new Hugenberg, anyone who has come to see that the policies he represents are sending us at breakneck speed into the most grandiose, most undeserved plutocracy in the history of the world, must pass on the warning, in speech and print, from armchairs and rostrums. Surprising things can happen in the destiny of nations. A general will sometimes asserts itself, a change comes from nowhere and there is a shift in the balance of power. If this should happen, then everything will depend on knowing what is needed. What is needed is a new president of the Reichsbank. With Schacht in that office we will never find peace.

No marks for Dr Schacht   18 January 1930

On 13 January of this year of grace, the Caligula of the Reichsbank, Hjalmar Schacht, once more demonstrated his outstanding qualities. Only a few hours after arriving at The Hague[51] he had the following achievements to his credit:

1. deliberately exceeding his authority;
2. carefully orchestrating a campaign to discredit his own government in front of our opponents at the negotiating table;
3. indulging in a piece of publicity for home consumption under the guise of foreign policy;
4. provoking the conference powers to pass a resolution that he, Herr Schacht, was to be ignored;
5. arousing the unanimous indignation of the whole German government leading to their decision to take up the fight against him this time;
6. setting off a storm of protest against him from all over the world and destroying the last vestiges of trust foreign countries still had in him;
7. at last antagonising wide sections of the German electorate, important parties and the media;
8. suddenly making the long-ignored demand for a change to the statutes of the Reichsbank popular and irresistible;
9. ensuring that our opponents at the negotiating table agreed to such a change to the statutes;
10. at last convincing even the farthest corners of the country, by such grotesque and unintended results, that he is unsuitable for important missions, while giving new grounds to the suspicion that there are pathological elements in his make-up.

As an opponent of Schacht, one can only express one's gratitude for his support. It is truly moving, such industrious cooperation surpasses all expectation!

In order not to get bogged down in generalities, which Schacht and his lackeys love to indulge in, let us start by examining what we might call the legal position. First let it be noted that the letter to the chairman of the committee, Reynolds,[52] which unleashed this beneficial world-wide hurricane, was written on 31 December 1929, that is, on a day on which Schacht had already absolutely refused to go to The Hague as a German delegate. The offer had been made. He had refused. He graciously agreed to be involved as expert adviser for one particular topic alone, the organisation of the Bank for International Settlements. And that was simply a matter of technical preparation. The conclusions of this group of advisors were to be presented to the governments for them to use as they saw fit. The situation on that 31 December, then, was that Schacht had voluntarily declined to have anything to do with any part of the Young set-up apart from the Bank for International Settlements; and for that he had restricted himself to the role of a technical assistant for the preparatory work. Despite all this, on that 31 December he wrote the letter in which he went into questions, the ex officio responsibility for which had been offered him, but he had declined. He made the line he would take on the banking subcommittee dependent on certain changes to the original Hague Protocols, on changes to the liquidation agreements with England and Poland,[53] on securities against future sanctions – on matters, that is, that did not have anything at all to do with the Bank for International Settlements. He could have quite legitimately dealt with all these issues if, as the government had begged him, he had gone to The Hague as an official delegate. Since he had said no, for whatever reason, and since other negotiators had been chosen to deal with those questions, he was once more sticking his fingers in a pie which, by his own decision, was none of his business. Once more he was worming his way – without authority, by the back door – into an area which he had only just made a song and dance about leaving.

Mr Reynolds did not reply at all. But on 13 January, when Schacht the technical assistant entered the room of the other banking assistants, he asked him straight out whether he stood by what he had written in his letter. At that point Schacht, like every newspaper reader, was aware of what the official representatives of his country had done. He knew that they had settled the question of sanctions but had not raised his other 'private' points at all. While on 31 December he might well still have believed that he, albeit without authorisation, could perhaps lead the way for the authorised German representatives, on 13 January he knew that his unauthorised private 'conditions' were in complete contradiction to the official position on these negotiations. He could still take them back. He could still explain that he would convey his personal opinions to the ministers, but that naturally the final decision would rest with them, the sole plenipotentiaries. In that case he would have done behind closed doors what he later ended up doing anyway to the amused derision of the whole world. But this stickler for discipline stuck to his guns. Despite being delegated to work on *proposals*, proposals on one particular issue, he insisted on his *conditions* on quite different issues. Despite being no more than a clerk in this situation, he treated his bosses and their intentions as if they simply did not exist and pointedly set up on his own. This was the man who, after the meeting in Paris,[54] had hurled insolent abuse at newspapers which, at a particular point in the negotiations, had recommended a different course of action to the one he favoured. That, he raged, had undermined his authority as a negotiator and harmed the German nation. How deep must his concern for the authority of the current negotiators have been when he pointedly sabotaged their efforts, not as a newspaper critic, but as a clerk, not in distant newsprint, but *in medias res*!

But did he perhaps not want to do some good for Germany? Did he perhaps think that, despite having no authority, he could still push his personal conditions through? Did he perhaps think, despite contrary decisions having been adopted in Berlin – adopted in his absence! – and despite the ten days during which his conditions had been ignored by the conference, that he might perhaps still be able to draw the official delegates of his country into his campaign? Or did he perhaps think that the banking subcommittee would make representations to Tardieu,[55] Snowden and Mrozowski[56] on its own initiative, even though his conditions were not part of its remit? And that these men, quivering with fear at Schacht's energetic display, would retrospectively discard the results of weeks and months of negotiations at The Hague and in the various cabinets which had already been signed on ceremonial parchment? Anyone who maintains that Schacht really believed all that is suggesting that his mental derangement is worse than even pessimists suspect. There is a very public argument that has been going on for weeks between the government, that is involved in the negotiations, and Schacht, who suddenly burst in on them; there are treaties signed, sealed and delivered; there are people like Tardieu and the obstinate Snowden – and there can still be discussions about alternative arrangements? Even Herr Hjalmar Schacht doesn't claim that. He just peddles the stories, well known since Cuno,[57] about certain Americans who actually approve of his stance, even though they keep quiet about it. Why was there nothing to be seen of these helpers in Paris, nothing at the first Hague meeting? Those mythical Americans, those gold mines on the moon! Is the Reichsbank allowed to discount its own bills of exchange?

There was nothing for Germany in this, none of this was being put on for Germany's sake, unless it was something contrived by a seriously disturbed mind. If there was a rational idea behind it, it can only have been that of setting up something that would whitewash him in the eyes of the whole German nation: Herr Schacht had set conditions – exceptionally important conditions – conditions which would have made the Young Plan very palatable. Unfortunately no one would listen to him, all his efforts were undermined, his good work deliberately sabotaged. One thing one can say for sure is that he expected his subterfuge to cause less of an uproar. He probably thought his letter would hardly be discussed at all; only once the government had signed everything had he intended to wave it to the German nation, as proof of his good intentions, while at the same time, resigned but patriotic, accepting the new post at the bank that was being forced on him. We are all too familiar with this distasteful double-dealing, this pathetic juggling, coming out against something while still going along with it. In this case too he refused, for patriotic reasons, to take up the post at the Bank for International Settlements, but then allowed himself, for equally patriotic reasons, to be persuaded to take on the unpatriotic post; he didn't resign, which would have been another way out – presumably, following the example of great men, 'to avoid something worse'. Yes, he would certainly have preferred 'operation whitewash' to go ahead without causing any uproar – not at home, that is, but abroad, where one has to play the man of the world, with toasts to the 'imaginative' Young Plan and interviews about the 'harmonious atmosphere'. But since Mr Reynolds – another of his secret American allies! – had been so unkind as to set off an uproar, a stormy and not at all allied uproar, and since he had insisted on immediate explanations and would not tolerate any devious temporising, the sudden darkness that descended over foreign parts was counterbalanced by all the more dazzling fireworks at home. It was not what Schacht had intended! Schacht would have won the day! The spineless Republic had let him down again!

Is this finally the end of the constant intrigues, the double-dealing, the weasel words, the manic self-importance, the scheming? Those who even today still believe it is just a technical question, a formal question, a question of the statues, are labouring under a delusion. The statutes of the Reichsbank are a very real problem and that for many reasons, above all because we must never have another Schacht. At the moment, however, everything revolves around the *person* of the president. The statutes of the Reichsbank could be even worse, but the situation might well be bearable with a different president; the statutes of the Reichsbank could be improved: with Schacht as president the situation would still be intolerable. Insofar as a change in the statutes is a prerequisite for throwing him out, they are naturally at the heart of the problem. But all those who imagine Herr Schacht can be tied down with fancy legal arrangements and thus remain in office, are deluding themselves. The very fact that he has come to be regarded throughout the world as a clown, the epitome of disreputable deviousness, means he can no longer be tolerated at an important point of contact between Germany and the world. How can he, a man who was arranging for his international reputation to be praised in the German ghetto while the most important foreign newspapers were already – even before the Hague debacle! – describing him with such harsh words as 'arrogant', 'dishonest', 'suspicious', how can he, after this new bombshell, after this new piece of duplicity, mercilessly exposed by an American of all people – how can he continue to work on the international stage without being hindered at every turn by a hundred suspicions and ironic whispers? How can the people in a world bank trust him when he only joined it after his arm had been twisted? Even if he had some reputation left in Germany, purely international considerations would make this man a burden ready for the scrap-heap.

Are the consequences of this to dissipate in wishy-washy legal formulations, as did those of the 1908 storm of protest against Wilhelm II? Is nothing to be done, apart from making him toe the line in this one particular case, by using the statutory powers to compel him to join the Bank for International Settlements, adding a clause providing for his dismissal should he break the statutes of the Reichsbank? It's bad enough that as the law stands at present he cannot be dismissed even if he does break the statutes. Hindenburg himself does not enjoy such divine rights; even for him there is a mechanism for dismissal should he break the law. But infringement of the statutes is not the danger this Caligula represents. In fact, he has hardly exceeded the rules of his own institution at all – unless his vainglorious throttling of foreign loans can be regarded as breaking paragraph 1 of the Banking Laws: for it states, with no distinction made between foreign and domestic sources of capital, that one of the three principal duties of the Reichsbank is to 'ensure the productive use of available capital.' Legal nitpickers, and there are more than enough of those in Germany, may find in that passage the means of demolishing the wretched 'advisory service' (Beratungsstelle) once and for all.

But apart from that 'interpretation', Caligula Schacht has never infringed the statutes. Even the Gold Discount Bank, from which this moraloholic evidently pockets a second, undisclosed salary beside his 340,000 marks from the Reichsbank, does not demonstrably breach any of the Reichsbank statutes. That is not what needs to be stopped, then, that is not how we can put the watchdog on a leash. The harm caused by Schacht's activities, although made possible by the power of the Reichsbank, was done in areas *outside* the Reichsbank, in politics and the wider economy, well away from the regulatory function of the Reichsbank. It was based on the citizen's right to freedom of expression and political activity, although the citizen exercising this right was immensely powerful because of his position in the Reichsbank. Dismissal for infringing the statutes would therefore only be a possibility if a paragraph were added to the statutes forbidding the president of the Reichsbank, unlike all other Germans, to indulge in any public activity or expression of opinion which was not expressly required by those statutes. Something like that could be discussed, although at best it would be a somewhat elastic provision and it would probably be impossible to find the parliamentary majority necessary for such a change to the constitution anyway. But without that, what would be the point of the milk-and-water regulation that the president of the Reichsbank must observe the statutes and can be dismissed if he infringes them?

'But the Reichsbank is meant to be independent. Despite everything, the rest of the world insists on it and surely we too must insist on it after what we went through during the inflation? So how can the president be made subject to outside interference?' This question is a stumbling block even for dyed-in-the-wool Schacht-haters. Even in governmental circles this secret seems to paralyse their power of decision. Has no one yet realised that in this context there are two quite distinct dimensions to the word 'independence'?

The independence we need, the independence that will protect us from another bout of inflation, resides in the series of regulations that forbid the Reichsbank from purchasing government bonds and bills of exchange or to lend it more that 100 million. The opposite situation was the cause of the collapse of the currency. These new regulations prevent it. Never again can the Reichsbank, never again will the Reichsbank help the government out by printing money.

But alongside this independence in affairs of monetary policy, there is also an institutional independence: the autonomy and immunity to dismissal of the president and the interpolation of an autonomous and similarly immune committee to appoint the undismissable president. This institutional arrangement was seen as strengthening the Reichbank's independence in monetary matters, as an exceptional safeguard after an exceptional aberration. But it is precisely the German example which should have taught us how little use this independence is as protection against inflation. It was not post-Dawes that the immunity to dismissal of the Reichsbank president was introduced, but in 1922 – to protect the currency! It was in that year that, in order to bolster his authority vis-à-vis the government, legislation was introduced making Havenstein[58] president of the Reichsbank for life. And still we had the apocalyptic frenzy the following year. So experience does not suggest there is any value in this institutional safeguard. And rational consideration brings us to the same conclusion. A government is either determined to respect its laws and international obligations, or it is determined to break them. If it is going to respect them, then it cannot make holes in the banking laws. If it is going to break them, it won't be put off by the institutional obstacles. It is neither more difficult nor more dangerous, nor will it have more serious consequences for a government, to infringe institutional arrangements by chucking the president out, than to renege on its international obligations by forcing the bank to print money. It was at The Hague that the time had come to make this clear. The mood was favourable from the very first day and completely open to it after Schacht's escapades. Will it be exploited? Will they be bold enough to accept the challenge which their opponent had no compunction about throwing down openly? Will they offer further safeguards in monetary matters as a quid pro quo for the ceremonial abolishment of the bank's institutional independence?

As this is being written, no one can see clearly what the delegation and the government are planning, what they are trying to achieve. If that should be less than the elimination of all this humbug about personal autonomy, the elimination of the president's divine status, the elimination of all this palaver with the supervisory board, then it will be less than is necessary, also less than reliable opinion suggests is achievable; it would also raise many questions about whether a treaty which quite unnecessarily leaves so many important problems with such poor solutions deserves to be ratified at all.

The Liberation of the Reichsbank   15 March 1930

So that's it! The pen that has spent months in the front line fighting against him can withdraw to the idyllic pastures of the obituary. For the man who is leaving us is a dead man. He resigned, like Ludendorff after the 1923 putsch. Now and then, here and there, we will still hear little stories about him, but as a factor in the corridors of power Doctor Schacht is finished, both as a real factor and as an illusory one. Some people refuse to believe it. They fear that he still has an ace up his sleeve, that some intrigue, some alliance, some precautionary measure prepared in advance will soon come to light which will transform the apparent downfall into a triumph. They are wrong.

All the things this pathologically ambitious man ever managed to plan were a thousand times easier to accomplish from the springboard of the Reichsbank, with the instrument of the Reichsbank firmly in his grip, than as a private individual. It is impossible to think of any project the preparation for which would have been hindered by the fact that the man pursuing it also had the resources of the central financial institution at his disposal. It is absurd to imagine that a fight would have a greater chance of success if it opened with the surrender of weapons that had already been captured. Schacht-out-of-office is only a shadow of Schacht-in-office. In reality he is only a tiny fragment of what he was until a few days ago. And what is he in the imagination – not in his own, of course, but in that of his contemporaries? He must have felt it when his last ploy, the ploy of offering his resignation, failed so utterly; and he will feel it even more strongly in future. For it was on lost illusions that he came to grief.

Uproar in America, protests from Washington, from financial circles in New York – that is what this Morgan-toady expected when he wired his intention to resign to Owen Young on 20 February. Uproar in Germany, pleas from industry and commerce, from politicians – that was what this saviour of the Fatherland expected when he set off the bomb a second time at the central committee of the Reichsbank. If it worked he would be able to set conditions for his patriotic self-sacrifice of remaining in office – so-called 'indispensable' conditions – and take one more step towards omnipotence. But those in whose faith in him he still put his faith, had lost their faith. The illusions, about which this illusionist still harboured illusions, had vanished at the sight of his latest posturing, blown away in the icy wind of the irrefutable indictment. Just as an employee who, imagining he is irreplaceable and believing his resignation to be the ultimate threat, is stunned to hear his boss say, 'Fine, off you go, then,' so Schacht was stunned to see his resignation accepted, without cries of despair, without uproar, with no attempts to persuade him to change his mind – politely, coolly, indifferently. Five minutes later his successor had been chosen, they didn't even bother with the ceremonial details.

What effectiveness can a man still possess who had so wasted the nimbus that used to surround him, that the sighs of relief when he left were clearly audible? What new nimbus can form round him, after the failure of this last ploy, after the laughing stock he became by shooting himself in the foot? The man is dead. Dead and buried. Tripped up in the ever more complicated net of his subtle scheming. He can replace Hugenberg's financial wheeler-dealer Bang. He can wallow in the hysteria of some nationalist sect or other in some old- or new-fashioned Tannenberg League.[59] He has nothing more to give on the big stage: his asset, the Reichsbank, gone; the bubble of his international reputation burst; finished for the great, finished for the small; fooled by the ghosts of delusion – sliding down into the shades of has-beendom, to join Wilhelm and Erich who went before him.

There is one danger that the man who comes after him – in better health than Schacht, smarter and more stable – will not succumb to: the danger that Schacht's influence will continue. Since Luther used the Enabling Law to make economic policy, since he had discussions with the most powerful men on the globe during his time as Chancellor, he belongs to the elite and he knows it. There will not be a repeat of the Helfferich/Havenstein case. Herr Luther does not share powers he already has; he will not turn himself into an acolyte when he is the undismissable ruler. It is another danger that threatens both him and us, the danger that his political ambition too will see the Reichsbank as a mere intermediate station, rather than a final destination. He was never a politician in the sense of a party apparatchik, has never identified entirely with any party line. But since he appeared on the scene, he has striven energetically and single-mindedly for power within the state, for the extension of his political influence. Moreover the president of the Reichsbank has very little to do; his day's work can be done in two or three hours and it must be sheer torture for an active person to have to restrict himself to this expected lofty inactivity. That this temptation, which is inherent in the nature of the position, coincides with the temptation inherent in his own character – that is the cloud hanging over the head of the new president.

A repeat of the Schacht case is not impossible, a repeat of the adulteration of the bank's aims with private aims, of a perversion of the institution, whose interests its head is supposed to serve, into an institution to serve the interests of its head. The question is, will Dr Luther be content with what he has; will he see this as the summit of his ambitions; will the attraction of the eminent appointment for life, the high income, the important task seem sufficiently fulfilling to the 50-year-old so that he will forget dreams of higher things and avoid the risky ventures his predecessor praised? If he does, he could be the man we need. For touches of originality, strokes of genius, heroics are not what is required of the head of the Reichsbank. By selecting an economic outsider, a novice in matters of banking, credit and the business cycle, those who chose him voted against the fiction that was maintained for so long in the case of Schacht: against the fiction that the head of a president of a central bank must have been anointed with divine grace, and that, therefore, Schacht's head must have been thus anointed. The choice of Luther signifies a return to the principle that the president is a civil servant, evidence that a good organiser with an open mind and a stable temperament is sufficient to deal with the few technical matters that lie within the remit of a central bank. Whatever theories are concocted in the future, for the moment we are sticking to the principle that the central banks of all countries have nothing more to do than to pull a few levers: lower bank rate when money is constantly on offer, raise bank rate when money is constantly in demand; sell off gold when the exchange rate goes down, buy in gold when the exchange rate goes up; make credit available during an economic downturn, restrict credit when the economy is overheated. Neither a Solomon nor a Ricardo is needed for that; 'that' is basically protecting the currency, which shallow propagandists liked to make into a kind of Zeileis mystery;[60] 'that' is also the 'confidence from abroad', which depends on the honest and exclusive way the institution is run, not on the person of the president and least of all on his self-praise.

A so-called genius can only demonstrate that he is one when he does not cross the prescribed boundaries which, in reality, do not demand genius, when he involves the Bank in things which are none of its business: public finance, foreign loans, share prices and whatever else. It is precisely this that must come to an end. If Luther does manage to put an end to this period of presumptuousness, if he restricts himself to his proper task of setting the rules, he will— although he doesn't come from an economic background and although no economic diamonds have been polished in his intellectual workshop – prove to be an excellent president of the Reichsbank. Let us watch and wait.

An imaginary speech by Brüning   20 September 1930

After the resignation of the Müller cabinet in March 1930, President Hindenburg, at Schleicher's suggestion, gave the Centre Party leader, Heinrich Brüning, the task of forming a government. Brüning did not even try to form a government with a parliamentary majority. The 'Hindenburg cabinet' left no one in any doubt that parliament would be dissolved and laws passed by emergency decree if the Reichstag should pass a vote of no confidence or reject proposed legislation. Initially this threat proved successful: tax legislation and an agricultural programme were passed by the Reichstag and a motion of no confidence from the SPD and KPD failed. But in July 1930 there came a trial of strength which Brüning lost. Despite his threat to use Article 48 of the constitution, which gave him emergency powers, his bill to stabilise the country's budget, which followed a rigorous deflationary policy, was rejected by 256 votes to 193. The emergency decree, to enforce adoption of this law, was likewise rejected two days later, which led to the Reichstag being dissolved once again. At the elections held on 14 September 1930 the middle-class and left-wing parties lost a considerable share of their vote, all of which went to the extremist parties. The NSDAP increased its vote from a bare 800,000 (2 per cent of the votes cast, 12 seats) to over 6.4 million (18 per cent) and with 107 seats became the second largest party in the Reichstag after the SPD. Brüning's cabinet remained in office, but could no longer count on the support of former allies such as the DVP. The SPD, however, decided to continue to tolerate Brüning in order to support the fragile coalition in Prussia (Centre Party and DDP under the Social Democrat prime minister Otto Braun). More determined opposition by the SPD might well have been capable of preventing the 'presidential cabinets' and the steady erosion of democratic standards.

The economic situation in Germany deteriorated rapidly after the winter of 1929/30. Unemployment rose from 1.3 million in September 1929 to 3.3 million a year later and reached 4.3 million by September 1931, an unemployment rate of about 23 per cent. In 1932 the German national income was 42 per cent below the level of 1929, while in Britain it only fell by 15 per cent and in France by 16 per cent. The USA, however, was as badly hit as Germany (minus 40 per cent). The budget deficit rose accordingly, reaching 1.1 billion Reichsmarks in the financial year 1931, about 1.6 per cent of gross domestic product, and threatening to rise even further. The comatose German capital markets made it increasingly difficult to finance the budget deficit through bond issuance. Brüning therefore cut back government spending even more stringently, with the result that between 1928 and 1932 it fell by 25 per cent, from 8.4 billion Reichsmarks to 6.3 billion. It is no surprise that such a slump in demand made the deflationary trend even worse. Given rising unemployment, the deficits of the Unemployment Insurance Office (Arbeitslosenversicherungsanstalt), which had already caused difficulties for the Müller cabinet, were naturally a particular problem. The Ministry of Finance therefore proposed to eliminate the government subsidy to the Unemployment Insurance Office and to raise instead workers' and employers' contributions by 2 per cent to 6.5 per cent of gross wages. One year previously the grand coalition had collapsed over a 0.25 per cent increase. In the subsequent debate in the Reichstag, Brüning declared that it was not his intention to reduce real wages in Germany at all costs, but he pointed out that given international deflation, a parallel price adjustment in Germany was unavoidable. In his speech in the Reichstag Brüning expressly linked his foreign and economic policy. Only if Germany could 'put her own house in order' could she profit from the measures which were available by treaty 'to counter danger to the economy and currency'. Here Brüning was alluding to the right granted to Germany in the Young Plan to apply for a moratorium on those parts of the reparations payments which could be deferred, if the economic situation should justify it. However, by 'putting their own house in order' Brüning understood bringing about German inability to pay, which he hoped would lead to the reparations payments being abolished altogether. As he admitted years later in his memoirs, he was prepared to accept an even worse depression to achieve that.

After the disappointment of the grand coalition, which had not shown the energy necessary to push through the economic programme it had presented to parliament, Brüning's recovery programme was implemented by emergency decree on 1 December 1930 and was approved by the Reichstag by 293 to 253 votes, the support of the Social Democrats guaranteeing Brüning the necessary majority.

An Imaginary Speech by Brüning   20 September 1930

Ladies and gentlemen.

When a new cabinet presents itself to parliament, it is usual for it to begin by thanking its predecessors. Since I am succeeding myself, I am relieved of a duty I would find it impossible to fulfil. (Ironic applause.) As you can see, honourable members, at least we are agreed on that. Although I am sure the elections were not simply a response to the mistakes of the previous cabinet, we clearly did make bad mistakes. But I would hope that the openness with which I admit this here today will show that we are determined to use a different language from now on, a courageous and open language, both among ourselves and to others; I hope it will also show that we have learnt the lesson of these elections. What this lesson is can be quickly said. The previous government considered reforms which, had they been carried through, would certainly have improved conditions. I still believe that today. But the mistake we made was in judging the pace at which we allowed ourselves to work. We underestimated the degree of despair that had already taken hold of the starving sections of the population; and we overestimated the readiness of those who were suffering and apprehensive to take on trust our preparations and public announcements. That was our main mistake and in it lies our main lesson. We no longer have the time, honourable members, to proceed at the careful, measured pace at which, under normal conditions, a government ought to introduce far-reaching measures. We are compelled to make our decisions as quickly as possible, even at the danger of it later being said of some measures that we could have devised something better. We are furthermore compelled to make the period between our decisions and their embodiment in legislation as short as possible, even at the danger of temporarily having to replace normal parliamentary procedures with a summary process. These are the first conclusions, as regards practical politics, that we must draw from the result of the elections.

But in starting by bringing to the notice of the House the overriding importance of the time factor, I am getting ahead of myself; first of all I need to explain how the government, which was announced yesterday, came to be formed. Permit me to take you through the thoughts I presented to the President on the day after the election. On that day the situation was that the parties which describe themselves as 'revolutionary' had received a total of 39 per cent of the vote: the Communists have 13.3 per cent, the National Socialists 18.7 per cent (Interruption: 'Until next time!') – you will see in a minute that I, too, think things will fortunately be different next time – and the German National Party 7 per cent. If 39 per cent of an electorate have declared war on the state in which they live, then that is without doubt an extremely explosive situation, a situation which can lead to all sorts of surprises, especially when this huge minority is better organised than the majority. For the moment, however, we must consider the fact that the revolutionary minority of 39 per cent is faced by a non-revolutionary majority of 61 per cent which, therefore, has a better claim to represent the will of the state. (Interruption: 'Are they of one mind?') The honourable gentleman's sharp eye has spotted the point at issue. Even his minority is not of one mind when it comes to doing anything other than putting a spoke in someone else's wheel. As will be seen, as soon as they have to do something positive, they will split into two bitterly hostile groups of 26 per cent and 13 per cent. But the question 'Are they of one mind?' is certainly justified in relation to the numerically substantial but substantially divided majority. Well, what I suggested to the President was to make that question the object of a practical experiment. If you like, the cabinet I am introducing to you today is the living embodiment of that question.

That the question had to be posed in the form of a *fait accompli*, honourable members, was the second necessary decision with which I presented the President. After the unfortunate experiences we have had over the last few years, it seemed to me pointless simply to say, 'Despite everything, we could – we must – try to form a non-revolutionary majority,' and then hawk the idea round the parties: 'Wouldn't you like to join us? What are your demands?' At times the amount of political good sense demonstrated by earlier episodes of this kind came so close to zero as to seriously undermine my belief in democracy. (Interruption: 'Why do you still believe in democracy, then?') When I look at you, I see I have no other choice. (Commotion) So I felt that all I could expect from setting in motion the cumbersome machinery of party bargaining, arousing all the parties' desires and sparking off a competitive hullabaloo between the various parties' programmes, was complications. In a situation such as we are faced with today, in which at least six parties – some of them quite small and unsure of themselves – have to be brought together to produce a majority of a little over 50 per cent, in such a situation it seemed to me very much doubtful whether the old ritual of negotiation would lead to a successful outcome. At the very least this method – and that was the second reason for creating a *fait accompli* – would have taken a long time. Finally, I suggested to the President that the despised spectacle of weeks and weeks of haggling to and fro, flogged to death in all the newspapers, would itself be a cause of further radicalisation, while the sole task facing the new government was to combat the causes of the radicalisation that had already taken place. (Interruption: 'You won't succeed.') I know you'll do your best to prevent that.

The consequence of all this was that the Centre Party and the Social Democratic Party (widespread commotion) would have to form the skeleton of the new government and we would have to leave it to the other groups to decide whether and in what way they would join the front formed by these two great powers for the defence of the Republic. (Noise. Shout: 'But you chucked the lefties out.') Honourable members, I will talk about my previous and present attitude to the Social Democratic Party at a later point and with all the openness I promised earlier. First of all allow me to continue my description of what we might call the historical development. After this discussion with the President, I summoned the prime minister of Prussia, Otto Braun,[61] as representative of the Social Democratic Party. Herr Braun was convinced of the need for a joint effort by our two parties, but he strongly resisted becoming personally involved. His reason for that – and we all know too well how true this is – was his indispensability within the present coalition governing Prussia. But he himself had to admit that he could not think of another figure he could approach in his party with the kind of authority that is most urgently needed for the task at hand. It was a struggle to persuade him to take on the immense amount of extra work he will have to take on if, as well as being prime minister of Prussia, he is now to run the ministry of the interior and take over the role of deputy chancellor.

As you can see, honourable members, the cabinet stands before you as an actual fact, resting on two towers: the Centre and the Social Democrats, ready to let any suitable party share its work, but not ready to bargain with anyone about personalities or programmes. The basic features of the programme, which we must carry through with all possible speed, have been agreed between the leaders of the two largest parties – the forces that are indispensable for the emergency programme of economic recovery have settled on the course. That leaves you with the question whether you are willing to grant us your allegiance, which means supporting us, or are unwilling to support us. It is just the initial recovery measures that you will have to accept immediately, without changes, without prior discussion. If you reject them, I herewith formally announce that they will be brought into force using Article 48, which was never more justified than at this moment. (Uproar lasting several minutes. Herr Thälmann:[62] 'What do the Social Democrats say to that? Where are their constitutional principles?') Gentlemen, gentlemen, I am not the Social Democrats' spokesman and you are aware that there were strong differences of opinion between us regarding Article 48. But is it surprising that even those who did not recognise the danger to public order when confronted with the previous parliament, should have changed their minds seeing this new parliament? We will regard your attitude towards the initial recovery measures as a test to see whether it is at all possible to make one last attempt. If you reject them they will, I repeat, be promulgated as emergency decrees under Article 48. If you insist on annulling this presidential emergency decree as well, our conclusion will be that this last attempt to counter the exceptional mood of the nation, which showed itself so alarmingly in the last elections, by speedy and energetic action to deal with its material causes, has failed.

There is, honourable members, a theory of 'self-destruction'. According to it radicals should be allowed to come to power so that they will show that 'they can't do it any better, either', so that they will be shown to have 'run out of ideas' and will suffer an inglorious defeat of their own at the next election. The theory has its attractions, honourable members, but in our particular case it is too reckless. (Interruption: 'Weren't you being reckless when you explored the possibility of a coalition of the moderate parties with Treviranus?')[63] What would be the point of experience if one weren't permitted to make use of it? Moreover – and here I am returning to the question of my relationship with the Social Democrats – moreover there is a difference between the attitude I take towards a partner, even if I intend to separate from him, and that towards an enemy who makes no bones about wanting to destroy me. The previous administration believed it ought to carry on for a while without the Social Democrats. It considered a coalition without the Social Democrats to be more internally homogeneous, that is, better capable of acting more swiftly and more decisively; finally, given the mood widespread in certain circles, it seemed to be less 'suspicious' and therefore less inhibited. But, honourable members, there is a fundamental difference between separating from a partner of many years with a feeling of mutual respect, in order to try and go my own way for a while, and inviting a mortal enemy of many years into my house and entrusting him with the greater part of my goods and chattels in the hope that he will be nice. The gentlemen on the other side of the house will confirm that they have absolutely no intention of being nice (Cries of 'Quite right,' from the National Socialists) and I think I am justified in saying that they are quite incapable of being nice. For they would have to give something to their supporters, whom they have won over with such unbridled promises, and as their coalition partners, we would be presented with the choice of either refusing them that something – and then they would always be able to point to that and there would be no talk of them having 'run out of ideas' – or granting it to them, and we think too much of Germany for that. (Uproar among the National Socialists)

Let me put it this way: whether we governed with or without the Social Democrats a few months ago was a question of practicalities; whether we ought now to govern with or without the National Socialists is perhaps a question of life and death. The moment we recognise this party – which we consider a passing phenomenon – as being what you might call socially acceptable, we transform its transitory existence into a permanent one. It will become profitable for civil servants, members of the armed forces and the police to belong to that party, and when a movement can take root in the fruitful soil of personal interest and profit, then even the absolute lack of real ideas, which under other circumstances would mean it would quickly wither away again, is replaced by the nourishing dung of these material interests. We consider the Social Democratic Party, with which we have significant differences, a well-founded organisation and a permanent feature of political life here, we recognise its right to exist, even when we believe we must follow a different course. We do not consider the National Socialist Party a well-founded organisation, but one that is susceptible to a return to the void from whence it came, and therefore we refuse to grant it the recognition, that collaboration with us would bring and give it the opportunity of establishing itself. That, honourable members, explains why we parted company with the Social Democrats a few months ago and why, now that the situation has changed immeasurably, we are joining forces with them again. And that also explains why we refuse to go along with the 'theory of self-destruction'. I would ask those who thought up this fundamentally mistaken game theory to think again and ask themselves whether they wouldn't be dragging a Trojan horse into the city which, as is well known, only became dangerous once it was inside the walls.

On the other hand, the new administration cannot bring itself to follow the suggestion that they should use their executive powers to combat the revolutionary radicalism on the left and the right. We refuse to recommend to the president that he suspend civil rights under Article 48 and on that – perfectly legal – basis dissolve those parties, confiscate their funds, ban their newspapers, bar their candidates from elections and other such dictatorial measures. I will not deny, honourable members, that I am not one of those democrats who sees our democracy as a kind of lamb whose only defence when the wolves approach, teeth bared, is to baa beseechingly. Our constitution recognises a state of danger and allows a whole series of measures to combat such danger. I am not at all against using each and every one of these measures, when and where appropriate. At the present moment, however, and in the present situation, the measures that Article 48 would allow seem to me of no use, apart from one: to promulgate laws without the approval of parliament if necessary. For, honourable members, the present situation is not a cause but an effect, an effect above all of the recession, which is threatening to get even worse, and what we have to do is to remove this cause. We have to do that by means of legislation, a whole system of legislation, and if parliament is so unreasonable as to stop us putting the legislation through quickly and in unadulterated form, then I consider it right to introduce it by decree. But I see no advantage in any other measures – at least for the moment, as the struggle is still at the ideological rather than physical stage. We must plan for the long term and in the long term prohibitions, repression and terror do not harm but demonstrably aid those against whom they are directed. Let us attack the causes – excessive prices and costs, excessive taxation and unemployment – let us make one supreme effort to give the nation better living conditions and hope for the future; the extent to which we succeed will bring about a parallel reduction in the wave of radicalism. It does not redound to the credit of previous parliaments that they did not have the energy to tackle the recession when the only point in doing so appeared to be to help the people who were its victims, not wider questions about the state and society. But at least now that the fate of our collective order is under threat, which many seem to find so much more important than the fate of individuals, we are determined to recognise what is required of us.

To meet just this one challenge is the task this government has set itself. It will keep the country running, but all its creative work, all its legislative work will be concentrated solely and exclusively on the struggle against the three horsemen of the apocalypse – excessive prices and costs, excessive taxation and unemployment. By doing that, it will not only keep potential sources of conflict to a minimum within the cabinet itself, but it hopes that such a limited programme, easier to keep free from ideological differences, can be carried through the House more quickly and with less conflict. This government regards itself as an emergency government and it is asking you to regard yourself as an emergency parliament. Germany will not lose that much if we put off all the things we so urgently desire – in the cultural, social, political, religious, educational and legal areas – for six months. History is very long, honourable members, we'll still get there in time. For the moment we must put off the splendid feats we could doubtless accomplish during the next few months (laughter) in order to focus on the more primitive details and I am sure that once that is done we will be able to set off on the road to ultimate perfection with all the more freedom and inspiration.

So now, honourable members, if you have the courage to dash the hopes of an administration that is calling on your support in such an emergency, then show it. When I step down from the rostrum, the clerks will hand out the text of the first economic recovery laws, which the finance minister will explain in more detail tomorrow. The most urgent of these laws requires the extraordinary measure of converting the short-term debts of the country – at the moment roughly 600 million, consisting of bank credit and short-term treasury bills – into a 7½ per cent bond with a maturity of 20 years. Creditors will receive bonds to cover their claim, which will even contain the possibility of further price increases and free the state from all repayments which are such a burden on this year's budget. That will release the funds to allow us to achieve a balanced budget, whatever the situation in the economy, even with the most unfavourable revenues from taxation, and devote our full attention to the larger problems. I'm sure the House will join me in welcoming the readiness of the banks, after some hesitation, to agree to convert their claims on the state into a bond. While that involves no significant material sacrifice, it does involve the sacrifice of hallowed principles and I believe it will set a good example for the way we ourselves must now proceed. For in the course of the drive for economic recovery we too – all of us, honourable members – will perhaps be asked to make non-material rather than material sacrifices: sacrifice of principles, dreams, prejudices and commitments. That is, as is well known, difficult for politicians because the so-called prestige of individuals and groups is tied to them. But I believe we will harvest greater prestige if each and every one of us declares, out loud and with pride, that that for the next few months we are leaving all that behind us for the sake of the country. I cannot say how great the shock to your principles will be when you hear of the further draft bills: the 20 per cent of every saving that will go to the servants of the state, *Länder* and municipalities who implement them on their own initiative. (Great agitation.) I hope you will not feel the end of the world is nigh when you read the third draft bill, the purpose of which is to abolish all income tax on earnings up to 4,000 marks. (Enthusiastic cries of 'Hear hear!') – Yes, honourable members, collecting taxes in that income range requires several hundred officials and if, instead, we increase some of the existing indirect taxes, we save all that at one blow. (Interruption: 'And what about the tax officials?') We will pension them off, instead of paying them their full salaries for pointless and tedious work; moreover a freeze on all new civil service and local government appointments will make it possible to reabsorb them gradually. As I said, honourable members, I don't know how great your horror will be at such revolutionary measures – or at the unheard-of proposal that all manufacturing enterprises that can prove by the end of the year that they have lowered their prices for the domestic market will be guaranteed a subsidy from the state, calculated on the amount of the reduction, to add to their dividends. (Tumultuous cries from the Communists.) Yes, honourable members, we want to get the market moving again, and that as quickly and using as many different methods as possible – (Interruption: 'What about the cost?') According to our calculations, in the medium term the cost will be less than that of unemployment benefit. (Further unrest.) Allow me a word, honourable members: we anticipated this response, it is part of our programme. We believe that, given the mood in Germany at present, the fact that the programme for economic recovery will cause a sensation in the country is very important psychologically. But since the finance minister and the minister for trade and industry will go into the draft legislation and the circumstances surrounding it at much greater length and with much greater knowledge, I will refrain from further detail and ask once more for your understanding for this historic moment.

We are faced, honourable members, with a decision. We are faced with a decision which is much harder than the decision about whether tomorrow Germany is to be governed according to this or that political programme. We, who are trying to exorcise the spirits of despair and set the mind of our nation back on the road to recovery, are convinced that the political programme that would be followed, were we to capitulate, would be disastrous. But we have to admit that it is a political programme. Germany would survive it and anything that was trampled underfoot could spring back up again after a few years. However, it is not simply a programme for

Germany's internal affairs alone which it is our task to prevent – our country's position in the political fabric of this continent will be decided over the next few months! Do not delude yourselves, the whole future not only of this country, but of the continent depends on whether the current administration in Germany can continue or whether its place will be taken by a fanatically nationalistic regime. 'It'll never get so bad that it comes to a real war' – that may well be the case, honourable members, even Herr Hitler might perhaps not proceed in such a narrow-minded manner, though he might well find it difficult to curb the spirits he has roused. But will we achieve anything by doing everything we can to exclude this ultimate and most horrible possibility because it is unthinkable? There are penultimate and equally horrible possibilities which are most assuredly bound to come about, namely infecting the whole world with precisely that selfish nationalistic spirit which bears so much of the blame for the troubles besetting the world. Do we not say every day, honourable members, that it is the excessive number of borders, the cramping of international trade within ever more confined spaces, the customs barriers, behind which nationalistic concerns lead to industries and crafts being artificially cultivated – that it is these developments which are mainly responsible for the seizing up of economic activity and the drying up of more and more means of earning a living in almost all countries? We are standing, honourable members, at a crossroads which will determine matters for centuries. We can take the road that will put us in the vanguard of dechauvinisation, a road that never offered better prospects than today – or we can take the other road, the one that will heighten distrust even more, inflate the vanities even more, make the national ghettos even more stifling. It is up to you, honourable members, to decide which of these roads we will take. The government that comes before you today is determined to work with all its passion, all its strength, to remove the mental and physical prison walls in Europe. It will also take the lead in this programme of recovery of the continent, as it has in its programme of domestic recovery; it will if necessary, if other measures get nowhere, demand popular referendums on this crucial question. If you follow our lead, you will have decided to support this programme; if you refuse to follow us, honourable members, do not deceive yourselves that you will be putting the fate of the country in the hands of those who will take it in the other direction and the curse and contempt of our children and our children's children will be upon the generation that murdered their future.

Of course, if there were to be war... 6 June 1931
The collapse 18 July 1931

In March 1931 Foreign Minister Curtius, with Brüning's approval, negotiated a German-Austrian customs union which was regarded on all sides, including the German, as the first step towards Austria's incorporation in Germany (just as the creation of the German Empire had started with a customs union). The reaction of the Western powers was furious, the League of Nations condemned the project as an infringement of the Treaty of Versailles, and Curtius' career came to an abrupt end. There was unrest on the international financial markets. Germany had raised short-term loans of more than 12 billion Reichsmarks from abroad which could be called in at any time if the mood changed for the worse. The collapse of the Austrian Creditanstalt in May, after an agricultural crisis in Eastern Europe which had lasted for years, and the withdrawal of French loans in May, there followed a series of bilateral withdrawals of credit in Central Europe, which seriously endangered German liquidity and caused regular panic among investors. By June 1931 the Reichsbank had lost over a billion of its reserves of gold and currency and was coming close to the prescribed (gold) cover limit of 40 per cent of the money in circulation. On 13 June the Reichsbank raised the bank rate by 2 per cent, but the exodus of capital simply continued since the crisis had political, not simply economic causes. Some estimates put the withdrawal from reserves during 1931 at 4.8 billion, and that despite the fact that Germany's current account balance showed a surplus of almost one billion Reichsmarks. Where was Germany to find the 1.7 billion for the annual payment under the Young Plan?

In this situation Brüning presented a new emergency decree to the nation on 5 June. 'We have reached the limit of the privations we can impose on our people,' he announced before he set about imposing further heavy burdens on the population. On the day before the visit to England discussed by Schwarzschild, he also demanded that 'Germany should be relieved of the unbearable liability of reparations.'

Following the dramatic financial crisis, which was exacerbated by the collapse of the Danat Bank in July, Brüning could record at least one success: on 1 July 1931 the Hoover moratorium on reparations payments came into effect. On 13 July Germany suspended payment of all private foreign debts and two days later went off the gold standard, the international currency system based on fixed exchange rates and convertibility into gold which had been in force, with a few interruptions shortly after the First

World War, since the late nineteenth century. At conferences in Paris (19–20 July) and London (21–23 July) the German government managed to reach an agreement to suspend repayment of an international loan of $100 million due in June 1931 and a moratorium on the repayment of short-term foreign loans. At the London conference, a commission of the BIS headed by Walter Layton (editor of The Economist) and Albert Wiggin, an American banker, was set up to analyse the state of Germany's short-term loans. Although the Wiggin-Layton Report never directly mentioned the problem of reparations, indirectly it supported the idea of a one-off final payment as the best solution for Germany's debt problem. It was indeed the case that the economic situation did not permit the punctual and complete payment of the 1931 reparations liability. However, the hopes of the Allies, above all of the British, that that would mean they would get a larger proportion of their private loans repaid, were disappointed. The drain on the currency continued. During the moratorium, which was initially limited to six months, Germany lost a further 2 billion Reichsmarks from her gold and currency reserves.

The French fear that a moratorium on payments, even if it were limited to one year, would be the beginning of the end of any kind of payments, proved to be well-founded. Britain went off the gold standard in September 1931, leading to further currency outflows from Germany and strengthening Brüning's call for a complete cancellation of all reparation payments. Following the Beneduce report by the BIS in December 1932, the Allies agreed to convene in Lausanne in July 1932 to settle once and for all bilateral private and official claims among the Allies and Germany. There the Young Plan was abandoned and Germany committed herself to the payment of a final sum of 3 billion Reichsmarks in 1935. However, the Lausanne agreement was never ratified by the Allies, and Germany stopped making any payments after 1934 (payments eventually resumed in 1995 following German reunification).

Of course, if there were to be war . . .   6 June 1931

In the course of the next few days the German chancellor will enjoy the privilege of staying in one of the most delightful and civilised country houses in Europe. He will, like so many heads of state before him, admire the historic lawn; and he will probably be filled with even greater admiration for the gesture of Lord Lee,[64] who presented the house to the nation, together with a substantial allowance, for the use of the prime minister. The radical changes in society meant it was likely that in future the highest office in England would be held by men who were not independently wealthy and he wanted to provide a place worthy to receive dignitaries and for him to relax in cultivated surroundings. The first servant of a country whose plutocrats had, since time immemorial, lacked not only any of the social graces but even the most rudimentary willingness to make sacrifices for the public good – of a country whose richest inhabitants traditionally displayed their patriotism solely by deploring the unpatriotic greed of the poor – the first servant of such a country must surely be sent into quasi-religious transports at the sight of Chequers, and even if he will not dream of mentioning them, Herr Brüning will observe this symbol of the difference between the two countries with the heightened interest one reserves for exotic sights.

Unfortunately it matters little what refreshing or instructive impressions the German leader will gather for his private hoard of memories. The nation he represents is hoping for more concrete results and nothing characterises the truly breathtaking speed at which its collapse is proceeding than the fact that the purpose his journey was originally intended to serve has already been completely forgotten. As readers will recall, the invitation was issued in March, immediately after Herr Brüning's stroke of genius: a customs union between Germany and Austria. And at the time we were living such a high life, with such high-powered ideas, that we saw no other purpose in the meeting than to steer this vital project into the safe haven of international acceptance. The concerns of March! Where are they in June? Gone, like the snows of yesteryear! In June, lashed by a new financial cyclone, even more tightly stuck in the strait between the Scylla of economic decay and the Charybdis of political cannibalism, in June it is the immediate and urgent question of the suspension, the cancellation of reparations payments which is to be discussed at Chequers. Any delay is dangerous, it must be operative by tomorrow, otherwise everything will collapse. What a country, what an elite, what a government to have no idea in March what matters will be like in June!

Now the house is on fire and Ramsay MacDonald is supposed to put it out. What influence can he have in a world of gaping deficits everywhere you look, small deficits, large deficits, and the worst – no less that four billion marks – in God's own country, which takes the lion's share of reparations. Let us hope he does have influence, more influence than a sober assessment would suggest. These are no longer the days when the campaign against reparations is the preserve of those defeated war-horses who hope to gain a belated victory by the back door, so to speak. When the world economy is in the throes of the most terrible convulsions, when we have a schedule of repayments which has no provision for differentiating between good and bad times – in such conditions things that would be bearable when business is booming are pointless torture and actual murder. It would be best for all concerned if a miracle happened and the machinery could be switched – very quickly, much more quickly than the moratorium envisaged in the Young Plan allows – to crisis mode. In politics the horrors we will be faced with if this does not come about are a vague cloud on the horizon; in the economy they are a very immediate threat. But even if this were to come about is it not true, has our Chancellor himself not said, that no one should delude himself into thinking that Germany's problems would disappear if we no longer had a pfennig of reparations to pay? And did he not say that back in December, when the domestic situation was not even remotely as bad as today? The extra burden of the annual payment of 1.7 billion on Germany's economy is just as great today as it was then, but the economy is now ailing to such an extent that one can confidently assert that even if *freed* from the burden of reparations, Germany would not be any better off than it was *with* reparations only a short while ago. What will the situation be like in a few months' time? What will it be like if the domestic economic decline, the continuing *progress* of which cannot be blamed on the political pressure *which has stayed the same* – what will it be like if the decline continues at the same pace?

This is the point at which all our illusions fade and we can see that even the swiftest and most radical reduction of reparations would mean nothing more than a *new stay of execution*, nothing more than a *return to the economic situation of the previous autumn or winter*; once more we would find ourselves on the same springboard, from which Herr Brüning fled to the ivory tower of his laissez-faire defiance, instead of taking the plunge. Once more we would have a relatively decent chance of extracting ourselves from the vicious circle of continually rising taxes and falling income, from the madness that is destroying the economy, and taking the course, which could have been taken before but which was blocked by the blind obstinacy of second-rate would-be captains of industry: to bring together in an organised fashion all the idle machinery and idle workforce. One more chance, but no more than that! Given the speed of the collapse in which we are caught up, even the *cancellation* of reparations would only mean a few months' reprieve to sort things out. If we continue to muddle along, the sentence that is hanging over us if we fail to revive economic activity will be carried out in a few months' time. Even if he were more powerful than he is, that would be beyond the power of the Master of Chequers. The decision resides with Chancellor

Brüning alone, in whose hands more power to solve this has accumulated than in the hands of any of his predecessors, and yet he refuses to use it.

Since he likes to go on about his experiences as a soldier in the trenches, since he is fired with enthusiasm for all things military, perhaps the question *What if there were to be a war tomorrow?* might appeal to him. Our Herr Brüning cannot deny that nowadays war is an industrial business, that waging war does not simply mean mobilising armies but getting every last machine working. Is the German chancellor willing to maintain that even if war were to break out tomorrow our factories would still be working at half capacity, our workforce on half time? Does he seriously think that the much-trumpeted 'lack of capital', or any of the other official reasons for the crisis, would mean that half our industrial capacity would still be lying idle, even in such an eventuality? If our chancellor does seriously believe that, then he might as well send the army and the navy to the children's playground; every pfennig he spent on it would be money thrown away. For an army which only has *half* the resources of the industrial capacity of its country behind it when the chips are down is the pitiful shadow of an army. But of course no one believes that, not even the chancellor. He knows, as we all know, that if war were to break out today, suddenly everything would be possible. Suddenly every wheel would start turning. Suddenly even women and girls would be sent to the factories as part of the 'patriotic labour service', and not without wage rises all along the line. Suddenly, despite the 'lack of capital', not only would there be uniforms, boots, blankets and kitbags to provide for those who can hardly afford a shirt today, they would also have to be equipped with those bullets, grenades, shrapnel and gas shells, whose economic function is to explode in thin air. I repeat, if that were not possible, the army would have to be pensioned off and those who keep harping on about our willingness to defend our country locked up in a lunatic asylum. But of course it is possible, it will be possible. And now my question to the Chancellor: if it is possible to organise and finance the production at maximum capacity of items which explode and disappear without trace, why is it not equally possible to organise and finance at least the medium-capacity production of goods which are highly desired and highly durable? As long as there is no proof that the piece of paper known as a declaration of war possesses some mystical economic creative power, as long as there is no proof that this piece of paper can conjure up from the bowels of the earth funds which can be conjured up by no other means – as long as that is the case, it must be accepted that what is possible for unproductive purposes must also be possible for productive ones. The sole difference lies in the will, in the intensity of the will and in the methods by which it is carried through. But is it Chancellor Brüning's opinion that trivial matters such as saving a country and resolving the most serious economic crisis of all times do not justify the same exercise of will as going to war?

It is the *will* that is lacking, that is the whole point, the whole problem and the whole shame. Today the German economy can still feed and clothe the nation, even if in the form of charity and in some sections very inadequately. The one thing that is essential is the creation of a supplement, an improvement for the inadequately fed and clothed sections. To do that we have an immense amount of extremely underused plant and land available, as well as the workforce to run and till both. And you claim that the same methods that are employed in wartime for the production of material that is to be thrown away cannot be employed to organise this tiny increase in the production of necessities? That is stupid. All the means of production are in place already, they do not have to be created, as they do in Russia. We also have most of the raw materials, and those that would have to be imported from abroad for the relatively small additional consumption could easily be paid for with the increased exports, which will be made possible by lower prices – lower prices which would result from producing in larger quantities. All that is true, it all adds up. There is just one factor missing: the government refuses to play its part. It refuses to recognise that Germany is in at least as great danger as we would be if we were at war. It refuses to calculate the amount of supplies needed and to issue directives for their production. It refuses to dictate to companies, let alone put them under state control, as Lloyd George did to more than 5,000. It refuses to do anything about the economy, apart from one thing: cutting consumers' disposable income *even* more, in order to remedy that figment of a deranged and disgruntled imagination, a 'lack of capital', thus condemning even more capital to lie fallow. And those who demand this, who persuade the government to accept it, are themselves degenerate capitalists, sclerotic capitalists wringing their hands as they bewail the fact that they cannot use their factories, their buildings and machines – that is, their capital – to full capacity, while at the same time screaming that wages and salaries must be lowered so that *even* more capital can be created – that is, even more factories, buildings and machines. There you have Germany's economic policy under Brüning. One is tempted to recall the Latin axiom: Whom the gods would destroy, they first make mad.

There is a war taking place, an economic war on all sides. Herr Brüning, to use an image close to his heart, is setting off for the front, for the Reparations Front, the importance of which must not be underestimated, it is as great as that of the Salonika Front in the World War. No one can predict how successful he will be. But no one should be in any doubt that the final decision on survival or collapse will not be made over there but in his home country. Nor should there be any doubt that everything that has happened so far – or, rather, everything that has *not* actually happened – has done nothing to slow down the collapse, only accelerated it at a feverish pace. We would love to be optimistic, but the anti-economic politician Brüning, together with his coterie of country *Junkers* and steel barons, manages to curdle even the milk of human kindness.

The Collapse   18 July 1931

I

It has happened rather more quickly than even the most miserable pessimist could have foreseen. But it was bound to happen and it has happened. When a house is full of damp and dry rot, it is impossible to say precisely when the collapse will come or at which place it will begin. That is entirely dependent on chance. The Danat case in Germany was a matter of chance, the type of phenomena that followed were a matter of chance. The collapse could just as well have followed on from some other event, could have taken some other form. But what was obvious to those with eyes to see was that the appalling economic policies pursued in this country over the last years were bound to lead inexorably to the most abysmal crash. And now it's here! Money and credit, 'the oil that lubricates the economy', are draining out like oil from a leaky engine. The parts screech as they grind against each other, some aren't even working at all, the system is threatening to fall apart *en gros* and *en détail*. We don't know what can be produced or bought tomorrow, what work or pay there will be; we don't even know how the exchange of goods between town and country, the bare provision of necessities, will function. The chaos of the final stage of deflation – different in cause, but not much different in effect to the chaos of the final stage of inflation! The machinery, workforce and raw materials are waiting – and there is *no money there* to bring them together. Do they realise what it means for a wretched technical device to plunge a nation of 65 million into despair, misery and turmoil? Do they realise what a monumentally colossal degree of stupidity was necessary to get us into this mess for that *sole* reason.

II

It is extremely difficult for anyone unacquainted with the fundamental principles of money and credit to get a clear idea of what has happened. They will never comprehend what has taken place – above all they will not realise that in the final analysis it is all about *gold*, gold that Keynes scornfully describes as 'an object of oriental splendour, it is true, and one to which Egyptian and Chaldaean bank directors attributed magical properties, but not otherwise useful in itself.'[65] Equivalent to gold is currency, that is, notes for which one receives, on request, gold from a foreign central bank. Since in economic terms they are the same thing, since the significance of currency comes from the fact that it represents gold, it will not be mentioned in what follows below, it will be subsumed in the concept of gold.

This gold, then, this object of oriental magnificence, is something that Germany has managed to lose during the last few weeks. Foreigners who had lent it to German banks against interest have been demanding it back in ever greater amounts; the banks had to hand over thousands of millions of it, out of their own stocks and those of the Reichsbank – and suddenly there was almost none of the commodity left, to which Egyptian and Chaldaean bank directors once attributed magical properties. So, what's bad about that? What difference has it made? In fact it has made *no* difference. At least it *ought* to have made no difference. Unfortunately in 1924 Germany had a bank governor called *Schacht*, who was just as Egyptian or Chaldaean as any of his predecessors on the Nile or the Euphrates. This man, who had gradually risen from a position of reporter on the *Kleines Journal* and had little comprehension of theory, recalled the ancient view that all chic money had to be 'covered' and covered by chic gold, of course. At the time Germany had a very fine and very sound currency *without* gold cover. It was, as you will remember, the Rentenmark. There was nothing behind it, it had no cover at all – the presumed cover with land and property was naturally merely a figment of the imagination. No one could go to the bank and exchange a note for land and property. It was, therefore, money that was completely uncovered, above all money that was not covered by gold – and yet it was sound money. All it lacked was the pedigree chic money ought to have, and Dr Schacht wanted the money which had the honour of being governed by him to be ever so chic. Thus in August 1924 we had the famous 'underpinning' with gold, for which purpose the so-called Dawes loan was raised, the proceeds from which were stored in the cellar of the Reichsbank in gold bars – not without a round 90 million marks having to be paid annually in interest. Suddenly our currency,

59

which until then had merely been sound, was chic. An internationally binding law was passed stating that in future for every German mark in circulation there must be 40 pfennigs of gold in the cellar of the Reichsbank. And a massive propaganda campaign drummed it into the Germans that until then they had actually had a poor currency and only now that there was, thanks to Schacht, that object of oriental splendour stored in the cellar, had it turned into something proper, something that was up to standard.

Since then, in international law and in the home-bred prejudices of the population, the mark is chained to the presence of gold. Whether the economy is booming or depressed, whether a lot of money is required or a little, there can only be two-and-a-half times as much in circulation as we have gold in the cellar. If, for whatever reason, our gold holdings decrease, then the amount of money has to be reduced correspondingly. Since, however, the supply of credit by the banks must bear a certain relation to the amount of money in circulation, that would mean credit would have to be restricted as well. Consequently every reduction in the stock of gold triggers a deflationary spiral across the board. And if it should happen that the Reichsbank had no more gold at all – a state that was not far away during these last weeks – then the last mark note actually ought to be withdrawn and the last credit cancelled. In that case people would have no choice but to return to the barter trade of prehistoric times and anyone who was hungry would have to go out into the country and see whether a kindly farmer would swap him a sack of potatoes for a pair of old boots. As long as he still has some old boots, of course. Once he has none left, he will have no choice but to lie down and starve to death, a currency martyr, resigned to his fate and comforted by the knowledge that he has not infringed the principle of gold coverage.

III

After this digression on matters of principle, it is necessary to devote some time to a survey of the course of events. The best and simplest way to do this is to follow the trail of the Egyptian bank governor, Herr Hjalmar Pharaoh Schacht. The following stages are to be noted:

1. The Egyptian bank governor ties the German currency to gold, that is to a commodity that can *only be obtained from abroad*. He guarantees that only two-and-a-half times as many marks as there is gold in the Reichsbank cellar will be in circulation in Germany. By doing that he

makes not only the currency but also the credit system – that is, *the rise and fall of the economy* – dependent on the presence of this foreign commodity.

2. Having done this, the Egyptian bank governor *prevents* this foreign commodity from coming to Germany in sufficient quantities and in a form in which it cannot be recalled. The Pharaoh that he is issues his *curse on foreign loans*, which at that time were readily available on terms of 30, 50 or 100 years. Thus he renders it impossible for the commodity, on which he has made the German economy dependent, to take up permanent residence in Germany. (He does this because otherwise it might facilitate the payment of reparations, i.e. by returning a fraction of the transferred commodity.)

3. Since the result of this is that the gold held in reserve is permanently less than the amount required for the money and credit needs of the German economy, which is booming, the banks find a way out by borrowing the same sums the Pharaoh's decree prevents them from taking up on a long-term basis, in short-term loans that can be recalled at a month's or three months' notice. The commodity, on the presence of which Schacht has made the German economy dependent, is now always available in sufficient quantities, but it can be recalled at any moment, it is insecure.

4. After things have reached this stage, the Pharaoh goes into politics, fomenting resistance and supporting the tearing-up of the treaties, thus helping to create such political tension that no capitalist is willing to leave his money in Germany. The commodity, on which he has made the German economy dependent and which he has prevented from taking up permanent residence, is driven out, since it is only here on short-term sufferance.

To sum up: four phases, none of which fits in with the others. First phase: the hoard of gold is artificially made the basis of the economy. Second phase: the hoard of gold is prevented from regenerating itself on a permanent basis. Third phase: all we are left with is a hoard of gold borrowed on a short-term basis. Fourth phase: the borrowed hoard is driven out of the country.

We could add three further phases. Fifth phase: Herr Dr Luther, the Pharaoh's successor, rushes round the world like a flying Dutchman to put together – on tick – a replacement hoard for the one that was driven out. Sixth phase: he fails; the economy, which is tied to the presence of gold, collapses. Seventh phase: having let things get this far, they go back beyond phase one and in effect delete the Chaldaean's chic creation, either by the creation of a new Rentenmark or by reducing the level of gold coverage in stages; suddenly it can be done, whereas it was impossible as long as we were just a tiny bit better off. But those are phases which have to be examined separately. What concerns us here is simply to bring out the truly sickening to'ing-and-fro'ing to no effect, economic charlatanism whose perniciousness is only surpassed by its brazenness.

IV

Of course, during the last year Herr Schacht has been too powerless for his chauvinistic but broken trumpet, with which he hoped to gather a new squadron of old war-horses round him, to have much effect on its own. Our German Cincinnatus on his pig-farm in Finow was only one voice among the Hitlers, Hugenbergs, Seldtes,[66] Seeckts,[67] Mackensens[68] and all the rest of the private freedom fighters. Yet this whole band, for all its nuisance value, would not have set the world's nerves jangling to such a degree that it eventually resulted in the most turbulent capital flight from German investments, if the German government *itself* had not taken the stage in a similar role. What point is there in denying, even today, that once again they set out on the grand venture of erasing the defeat of the World War and undoing its effects in at least four areas: the effects of reparations in the financial sphere; of the restrictions on the army in the military sphere; of the Polish border in the territorial sphere; of the prohibition of an *Anschluss* with Austria in the national sphere? And what point is there in deluding ourselves about the fact that the result of these policies – which took us in theory to the very brink of a war which in practice we were incapable of waging – is the same as that of similar policies pursued by Herr Cuno, with the one difference that the latter ended in hyperinflation, the former in hyper-deflation? It is an absolute mystery how anyone could expect such policies to be successful. It is simply impossible to imagine what is going on inside the heads that produced them. There are only two assumptions on which they could have based them: either that France and Poland would *voluntarily* relinquish the factors which assure them the material superiority over Germany that they gained in the World War; or that the *other great powers* would exert such unbearable pressure on the two countries that they would simply be forced to concede. It is impossible to assume that anyone really expected them to give way voluntarily; it was precisely the most virulent revisionist section of the press which repeated 20 times a day that France, like the tyrant she was, insisted on her material power and was the untameable wolf of Europe; how could such views be compatible with the expectation that she would suddenly and of her own free will behave not like a wolf, but like a dove? And how could even those who had a more accurate view of our neighbour beyond the Vosges imagine that France would voluntarily give up some of her power at the very moment when she felt, in view of developments in Germany, that she needed that power more than ever? It is inconceivable that ministers could have harboured such an ultra-pacifist view of France and Poland.

That leaves the confident expectation that 'the world' would help us, that the great powers would put pressure on France so that she would feel the need to escape from her 'isolation'. We admit that we ourselves believe that in the spring of 1930, at the start of the 'new dynamics', the hopes placed on 'the world' were not entirely illusory.

Was even this second expectation not shown to be false in the spring of 1931? Had it not by then become apparent that in the turmoil of the world economic crisis every country was crying out for peace and quiet, no new crises, for God's sake ? Had not even Mussolini, who until then had certainly not been averse to kicking up a fuss, become the quietest, most unassuming, most warm-hearted, most categorically pacifist of Europeans? Had they not seen that the disturbance caused by the announcement of the customs union had roused all governments to unanimous opposition? Was it not obvious that no support could be expected for any movement, any campaign that was aimed at overturning *another* aspect of the world order, at setting off *another* landslide, at adding *even more* unrest to what there was already? They didn't see it until they found themselves confronted with the complete opposite of what they had hoped for: the general exhortation from London, Washington and even Rome to satisfy France's political aims was not evidence of anti-Versailles pressure on France, but of pro-Versailles pressure on Germany. It is not France that is having her arm twisted to give Germany another item of her war booty, it is Germany that is having her arm twisted to switch off her campaign for revision and give pledges that she will not start it up again in the foreseeable future.

That is the outcome of a campaign that was a straightforward repetition of the Ruhr conflict and led to the same result. 1918 – 1923 – 1931 – the same war undertaken with insufficient forces for a completely unattainable goal. Economic catastrophe the dark and bitter end. Germany totally isolated. With no alternative but to sue for peace under much worse conditions than would have been obtainable only a few weeks earlier. Not to mention the good fortune that we hadn't plunged into the hopeless war at all!

V

But even the campaign for revision would not have been enough in itself to take us to the peak of this catastrophe, to the abyss of this economic apoplectic seizure, if it had not been accompanied by scandalous, hare-brained policies that amounted to internal self-mutilation. In fact foreign and economic policy seemed to be vying with each other in a race to see which could ruin Germany sooner, and it is difficult to say now which of them deserves the prize. They were both lightning-fast horses, with riders who gave their all. The nature of the economic policies has so often been described in these pages and we have so often, and with growing certainty, explained why they are bound to end in a terrible collapse, that no lengthy repeats are necessary. A brief summary will suffice:

1. The healthy parts of the economy have been starved of funds in order to maintain the feudal power of the owners of hopelessly uneconomic large estates.
2. The healthy limbs of the economy have been subjected to further constant bloodletting in order to preserve the plutocratic power of the owners of our hopelessly uneconomic heavy industry.
3. Despite the fact that the country has an unprecedented wealth of machines hungry to produce and people hungry to buy, no attempt has been made to bring the two together; on the contrary, repeated reductions in wage income have curbed sales more and more, thus tearing people and machines ever further apart. Instead, preference has been given to the 'accumulation of capital'; in theory that ought to have meant investment in more idle machines, in practice it meant setting up accounts worth billions with banks abroad.

Year by year each one of these gigantic operations has done infinitely more harm to the German economy and its output than the annual amount of reparations. These operations, all of which are a German speciality, are the reason why the German situation is not comparable to that of any other country. They blame the world economic crisis, but there is a difference between the difficult conditions in many other countries and the horrendous collapse we are experiencing. This difference is almost entirely due to the consequences of our foreign and economic policy summarised above. I would estimate the reduction in income resulting from the three operations I described to be at least 10 to 12 billion marks a year – a reduction, that is, in income *over and above* that caused by the world economic crisis and brought about solely by our own wrong economic policies. On top of that comes the flight of capital resulting from the psychologically unnerving combination of a worrying foreign policy and an ever more discredited economic situation; 7–8 billion of gold has gone, probably a third of that German capital, two-thirds foreign loans. Add the amounts together and compare the result to the 1.7 billion of reparations, the third special case affecting Germany. Anyone who can read, anyone who can understand will see that almost everything in the German crisis that goes beyond the world crisis was self-inflicted and avoidable.

VI

There is no doubt that a wrong solution will be found. Already they are taking sides in the most stupid manner imaginable. For weeks now we have been arguing, with Cassandra-like despair, that the wheel of misfortune can only be stopped by an increased supply of credit and an increased amount of money in circulation – n.b. if it is properly used: for consumption. At the time the Reichsbank still had its full complement of gold and the operation would have been possible without the coverage ratio dropping below the formal minimum. Later, but still long before the final collapse, they were told again and again in these pages how incredibly suicidal it was to insist on sticking to their superstitious belief in gold and jettison the economy rather than the principle. At that time it couldn't be done. Impossible! Madness! Bolshevism! But now that the economy has suffered its apoplectic seizure, it suddenly can be done – because it has to be done. Call it what you will, Rentenmark, *Binnenmark*,[69] lowering of the minimum coverage ratio, it all comes down to the same thing, liberation from the gold standard, something all Herr Luther's flights round the world could not achieve.

But as this gradually becomes clear, the belated, correct understanding is already being placed on blighted, rotting foundations. Since a currency liberated from gold would put an end to our dependence on foreign countries, since it is a domestic matter, many see it as something that relieves us of the need to make any change at all in our foreign policy. Off the gold standard? Then we don't need the nasty world outside any longer, then we can go on playing at 'new dynamics', then we can go on holding parades, then we can go on pursuing the economic policies that were so efficient at increasing the general impoverishment, the better to prepare for a dictatorship, then we can go on collecting the destructive domestic levies to support big estates and heavy industry! A fantastic invention! Let's do it! On the other side, suspecting this turn of events, is the correspondingly wrong opposite position. Of course we can't stick to the minimum gold cover at the moment. But we should only breach it a little bit, now of all times the demand for money must be kept below its customary level, we must get back to the gold standard as soon as possible, we must get more gold as soon as possible. What kind of reasoning is that! Is gold the only thing that connects us with the outside world? Are there not other links to it, apart from the one that runs through the cellar of the Reichsbank? Does the abandonment of the gold standard give us carte blanche for a suicidal foreign policy, for a perverse, flagellant way of running the economy? Is the gold standard a barrier to warmongering, to poisoning the international atmosphere and starving our own nation? In this country the clearest things become murky.

Our economy is a house that is rotten through and through. The cause is a combination of an obstinate foreign policy and an obstinate economic policy. By chance the first part to collapse was the wing housing the system of money and credit. It is now to be restored and the means of doing this is literally paper. But that does nothing to alter the fact that the house is rotten and if the causes are not addressed, another wing will come down with another loud crash in the near future. Renovation is not renovation if the root causes are not treated. The causes were there while we still had gold and they will remain as long as we do nothing apart from declaring our independence from gold. What an abysmal level of debate!

VII What level of debate?

We would be overlooking the decisive point if we did not bring up the question of whether Germany has any prospect at all of better times under the men who are in charge of its fate. It is not the government we are talking about here, although its mistakes, both great and small, are among the worst things ever done by any government to any country. Nor is it the President of the Reichsbank we are talking about who, entering on new terrain as a 50-year-old, was no more helpless when faced with anomalous events than might reasonably be expected. What we are talking about is the power elite as a whole, those 100 or 200 men who, in practice and usually without an official position, control events. I am not passing judgement on the intellectual level of the German nation in general, one never knows what is going on underneath the surface. Despite the pessimistic tones we are starting to hear from many university professors, despite the laments about the increasingly disastrous lack of talented newcomers in almost all areas, it is possible that the regenerative power of the nation as a whole has simply shifted to sections where it is invisible for the moment. We don't know, we can't check, we can simply hope.

But who could fail to see that among the so-called upper classes the intellectual level is lower than in Germany's halcyon days and lower than it still is in most countries? And, above all, who could fail to see that the thin stratum of those who ultimately have the decisive voice has failed miserably, as miserably as could be imagined, in its response to each and every difficult question it has been faced with over the last 20 years? It is not just the second generation, not just the generation of the heirs, for whom there is really no other designation than 'dim'.[70] They have co-opted people who match them, forming a whole class of diadochi whose intellects are too dull, whose education too slight, whose imagination too poor to be able effectively to accomplish what they need to accomplish. They helped bring about the war. They stopped us bringing the war to an end at the right time and with fewer losses – the proof is enshrined for ever in their memoranda about Longwy and Briey.[71] They thought the inflation and the resistance to the French occupation of the Ruhr were strokes of genius. They made wrong investments all along the line. They supported Herr Schacht's risky ventures, as well as those of Hitler and Seldte. With plant lying idle, they issued calls to curtail demand – simply a recipe for economic paralysis. They supported the crazy agricultural policies, they financed the propaganda campaign against France, they piled up debts that can never be repaid and in none of their supervisory boards did they have any idea what was really going on – is there a more complete record of incompetence, a more demonstrably abysmal level of intelligence than that of these people, whose fingers spin the thread of Germany's fate?

Unfortunately no one knows where we might find better successors. It is only logical that another of the achievements of these gentlemen is that those next in line, whom they have put there themselves, are *even* worse than their superiors. Even blanker expressions, even more vacant stares, their so-called thinking of even more block-headed banality. What we do have to accept, and shudder at the thought, is that with such an 'elite', with such a clique of sub-mediocrities as leaders, the nation has been sold down the river. It is still the head, not any other instrument, that rules the world, and it is an illusion that Germany's ruling class is equipped with that part of the body. It is physically, but that is not enough. At most it can be used for hitting against brick walls. As long as that is the kind of 'elite' we have, the prospects look bleak for the country and its people.

Hail Adolf   21 November 1931

Let him have a go   30 April 1932

At the elections to the Land parliament in Hesse on 15 November 1931, the governing coalition suffered a heavy defeat, while the left wing managed to maintain its percentage of the vote. On the day parliament was dissolved (18 July 1930), Hitler had declared that he was seeking a parliamentary majority via the ballot box in order to overcome democracy by democratic methods. His success in the Reichstag elections of September 1930 and in the subsequent Land elections confirmed that he was on the right course. In April 1932 Hitler had considerable success in Prussia (36.3 per cent), Bavaria (32.5 per cent), Württemberg (26.4 per cent), Hamburg (31.4 per cent) and Anhalt (40.9 per cent); after the elections the NSDAP provided the prime ministers in Oldenburg, Mecklenburg-Schwerin and Thuringia. At the presidential elections in April Hindenburg was re-elected (at the second ballot) with 53 per cent of the vote, but Hitler still took 36.8 per cent. It is no wonder that in the spring of 1931 there was a widespread feeling that Hitler was about to storm the palace. However, the percentage of votes for the NSDAP was never to rise much above that achieved at these regional elections. Schwarzschild's 'unfavourable' conditions (see 'Hail Adolf') materialised, and if he had not tampered with the constitution Hitler would presumably not even have achieved the 43.9 per cent of the last Reichstag elections in March 1933.

Initially Brüning was against including the National Socialists in a coalition, since he was afraid they would hardly be prepared to share responsibility for the deflationary policies that were necessary to bring about an end to Germany's reparation payments. Hindenburg was anything but taken with Hitler either, but General Schleicher, head of the Office of Ministerial Affairs, and the SA Chief of Staff, Röhm, made sure that contact between Hitler and government circles was not broken off. As Schwarzschild explains, his suggestion that Hitler could be neutralised by participating in government was dependent on a functioning democratic system which could cushion the shock of Hitler and absorb him without allowing him to exploit and, ultimately, destroy it. It is questionable whether those conditions still held in April 1932; certainly Schwarzschild's opinion was that they no longer held six months later (as can be seen in his article 'What do we want' of November 1932 [not included in this volume]).

Hail Adolf   21 November 1931

Hesse is an analogue of Prussia. For years the changes in voting patterns in the two *Länder* have run almost mathematically parallel, except that the *moderate* parties in Hesse have always done better than in Prussia by a few per cent and by contrast the *radicals* worse by a few per cent.

On the following pages the reader will find an exhaustive analysis, calculated in percentages, of the elections in Hesse and Prussia since 1919. We recommend our readers to study it, when convenient, for the *Land* elections have to be held in Prussia by May at the latest. And if we can still count on the democratic mechanisms enshrined in the constitution, the comparison with Hesse should enable us to come to some fairly certain conclusions about the way power in Prussia will be distributed in the near future.

To be precise, the way power would be distributed if the elections were to take place *now*. By May the parallel could of course be broken by unforeseen events, but for the moment we can leave aside consideration of how likely or unlikely a prospect that is.

What emerges first and foremost from this is the absolute certainty that the 'Weimar' Coalition that is ruling today would have been *even more decisively defeated* in elections in Prussia than it was last Sunday in Hesse, for Hesse was always more favourable ground for it, as the proportion of the vote it achieved in the two *Länder* shows:

Election	1920	1924	1924	1927/28	1928	1930	1931/32
Hesse	57.2	52.4	59.8	58.1	54.6	48.1	36.4
Prussia	46.7	40.6	48.4	48.0	48.7	41.1	?

If only 36.4 per cent is left of the exceptionally strong majority for the ruling coalition in Hesse, then it follows that in Prussia, where it has never actually achieved an overall majority, these parties would struggle to get more than 30 per cent.

The second important conclusion is that over the last ten years the true *socialist* (= Marxist) parties have proved surprisingly *immune to all trends*. There have been shifts *within* this grouping. Added together, the support for the Social Democrats, Communists and smaller groups has evolved as follows:

Election	1920	1924	1924	1927/28	1928	1930	1931/32
Hesse	43.0	38.8	40.6	41.2	41.0	40.2	39.2
Prussia	42.3	32.0	34.5	40.9	40.8	37.8	?

Hesse (%)	Constituent Assembly 19.1.19	Reichstag 6.6.20	Reichstag 4.5.24	Landtag 7.12.24	Landtag 13.11.27	Reichstag 20.5.28	Reichstag 14.9.30	Landtag 15.11.31
Weimar Coalition								
Social Democrats	44.3	30.3	29.5	35.2	32.6	32.3	28.9	21.4
Democrats	19.0	10.8	7.4	8.5	7.8	6.3	5.2	1.4
Centre Party	18.0	16.1	15.5	16.1	17.7	16.0	14.0	13.6
	81.3	57.2	52.4	59.8	58.1	54.6	48.1	36.4
Right-wing Opposition								
National Socialists	—	—	2.9	1.4	—	1.9	18.5	37.1
German Nationals	6.6	14.1	6.1	7.0	5.0	3.5	1.6	1.4
	6.6	14.1	9.0	8.4	5.0	5.4	20.1	38.5
Left-wing Opposition								
Indep. Social Dem. (Soc. Workers Party)	1.9	12.2	—	—	—	—	—	1.0
Communists	—	0.5	9.3	5.4	8.6	8.7	11.3	14.3
Comm. Opposition	—	—	—	—	—	—	—	1.9
Radicals	—	—	—	—	—	—	—	0.6
	1.9	12.7	9.3	5.4	8.6	8.7	11.3	17.8
Floating Groups								
German People's Party	11.2	16.0	10.8	11.8	10.7	11.3	6.7	2.3
Land League (Hesse Farmers' League)	—	—	14.3	13.2	12.7	13.4	7.7	2.6
Economy Party	—	—	1.2	—	—	1.3	2.3	—
Christ. Social. People's Service	—	—	—	—	—	—	3.6	2.1
Others	—	—	3.0	1.4	4.9	5.3	0.2	0.3
	11.2	16.0	29.3	26.4	28.3	31.3	20.5	7.3

Prussia (%)	Constituent Assembly 19.1.19	Reichstag 6.6.20	Reichstag 4.5.24	Landtag 7.12.24	Landtag 20.5.28	Reichstag 20.5.28	Reichstag 14.9.30	Landtag ?
Weimar Coalition								
Social Democrats	36.8	21.4	18.7	24.9	29.0	29.0	23.2	?
Democrats	17.1	7.1	5.0	5.9	4.5	4.5	3.2	?
Centre Party	21.1	18.2	16.9	17.6	14.5	15.2	14.7	?
	75.0	46.7	40.6	48.4	48.0	48.7	41.1	?
Right-wing Opposition								
National Socialists	—	—	4.9	2.5	1.8	1.8	18.5	?
German Nationals	11.3	14.1	23.1	23.7	17.4	17.4	9.2	?
	11.3	14.1	28.0	26.2	19.2	19.2	27.7	?
Left-wing Opposition								
Indep. Social Democrats (Soc. Workers' Party)	7.9	19.7	—	—	—	—	—	?
Communists	—	1.2	13.3	9.6	11.9	11.8	14.6	?
Comm. Opposition	—	—	—	—	—	—	—	?
Radicals	—	—	—	—	—	—	—	?
	7.9	20.9	13.3	9.6	11.9	11.8	14.6	?
Floating Groups								
German People's Party	5.1	14.8	9.3	9.8	8.5	8.6	4.7	?
Land League	—	2.0	—	—	2.5	2.1	4.1	?
Economy Party	—	—	2.0	2.5	4.5	4.5	3.7	?
Christian Social People's Service	—	—	—	—	—	—	2.4	?
Others	0.7	1.5	6.8	3.5	5.4	5.1	1.7	?
	5.8	18.3	18.1	15.8	20.9	20.3	16.6	?

Over the decade, then, 'Marxism', to eradicate which Herr Hitler and his Sancho Panza, Hugenberg, took up arms, oscillated around the same point. *A fact of quite exceptional significance!* In the first place it shows that the working class, taken as a whole, is clear and steadfast, and it proves beyond statistical doubt that Hitler's so-called 'workers' Party' *cannot possibly* contain a significant contingent of workers. It also shows that the opportunities for growth available to the right wing stop at this social boundary. If elections had been held in Prussia this week, the socialist vote would perhaps have fallen by 1–2 per cent, as it did in Hesse, but definitely not by more. What this tells us is that the sources of growth for the right wing lie solely in the *floating groups*: the middle-of-the-road middle-class parties *outside* the stable core of socialist and Catholic groups. Over the last decade these floating groups have shown the following development:

Election	1920	1924	1924	1927/28	1928	1930	1931/32
Hesse	16.0	29.3	26.4	28.3	31.3	20.5	7.3
Prussia	18.3	18.1	15.8	20.9	20.3	16.6	?

As we can see, there are only scraps left and it is these scraps alone that form the remaining reservoir of votes the National Socialists can swallow up. In a word: all previous experience suggests that the potential for growth of the right-wing will go no farther than just below or just above 50 per cent of the total vote. Under normal conditions, assuming the democratic constitution stays in force, the right wing will never be able to make significant inroads into the area the *'Marxists' plus Centre Party* occupied and still occupy and which is as follows:

Election	1920	1924	1924	1927/28	1928	1930	1931/32
Hesse	59.1	54.3	59.7	55.3	57.0	54.2	52.8
Prussia	60.5	48.9	52.1	55.4	56.0	52.5	?

If we subtract the maximum that remains available to Herr Hitler, we will see that his ceiling is roughly 50 per cent – assuming the constitution and the rule of law remain in force. Under the most *favourable* conditions imaginable, he might exceed 50 per cent by a few points, thus creating a perfectly legal situation which could keep him in power for years to come, regardless of further votes. If conditions are only slightly *unfavourable* to him, he will – again assuming the constitution is left inviolate – never reach the ominous 50 per cent which would allow him and his allies a free hand to do as they please.

The final conclusion of these reflections is that Herr Hitler's constitutional future depends on whether or not he is left to enjoy the favourable conditions in which he has been allowed to operate during the last few years. There are two ways in which conditions have worked in his favour so far: *the economic crisis has deepened from day to day; and he was not burdened with the responsibility*. He was not put to the test by being forced to take positive action. Our hopes of Brüning performing an economic miracle that would stop the supply of grist to the National Socialists' mill have vanished; for a long time to come, everything coming from that direction will work in their favour. There does not appear to be any other way of guaranteeing he will never reach the 50 per cent boundary than to force him to share the responsibility *before* he reaches it. We are still almost six months away from the Prussian and the presidential elections. It is still probable that the army generals are neither Hitlerish nor Brüningish, but simply general-ish. Hindenburg is still in office; he has taken his oath on the constitution and will no more break his oath than he can simply be pushed aside. Still to come is the obligation to sign the debt-rescheduling treaties, which are a real blessing for Hitler, who is not involved, and will be the first great defeat for those who are involved. If there is still any chance at all of maintaining the democratic constitutional mechanism for even just one more year, then political foresight demands that this year must bear the stamp of a coalition with Hitler. If, tomorrow, the National Socialists join a government which remains strong enough to prevent the violation of the constitution, the tide will recede in a few months and Herr Hitler can be pushed into the background again, using the means provided in the constitution which has just been saved. If they are allowed to keep out of government for a few months, then either they will quite legitimately pass the decisive 50 per cent barrier or it will be a hundred times more difficult than now to stop them using violence to remove the mechanism which lies between them and their goal of absolute power.

The arguments against this are obvious. It will not be a pleasant period. Even a minority partner in a coalition has to be given some room to manoeuvre, especially if the point is to get him to tarnish the aura surrounding him. But when the choice is between partial and temporary or total and permanent terror, the decision is not a difficult one. Eighteen months ago, even 12 months ago, there were other alternatives. Brüning held all the trumps. Now that he has thrown them all away, every one of them, now that he has wasted every other opportunity, every one of them, this perilous tightrope walk over the abyss is all that is left. Given what has recently become a tradition in Germany, we can safely assume that they will not undertake this in time either.

Let him have a go   30 April 1932
Politics is fate   28 May 1932

On 13 April 1932, following his re-election and on the advice of his army
minister Groener, President Hindenburg banned the SA and the SS on the
ground of their violent disturbance of the peace in Germany. For a brief
period it seemed as if Hindenburg had finally decided to crack down on the
violent agitation of the NSDAP. However, following the resignation of
Groener, on 13 May 1932, and after an intense campaign by his Prussian
Junkers, Hindenburg finally dismissed the Brüning cabinet on 30 May 1932,
after 26 months in office. On the following day Franz von Papen was
commissioned to form a 'government of national unity' in which he was
supposed to be not the head but a 'figurehead' for the ambitious new army
minister, Schleicher; the cabinet consisted entirely of conservative, mostly
aristocratic, civil servants with no political mandate. Papen was not
unknown – as military attaché he had organised industrial sabotage,
explosions and bomb attacks in the USA prior to 1917! Hermann Dietrich,
the vice-chancellor and minister of finance in Brüning's cabinet, explained
the motives for Brüning's fall as follows:

> The deeper reasons for the removal of Brüning lay in the fact that a social class
> that had previously lost its decisive influence in the state, namely the old
> Prussian aristocracy, is determined to take over power again ... Brüning tried
> to swing to the right, but didn't succeed ... so he fell from power because he
> disappointed the expectations of those gentlemen.

Hindenburg had blamed Brüning for the unexpected difficulties during his
re-election as president in April, and when a controversial agricultural
reform was proposed, his fellow aristocratic landowners persuaded him to
get rid of the Chancellor. For the rest of his life Brüning complained that he
had been removed from office 'a hundred metres before the finish'.
However, since he was the one who had introduced presidential
government, it should have been no surprise to him that the President could
dismiss the chancellor without giving any consideration to the state of
affairs in parliament.

The Reichstag was dissolved on 4 June 1932 and elections set for 31 July.
In a government statement that was read out on the radio, von Papen
attacked the Brüning government, rejected the 'welfare state that has
weakened the moral forces of the nation' and inveighed against 'cultural

74

bolshevism'. It was clear to all observers that Hitler had a hand in this, even if he remained in the background. The removal of the ban on the SA and the SS, which both he and Hindenburg desired, came on 16 June, when extremely bloody street fighting broke out between the Nazis and the Communists; in four weeks there were 99 dead, the climax being 'Bloody Sunday' at Altona, when a National Socialist march through the Communist districts of Altona resulted in 17 dead. The events in Altona gave von Papen and von Schleicher a suitable excuse for their long-planned action against the Braun-Severing government in Prussia, which since April 1932 had only been operating as a caretaker government. On 20 July the Prussian government was dismissed by emergency decree and within a short period all officials and land politicians with Social Democratic or republican sympathies were removed from office.

Schleicher was not only behind the Prussian coup, he was the key figure in the months before Hitler's seizure of power. His aim was an authoritarian presidential dictatorship without parliament which should also include the National Socialist movement, though only in a passive role. His idea of taming Hitler by involving him in the responsibility of government was doubtless partly prompted by his military ambitions, since he saw the SA as making a valuable contribution to his planned rearmament and consequently had no time for the ban on the organisation. He therefore promised Hitler, in an agreement of 8 May, that he would see to it that the government was dismissed, the ban on the SA lifted and new elections were held, as long as Hitler agreed to a national presidential government under von Papen's leadership. One of the reasons for the failure of Schleicher's idea of taming Hitler was that, like everyone else, he seriously underestimated his abilities. Basically he, von Papen and the rest of the 'cabinet of barons' must have thought that a common working-class Austrian such as Hitler would be easy prey for them once the chips were down. Schleicher's duplicitous manoeuvring during these crisis months harmed his credibility, so that when the decisive moment came, he could no longer rely on Hindenburg's support. Thus in January 1933 the President chose what appeared to be the less risky course of appointing the Hitler-Papen-Hugenberg cabinet. The broom of dictatorship was difficult to control once the sorcerer's apprentices, Brüning and Schleicher, had brought it out of the cupboard. One commentator summed up Schleicher's intrigues thus: 'ultimately he was prevented from averting a danger which would quite probably never have arisen had he not taken the steps he did.'

Let him have a go   30 April 1932

I

November 1931: the elections for the state parliament have been held in Hesse and the Hitler Party has had its greatest triumph yet. Their list managed to garner 37.1 per cent of the vote, even more than now, six months later, in Prussia. The result was analysed in the *Tage-Buch* of 21 November 1931, in an article which examined the voting trends in Hesse since 1919 and, since Hesse is an 'analogue of Prussia', showed them in parallel with those in Prussia. The conclusion was that '*all previous experience suggests that the potential for growth of the right-wing will go no farther than just below or just above 50 per cent of the total vote.*' Under normal, constitutional democratic conditions the right wing will clearly never be able to make serious inroads into the area occupied by the '*Marxists*' *plus the Centre Party*. Since in Germany election statistics are usually still given in absolute numbers rather than percentages, it has so far remained unnoticed that surprisingly the Prussian elections of April 1932 have once again confirmed this axiom.

The fact is that the Catholic-Socialist-Communist domain has once again proved absolutely inviolable. That group received almost exactly the same share of the vote in April 1932 as it did in September 1930. The share of the total vote obtained by the Centre, the Social Democrats, the Social-Democrat Opposition and the Communists was as follows:

Results for Prussia (%)	SPD	Communist Socialist Opposition	Total Marxists	Centre Party	Centre + Marxists
Federal Elections in Prussia					
June 1920	21.4	20.9	42.3	18.2	60.5
May 1924	18.7	13.3	32.0	16.9	48.9
Regional Elections in Prussia					
December 1924	24.9	9.6	34.5	17.6	52.1
May 1928	29.0	11.9	40.9	14.5	55.4
Federal Elections in Prussia					
September 1930	23.2	14.6	37.8	14.7	52.5
Regional Elections in Prussia					
April 1932	21.2	13.3	34.5	15.3	49.8

Elections in Prussia, 1919–1932 in percentages of the total vote

Prussia (%)	Constituent Assembly 19.1.19	Reichstag 6.6.20	Reichstag 4.5.24	Landtag 7.12.24	Landtag 20.5.28	Reichstag 20.5.28	Reichstag 14.9.30	Landtag 24.4.1932 Votes	Landtag 24.4.1932 Seats
Weimar Coalition									
Social Democrats	36.8	21.4	18.7	24.9	29.0	29.0	23.2	21.2	22.2
Democrats	17.1	7.1	5.0	5.9	4.5	4.5	3.2	1.5	0.5
Centre Party	21.1	18.2	16.9	17.6	14.5	15.2	14.7	15.3	15.8
	75.0	46.7	40.6	48.4	48.0	48.7	41.1	38.0	38.5
Right-wing Opposition									
National Socialists	—	—	4.9	2.5	1.8	1.8	18.5	36.3	38.3
German Nationals	11.3	14.1	23.1	23.7	17.4	17.4	9.2	7.0	7.3
	11.3	14.1	28.0	26.2	19.2	19.2	27.7	43.3	45.6
Left-wing Opposition									
Indep. Social Democrats (Soc. Workers' Party)	7.9	19.7	—	—	—	—	—	0.4	0.0
Communists	—	1.2	13.3	9.6	11.9	11.8	14.6	12.9	13.5
	7.9	20.9	13.3	9.6	11.9	11.8	14.6	13.3	13.5
Floating Groups									
German People's Party	5.1	14.8	9.3	9.8	8.5	8.6	4.7	1.7	1.7
Land League	—	2.0	—	—	2.5	2.1	4.1	0.7	0.0
Economy Party	—	—	2.0	2.5	4.5	4.5	3.7	0.9	0.0
Christian Social People's Service	—	—	—	—	—	—	2.4	1.2	0.5
Others	0.7	1.5	6.8	3.5	5.4	5.1	1.7	0.9	0.2
	5.8	18.3	18.1	15.8	20.9	20.3	16.6	5.4	2.2

Thus despite the immense temptations of the last 18 months, there has been no decisive change. Their share of the total vote is even better than in 1924; and if one looks at the result in terms of seats gained, they still have a majority of 51.5 per cent. It is a safe conclusion that nothing will happen in future either that will look anything like a landslide. It is a barrier on which the nationalist right wing, especially Hitlerism, makes almost no impression whatsoever. It can gobble up the middle-class parties and it could well be that the most rabid of the nationalist movements will eventually absorb the second most rabid. But the assertion that the brown tidal wave has no prospect of ever completely breaking through the black-and-red dam is more than ever justified. It may wash away a few extra marginal per cent, it may even finally just creep over 50 per cent, which, as we have seen, it did not manage to do this time. Hitler himself only reached 36.3 per cent and even counting all possible coalition partners would only make 48.7 per cent. But however immense, under the rules of democracy, the significance of these few per cent either side of the borderline between a majority and a minority, it is fundamentally important to note once more that under the democratic system Hitlerism and its appendages will always remain a matter of half the nation and never of the whole nation. As long as the democratic mechanism continues to function, even the maximum extension of Hitlerism will always remain within a limit which will mean that the slightest counter-current will send it tumbling back into a minority. Six months ago this state of affairs, which has once more been confirmed, led to the following conclusion: '*If there is still any chance at all of maintaining the democratic constitutional mechanism for even just one more year, then political foresight demands that this year must bear the stamp of a coalition with Hitler.*' The step was not taken, Herr Brüning thought it important to harvest the inevitable failures of his policies himself. Is it too late, now that the consequences have become evident, for a change of attitude?

II

It is completely wrong to ask the question of the moment solely in regard to those *Länder* which happen to have had elections last week. For the issues on which the campaigns were fought were not local issues, and it is not developments in popular opinion in the *Länder* that are demonstrated by the result. That may not be the case for a *Land* like Bavaria. The very singular result there justifies it going its own way in its own affairs; indeed, affairs in Bavaria have long gone in the opposite direction to the rest of the country. For the others, however, it was problems affecting the country as a whole – in foreign and economic policy – that were the key issues, often not even done up in local dress. It was problems affecting the country, not the individual *Länder*, which determined the way people voted, and the expression of the popular will in these regional elections relates to the previous and future policies of the national government. They are what produced that expression of will and what it aims to influence. The nationalist vote comprising 48.7 per cent of the electorate, including the 5.4 per cent per cent of the floating groups, who are doomed to be gobbled up, is a model which is to be applied to the country as a whole. It is on the national level that we find the problems to which the nationalist parties owe their existence, and that is where the decision how to respond must be taken. Matters will not be decided, nor even influenced in any meaningful way, in Prussia or the state governments alone. If a change in the procedural rules of the Prussian parliament is once more used to keep the Nationalists out of the Prussian government, that will do nothing at all to stop them forcing their way into the national government tomorrow.[72] If, on the other hand, they are taken into the Prussian government, no failure will be blamed on them, since they will be able to point out that all important decisions are made by the national, not the regional government. If one takes the result of the Prussian election as the last signal that German nationalism is 2 per cent away from a majority, it is clear that the conclusion to be drawn must be a conclusion in the realm of national politics. They can do what they like in Prussia, they can offer Hitler seats in the cabinet or not, the die that will decide our fate, which includes Prussia's, will be cast at the national level, and there, as has been demonstrated, the clock stands at two per cent to midnight.

What is still possible? Since for by far the largest part of their supporters Nationalism, which has pushed its strength up to 48.7 per cent of the vote, is not a positive product of burning idealistic faith, but a negative product of burning economic hardship, it can only subside – but will it subside? – once the economic situation improves, or once the Nationalists have shown themselves incapable of stopping things getting worse. The logical conclusion is that there are only two methods of combating it remaining:

— either the economic recovery must be brought about while the Nationalists are still not involved in the government,

— or the Nationalists must be brought into the government while the economic situation is still getting worse.

So far the alternatives are clear. The difficulty only arises when we consider the dual role of Nationalism, which is not simply the beneficiary of the economic difficulties but also the decisive factor in their cause. Nationalism is not only a typical war profiteer, it not only profits from the economic devastation, which has descended upon the whole of Europe and the world as a consequence of the Franco-German cold war; in a deeper sense it is, as is occasionally the case with war profiteers, the originator of this war, which it desired, which it wanted, which it demanded – until a government, which believed it could use this policy to unify the nation, actually adopted the policy the Nationalists were screaming for. This gamble in foreign policy, which led to the economic catastrophe, was brought about by what was at the time a relatively weak group; how can we then, when confronted by the same group, but incomparably stronger now, abandon this risky venture and thus lay the foundations of an economic recovery? It is certain that a Franco-German peace would also fuel European prosperity and that within a short time German nationalism would recede from its 48.7 per cent peak. But how can we make peace, when 48.7 per cent of the population demand an escalation of the war and when the least action that looks like capitulation would immediately bring about the triumph of the 48.7 per cent in some perfectly legal way? This, by the way, shows how Chancellor Brüning, that champion of the remnants of democracy, has pursued policies which have got him into the monstrous situation where he cannot go back or forward without abandoning democracy one way or the other. It is here that the disastrous results of this risky policy of trying to steal the Nationalists' thunder become apparent. But what also becomes apparent is that there is absolutely no possible way out other than a short period of straightforward terror. At the stage we have reached, where everything is on a knife edge, the boost of a Franco-German peace, the prerequisite for economic recovery and thus of a Nationalist slump, is only possible if the last remnants of democracy are set aside for the transition period, if all opposition, all counter-propaganda, all elections and change of government are suppressed with ruthless, autocratic force, if we are bold enough to use full dictatorial powers, backed up by bayonets and truncheons, to prevent the Nationalists becoming established at home, which will inevitably follow the liquidation of Nationalism as a force in foreign policy. For a few days it looked as if the ban on the SA might possibly be the harbinger of such an extreme turn of events, but if that was ever the intention, the remarkable events that have since taken place in the presidential palace show the lack of any practical possibility of such an heroic approach. Without going into detail, it is apparent that for the moment it is completely unthinkable that this combination of a peace agreement abroad and martial law at home could be the method by which our government would be prepared and able to bring about an economic recovery.

That leaves us with the second alternative. If the change – an anti-Nationalist change in foreign policy – that would lead to an economic recovery cannot be brought about *against* the Nationalists, then the continuation of the economic slump must be brought about *with* the Nationalists. They must finally be made to share the responsibility for the policies, which are nothing other than their own policies that have been imposed on us by them and their terror tactics. Since it is the Young Plan that is ruining Germany, since it is France that is ruining Germany, since that is the alpha and omega of the Nationalists' propaganda and since these new Teutons who would free us from the foreign yoke mainly owe their rise to the abuse they hurl at all those who tolerate such a shameful situation – well, since that is the case, let them be offered the *foreign* ministry, and with such a loud fanfare of trumpets that they cannot refuse. Let them be given the assurance that they can pursue whatever foreign policy they want. And let them choose from among the other ministries those that are closest to their hearts and that the arithmetic of the coalition will allow, apart from the ones that give them control of the army and the ministry of justice. Let them govern, but with the proviso that no changes can be made to the constitutional framework and that the few departments responsible for that must remain in other hands. The Lausanne Reparations Conference is in June. The new financial year begins in July. In Geneva the League of Nations might be playing at disarmament well into the autumn. In the winter the unemployment figures might reach eight million. Why should Hitler not participate in these delights? Why should the defeats which *his* policies – for it is his policies that have been pursued in key matters for a long time now! – have suffered and will continue to suffer be blamed on others, while they even give him the halo of a saviour? Why should the thousands of political IOUs, which he has signed for all and sundry and which fall due when he takes over the government, only be presented for payment when he is so powerful that he can simply have anyone who presents one arrested?

Handing over the powers of the state – it sounds drastic! But taking a party into a governing coalition is not the same as handing over the powers of the state – as long as Hitlerism remains nothing more than a party, a party with only 36 per cent of the vote; even with its appendages which, under present conditions, are likely to be swallowed up but could go in a different direction under different conditions, it is still only a party, not an omnipotent power. As things stand at present, Hitler has in practice 48.7 per cent of the weight of the German electorate at his disposition, since neither Hugenberg nor the other minor parties can resist the gravitational force of this huge negative mass. But the moment he becomes part of the government, we can confidently predict that traditional German loyalty will mean that the 36 per cent, now that they have suddenly become a positive quantity, are on their own. As things stand at present, Hitler can have nothing but successes; everything that goes wrong benefits him – and what can *not* go wrong, if one pursues Hitlerist policies? The moment he becomes part of the government, he will have nothing but failures, for as long as he is not omnipotent, he can do nothing but continue with the failed policies he has invoked and for the first time he will feel the consequences. As things stand, Hitler almost has a majority, and in a few weeks he will have more than a majority – he will have crossed the line between a mere party and an omnipotent power. The moment he is part of a coalition, when he represents one party among others, he will only have a third at his disposition, and within a few months a quarter at most. Is the choice between a necessary evil that we have to work our way through and a terrible fate, from which we may perhaps never escape, such a difficult one?

Politics is fate   28 May 1932

It is a year now – yes, only a year – since an economic plan entitled 'The emergency decree that never came' was published in this journal. The circumstances were similar to those obtaining at present. The banks were still holding firm against the run on them that had been unleashed from home and abroad, but all the time the German economy was slowly but inexorably sliding downhill. The emergency decree that the Brüning cabinet prepared in the last days of May and the first days of June 1931 may have been regarded by the general public as an instrument for economic recovery – unlike the emergency decree being prepared in these last days of May 1932, of which no one believes that any more – but anyone with eyes to see realised it was of an entirely different nature. Like everything the Brüning cabinet did (and will do) in this area, this raft of measures simply redistributed the economic and financial deficit, simply shifted the poverty from here to there and from there to here. The causes of our plight were not even remotely addressed. It was these causes that were to be dealt with by the credit expansion plan, which was put forward in the *Tage-Buch* article.[73] The purpose was to put an end to the decline in our economy itself, not just its social and financial consequences, and that *with purely economic* measures, albeit unusual ones.

The discussions on this plan went on for some time and it is clear that the ideas presented there were taken up in all kinds of later projects for creating jobs or stimulating the economy. But while the central idea – an artificial 'kick-start' by means of a credit expansion and public, as a substitute for private, enterprise – became increasingly popular, the readers of the *Tage-Buch* will have noticed that there has been a resounding silence on the subject in these pages. The anniversary of the article provides an opportunity to explain why. I have to confess that it is my conviction that all the plans – of this or any other type – to stimulate the economy have been overtaken by events. The decline of the German economy is a process which can no longer be arrested, let alone reversed, by *economic* means. There is no point any more in discussing economic measures, however 'radical' they may be. For some time now it is *political* not economic facts that have determined economic developments. And there is no economic medicine which would be strong enough and lasting enough to counteract the deadly miasma constantly rising from the quagmire of politics. People's understanding always lags behind events. Things that will be seen as a matter of course tomorrow appear monstrous today. But whether it is already accepted or will only be in several months' time, the truth is – and has been for several weeks and months – that any attempt to save the German economy is doomed to failure as long as it is exposed to the prevailing political conditions; even the boldest and most brilliant of economic programmes cannot halt its progressive decline as long as the political source of infection has not been dealt with. In this particular case the argument about who was right, Napoleon with his 'Politics is fate', or Walther Rathenau with his modernised version, 'Economics is fate', comes down, in an oddly modified form, on the side of the Frenchman, even though he lived over 100 years ago: 'Politics is the fate of the economy.'

The turning point in these reflections came when it became impossible to ignore the fact that the world economic crisis was not simply a particularly severe case of the normal capitalist trade cycle, but that *a political crisis of the utmost severity had been grafted on to the economic crisis*. The normal capitalist crisis contains its own antidote. Nonetheless, the recurrence of this phenomenon is certainly bad enough to justify the desire for a better economic system, one that is free of crises. However, it is undeniable, and we do not deny, that every capitalist crisis so far has of itself produced a recovery; and the claim that this time it is the 'final crisis of capitalism' – born of the stage of economic development itself! – stands in a complete vacuum as far as proof is concerned. It is significant that not even Marxist theorists take it seriously, only fragrant bourgeois pessimists. This crisis may well be much severer than preceding ones, and that may well be due to the latest stage of development of capitalism. It may well therefore be necessary to assist the self-healing process, to give it an artificial 'kick-start' – which was precisely the aim of all the plans, including the one elaborated in these pages. But then it became increasingly clear that, above and beyond that, this stage of a severe economic crisis – a stage which required the lightest of touches – had been chosen as the battleground for a decisive political struggle between two countries with a decisive place in the world economy: *the struggle began between Germany and France over the Treaty of Versailles*. It grew daily more bitter and ominous, more and more nations were affected by the offensive and defensive manoeuvres and were themselves compelled to resort to combative measures, thus grafting a huge extra-economic disruption onto the purely economic crisis, a disruption that completely paralysed the self-healing mechanism of a capitalist crisis. In this political situation it has become impossible for those forces to come into effect – with or without artificial assistance – which prevent a normal, purely economic crisis from becoming an endless vicious circle, one contraction engendering another.

Why has it become impossible? Because what solely and exclusively determines the ups and downs of the business cycle is the entrepreneurs' and investors' hope of gain or fear of loss. At bottom, no other factor exists, neither patriotism, nor hunger, nor poverty, nor 'need' – nothing but hope of gain and fear of loss. The moment a reasonable number of entrepreneurs start to believe, for whatever reason, that things will be better tomorrow, new supplies are ordered, new workers taken on, so that demand does actually grow, credit is on offer, and everything that comes from their belief confirms that belief, until suddenly the economy is working again and hauls itself back up to the peak by its own bootstraps.

It could be that the pessimism, which in earlier times led to crisis, is very firmly rooted – or at least the cautious attitude which does nothing rather than plunge into a risky undertaking. In such cases 'stimulation' can help. A reasonable number of 'artificial' orders can produce a tendency for prices to rise, which sparks off an increase in purchases, because every dealer wants to stock up while prices are still low. A reasonable number of 'artificial' orders also leads to workers being taken on and thus to a genuine rise in demand. Thus such an artificial operation can produce a real change in sentiment, which brings about the turn from stagnation to recovery – and that is the point of all the proposals for 'stimulation': their aim and intention is to create the trigger which turns fear of loss into hope of gain. But all that is only possible in the purely economic sphere, where entrepreneurs and investors are eagerly waiting for a glimpse of the silver lining on the commercial horizon.

It is a situation beyond our worst imagining when every post-stimulus dawn is immediately darkened by the storms of politics; when governments face up to each other with bloodshot eyes, determined to do anything that will damage the other, hitting out with the weapons of offensive and defensive laws, which create more and more economic havoc, furiously trying to see who can stick it out the longest. 'You don't invest when you're on a battlefield.' Not on an economic battlefield and especially not on a military one, which is what is lurking in the background. It is a situation which drums one single message into the head of every entrepreneur and investor: Get out of anything risky – get out of goods: prices are going to fall; get out of manufacturing: sales are going to plummet; get out of credit: the borrower won't be able to pay it back – get out of any kind of enterprise as quickly as possible, better no gain than certain loss! In such a situation, dominated by the fear of entrepreneurs across the entire spectrum, any attempt at stimulating the economy, which can only provide a moderate impetus in small sectors, is doomed to failure. In such a situation, all measures which attempt to repair *en détail* what has been destroyed *en gros* are doomed to failure. In such a situation the contraction is bound to continue unceasingly and unstoppably – unless, that is, the state not only uses the limited means it has at its disposal within a capitalist economy to stimulate the activities of what is the sole decisive factor, private enterprise, but also completely, or almost completely, takes its place; unless, that is, it takes over capital and means of production, no longer just encouraging others, but going into business itself; no longer just trying to foster the private sector's hope of gain but, leaving aside all considerations of profit, going into the business of satisfying people's needs itself.

But that would be to go over to communism, and with an economy that is fairly short on raw materials. It would, therefore, also be necessary to find the raw materials on which to base such an economy, which could only be done by close dependence on Russia. So now we have the full picture. Around 1930 Germany and the rest of the world entered a normal capitalist crisis; the struggle between France and Germany over Versailles, that was grafted on to the world economic crisis, and the ever more intense, worldwide consequences of this struggle for existence have destroyed the whole mechanism by which normal capitalist crises automatically engineer their own recovery. It is precisely this ever more fanatical political struggle with no obvious solution in sight that makes it impossible to stimulate the economy in ways that are still compatible with the capitalist system. Germany, and with it presumably the whole world, is clearly condemned to be dragged farther and farther down into destitution; and every measure, every programme, every plan and every piece of legislation designed to bring about a recovery, will remain completely ineffective, unless:

> *either* we make peace with France; that would at least restore the situation of a normal crisis of capitalism, release its powers of regeneration and allow the artificial stimulation of confidence among entrepreneurs within the framework of the capitalist system;

> *or*: we go over to a communist economic system; that would render superfluous entrepreneurs' hope of gain, which anyway has been irreparably broken in a situation that combines a severe economic crisis with a state of war; the state would take over the running of the economy and close cooperation with Russia would ensure a supply of industrial and agricultural raw materials as well as finished products for both countries.

Looked at dispassionately, there is no way out of our inexorable progress towards destitution other than either peace with France or the transition to communism; the time for plans, programmes and pamphlets is over. And the Chancellor, Dr Brüning, seems to be well aware of that, even though he is working on yet another emergency decree which, however, he obviously regards as nothing more than a measure to bring about another redistribution of poverty. Naturally he is not thinking about a transition to communism. As far as the link between the economic situation and Franco-German relations is concerned, however, he has spoken out in the clearest terms. If the discussions in Lausanne and Geneva do not lead to an accord – that is, if peace is not brought about between our two countries – then, the Chancellor said, the whole world will inevitably be plunged into even worse economic distress. Exactly! This resignation regarding the economic outlook as long as the current political situation continues, is only too justified – although it should be noted that it is not the same as political resignation, for in politics we always have free will; in politics any situation can be changed, as long as one has the courage and the clarity of mind and accepts the limitations of the possible. The Chancellor, though, does not appear to think that necessary, for he went on to say, with a touch of optimism in the blackest pessimism, that Germany would not be the first to collapse. In that he is unquestionably right.

Austria, for example, although not directly involved, will definitely collapse before Germany, however one defines 'collapse'. On the other hand, Germany will not be the last to collapse either; there appear to be countries that can hold out longer. But it is little comfort for people who are suffering to be told that people elsewhere are suffering even more. In the name of those who are already suffering unimaginably today, in the name of those who are condemned to even worse suffering tomorrow, I ask: to what end is politics being allowed to become the fate of an economy which these poor, tormented millions expect to provide a livelihood for them, a livelihood, nothing more?

Twilight	**31 December 1932**
Chancellor Hitler	**4 February 1933**
Caught up in the nationalist revolution	**1 July 1933**

In August 1932 Hindenburg was still refusing to appoint Hitler to the position of chancellor, even though, as Schwarzschild had foreseen, in the 31 July election the National Socialists had become the largest party in the Reichstag, with 37.4 per cent of the vote. Von Papen remained chancellor against all odds. The rejection of Hitler, and the tone of the official announcement, which was designed to emphasise the gap between the President, who represented the whole nation, and Hitler as the leader of a one-sided, totalitarian party, were a serious setback for the NSDAP. (Amongst other things, the 13 August announcement said: 'Hitler demanded the position Mussolini had after the March on Rome.') While the von Papen government fell to a National Socialist vote of no confidence on the day of the opening of parliament, doubts in the country about Hitler's reliability and seriousness as a politician meant that the Party lost two million votes – above all middle-class votes – at the subsequent elections of 6 November. However, it remained the party with the largest percentage of the vote (33.1 per cent; 196 seats compared with 230 in July) and Hitler managed to retain full control over his party, despite further losses in the local elections in Saxony and Thuringia. The composition of the Reichstag was such that no new coalitions were possible, with the result that the rest of November was spent in feverish attempts to put together a new government. Papen, who continued to enjoy Hindenburg's confidence, wanted to continue the presidential government with the support of the DNVP; he wanted at all costs to avoid an 'emergency' coalition of the NSDAP, Centre Party and DVP. But in vain. Hindenburg once more refused to give Hitler, who could now count on the open support of Schacht and the industrialists Fritz Thyssen and Albert Vögler, the post of chancellor, but, much to the disappointment of the aged President, von Papen was compelled to resign on 17 November, though he remained in the background as an influential adviser.

After unsuccessful negotiations with Hitler, Schleicher was appointed chancellor by Hindenburg on 3 December and charged with forming a new presidential cabinet. Schleicher's intention, in his so-called Querfront idea, was to create an alliance between the Army, professional organisations and the workers which would be outside and counter to the party system and give him a broad basis of support among the population. However, his plan had already failed by the beginning of January 1933, above all because of the unions' unwillingness to cooperate even though, amongst other things, Schleicher had rescinded the cuts in social welfare imposed by von Papen in September. In the meantime von Papen, with Hindenburg's consent, was sounding out the National Socialists. On 4 January there was an initial meeting at the house of the Cologne banker von Schröder. The feelings among Prussian landowners and industrialists from the west towards the NSDAP noticeably improved as they were unhappy with Schleicher's social and economic policies. And the National Socialists seemed to be gaining the upper hand again (on 15 January they won the regional elections in the little Land of Lippe). In this situation von Papen managed to convince the President, who had resisted Hitler's appointment as chancellor to the end, that there was minimal danger in conferring the power of state on the National Socialist Führer if he were 'framed' by a conservative majority in the cabinet, especially since von Papen had stipulated that he should have the post of deputy chancellor himself. Papen's colleagues had eight ministries in all, the NSDAP only three. A key role in this policy of taming the National Socialist tiger was supposed to fall to the Army and General Werner von Blomberg. Hindenburg made his appointment as the new army minister a condition of Hitler's assumption of the role of chancellor. However, the President was unaware of the fact that Blomberg was extremely sympathetic towards the NSDAP. Schleicher resigned on 28 January. Two days later Hitler was appointed chancellor and over the next four months he destroyed the democratic institutions of the Weimar Republic. Schleicher was to pay dearly for his attempt to control Hitler's rise to power – he was murdered on 30 June 1934.

Twilight   31 December 1932

Our annual review on the last day of the year had become more and more horrendous over the previous three years. *Economically*, a descent from difficulties to crisis, from crisis to paralysis and decay; *politically*, a slide into a more and more militant situation in foreign affairs and a more and more counter-revolutionary one at home; *intellectually*, however, a constantly growing inability to see the causes of this galloping process, a more and more frantic obsession with applying as medicine, in more and more unrestrained fashion, the very measures which caused the fever in the first place and which consequently forced it up higher and higher.

The developments in Germany during 1932 will be a supremely important area of study for future historians and politicians. There was such a stumbling final dash towards catastrophe, towards the mayhem of a fascist – of either the plebeian or feudal variety – revolution, with everything that it would entail: terror, hunger, barbarism, the disintegration of the country, that even today we cannot quite understand by what historical miracle our course was diverted almost at the last minute. We are so close to events that all we can do is attempt to understand the reasons for the miracle, a miracle of which it will one day be said that there have been few like it in the annals of the nations. That a turning-point has been passed is indicated by many objective signs and one would have to be totally lacking in nerves and instincts not to sense it in the very air as well. It is clear that at the end of this year of 1932 the *economic* indicators have for the first time stopped their long-established downward trend. It is clear that the *political* tide has changed direction and lost some of its violence. It is also clear that *intellectually* there has been a kind of awakening: some understanding of the sources of our desperate plight has appeared and a few of the crudest pseudo-theoretical misconceptions are starting to lose their masochistic attraction. Although developments never proceed in a straight line and although no one can say at what point they will run out of steam, for the first time for a long time this New Year's Eve 1932 has seen a break in the clouds appear on the horizon.

The dialectical inversion of 20 July

The point at which any process reaches the celebrated 'dialectical inversion' – that is, suddenly turns into its opposite – can never be determined in advance; it is hardly ever even perceived at the moment when it happens, but becomes clearer and clearer when looked at in retrospect. Only a few weeks after the coup d'etat in Prussia, these pages contained reflections wondering whether, under the given circumstances, the event had not proved to be a piece of good fortune for those who initially felt it as a hammer-blow; by now that has become a certainty. There can no longer be any doubt that 20 July, the day of greatest triumph for reactionaries of all shades, marked the beginning of their decline.

This may sound strange, since the *economic* circumstances, the ultimate basis of all political events, were not changed at all by what happened in Prussia. It becomes understandable, however, when one remembers that the success of the reactionary/fascist movement rested on the fact that the masses had been fed a quite specific interpretation of the economic conditions. In brief, this very nebulous interpretation was: it's the socialists' fault. The socialists are bleeding small businesses dry; the socialists are allowing, they even want, our enemies abroad to bleed Germany dry! This patriotic mythology, which could be – and was – applied both to the openly Social Democratic governments and to Brüning, who relied on their toleration, created the opinion among the masses to which the reactionaries and the fascists owed the army of followers they needed. Then came the day when the last Social Democratic government, the last outpost of the 'November criminals', was removed and in the places where they had 'ruled', or at least passively supported the government, the figures of the field marshall, the army general, the aristocrat, landowner and industrialist appeared on the scene. From that moment on this patriotic mythology – employed to conceal the true circumstances and find recruits for the reactionary/ fascist general staff – was bound to fade sooner or later. It was impossible to present Herr von Hindenburg as an anti-nationalist, Herr von Papen as a Bolshevik. The aunt sally of the socialist in his cloth cap had been blown out of the fairground booth of practical politics and the instincts that had been whipped up against that figure suddenly lacked anything to feed on. That left three alternatives. *Either*: having reached this high point they had to secure absolute and irreversible dictatorial powers; *or*: the redundant myth, which until now had brought them the army of supporters, had to be replaced with a new, equally effective myth; *or*: the wave would begin to drain away, the big question being where to.

Absolute and irreversible dictatorial powers have *not* been secured. The hands stretching out to grasp them were not strong enough to overcome the final obstacles, moreover they started to quarrel among themselves. Most important at that point was the furious resistance of the Bavarians, who were prepared to go to any lengths to prevent anything that smacked of a Prussoprotestant take-over; combined with many other difficulties, it prevented the representatives of the *old* ruling caste from carrying through the operation they had in mind. But an internal struggle for hegemony also broke out between the old and the new reactionary forces, between the aristocratic and the plebeian wings. It was a typical struggle, which ended up as a free-for-all in which it was every man – Hindenburg, Hitler, Papen, Schleicher, Strasser[74] – for himself, none co-operating with any other, producing an almost inextricable tangle of antagonisms, rivalries, broken oaths and calculations that didn't work out. The final result was a complete failure to pick the fruit at the moment when it was ripe, compounded by the danger that it might go rotten if left much longer. The conditions, which had been created by pressure from a misled public, were only exploited feebly, only to a minimal degree; without a fundamental change in the power structure, not to mention the constitutional situation, having been brought about, the main consequence was simply that the source of this misled public opinion was blocked up. The 'traitors', against whom the masses of the petty bourgeoisie had been whipped up into a crusading mood, had been toppled, leaving no further cause for a crusading mood.

New slogans, to replace the now meaningless 'November criminals' slogan, have not yet been found. On the contrary. The failure to seize power and the contemptible spectacle of the struggle between the rival leaders has produced effective counter-slogans to replace the empty 'November criminals' slogan. Thus as a consequence of the coup d'état in Prussia, which was meant to be just a beginning but was in fact an end, our third possibility is becoming reality: the consolidated mass of public opinion is starting to crumble visibly, the crusading mood among the massed battalions is on the wane, desertion is steadily increasing. In this situation, the possibility that was closer than ever between June and July (apart from the period following the 1930 elections) has been eliminated – the possibility of an *isolated National-Socialist takeover by force*. The much-talked-about Hitler putsch has lost any chance of success. The point at which a revolt can succeed is the point when the army, the police and the civil service are mesmerised and consider the victory of the revolt inevitable. A revolt does not succeed when the police, army and civil service, who by nature are not enthusiasts but simply want to be on the winning side, regard a collapse as likely. If one thing is certain, then it is that the conditions for a coup d'état by the National Socialists have gone and with them the possibility of a 'seizure of power' in the style which they still fondly imagine.

But, given the way things have developed since July, the prospects for even a dictatorship of 'national concentration' – that is a feudal/fascist duumvirate

– are getting worse with every day that passes. Even if the feuding parties were to reunite, there will be enough mutual distrust to render internal wrangling for power inevitable; that means that they will strive to use their influence over the masses to secure their position against each other, which further means that they will have to retain some form of democracy. Also the fact that, the more Hitler's magic fades, the more easily Herr von Schleicher will probably find it to gain and secure the office of president by means of a democratic election, points in the same direction. Given the need to look to the masses for support, to mobilise the masses, one must also take into account the fact that, as the National Socialist movement declines, the ideologies and slogans which were mainly emblazoned on *their* banners, will be discredited, among others their slogan demanding dictatorship. All of this, together with a number of other factors, leads to the conclusion that, even if it were to come about, the 'national concentration' would be neither willing nor able to deviate too far from the forms of democracy. It is not mere chance that Herr von Schleicher, who was certainly not uninvolved in creating his predecessor, Papen, and the events that took place under him, is now talking about 'all that nonsense about changing the constitution'. It is not mere chance that he has jettisoned the *political* issues, which were indeed leading nowhere, and turned his attention to *economic* matters. Once the ideologies, with which they attempted to exploit the economic problems of the masses for political ends, have become threadbare, once they have starved these ideologies of further nourishment by a coup d'état which is leading nowhere, allowing them eventually to wither, but have proved incapable of taking the coup d'état itself to its logical conclusion, it becomes advisable to jettison the ideologies while there is still time and get through the fog they created themselves back to the heart of the matter. The Schleicher administration's return to purely economic matters indicates their realisation that the period in which our economic worries, distress and panic can be exploited to create a mass psychosis, that seeks urgent relief in absolutism, is coming to an end.

The economic turnaround

As long as this remained a possibility, it is debatable whether these people were particularly interested in an 'economic turnaround'. Recently the dethroned Herr von Papen warned – appropriately in an after-dinner speech to the assembled magnates, industrialists and senior civil servants of the Herrenklub:[75] 'Once the people are once more sitting with cheerful smiles on their faces and full bowls of soup in front of them, it will be much more difficult to change the constitution than at present.' If the gentleman who governed us until a few weeks ago now uses this classic formulation, his logic compels us to assume that previously he was *acting* according to that maxim. That is, he was not particularly worried about 'full bowls' *before* the constitutional changes had been accomplished. There is at least no doubt that that was the view and the recommendation of a fair number of his influential advisers, even if the advice was only expressed in forms similar to Hugo Stinnes's recommendations for currency stabilisation – forms of determined resistance to anything that might improve conditions. It is probably wrong to assume Herr Papen shared the same determination, for the simple reason that he lacked the necessary intellectual clarity. All sorts of divergent influences were struggling for control of his heart and mind, and the resultant economic policies were as random, illogical and imprecise as, fortunately, were the political ones. It is also certain that he himself, had he stayed in office, would have drawn the same conclusion as Herr Schleicher has from the failure of his bid for full absolutism, from the way the coup d'état ground to a halt in the very early stages – the conclusion, namely, that it is time to abandon 'the nonsense about changing the constitution' and to harvest, if not the advantages of overthrowing democracy, at least the laurels of the economic saviour for himself and his class. However that may be, the first serious efforts are only being made now, under his successor. And the measures that are being rolled out at the moment are one of the signs of hope for the coming year.

As is well known, until only a few days ago there was still some disagreement about whether any measures should be taken at all. As far as practical matters were concerned, some commentators pointed to the symptoms of recovery which had undoubtedly begun to appear in the organism of the world economy – although in Germany it was more a question of the end of the downward spiral, than the beginning of an upward trend. As far as theoretical considerations were concerned, we were reminded of the principle of economic freedom, of the bane of 'interventionism', of the dangers of bad investments, of inflation and goodness knows what else. It would mean repeating a discussion that went on for a whole year if we were now to review all these arguments, which constantly changed in type but whose thrust remained the same. The fact is, that in the last days of the year the 'modernist' school of thought won a second and decisive victory. The first breakthrough was Papen's tax credits – a clear measure of *credit expansion*, although not set up in a very easily understandable way.[76] This first step meant the debate on inflation was as good as over; the artificial credit foundation had been created, the Reichsbank had agreed to provide credit against adequate collateral, and the mobilisation of this artificially created credit through an increase in the money supply was guaranteed – insofar as money is actually necessary for that, since the use of credit only requires a partial payment in cash. That meant that on the authority of the state – including that of the man whom even today old fogeys call the 'guardian of the currency' – the anti-inflation rampart of the fortress, which had been fought over for years, had been completely abandoned. Those who continued to defend the position did not notice that they were fighting in a sector that had long been abandoned, thus presenting a modern version of Don Quixote tilting at windmills.

The second door was still barricaded. The expansion of credit had been agreed and decreed with due pomp and ceremony. However, the new funds had been made available to the private sector in the hope of stimulating private production, private investment and private risk-taking. But in the uncertain conditions of a severe shortage of demand and a credit crisis it went against the very essence of private enterprise to increase risk, investment, production and order volumes beyond the present level merely in anticipation of a possible economic recovery. Even the balance sheets of the banks published at the beginning of December show a further decline in customer loans, which is convincing proof that at this point in time private enterprise is *not* yet willing to 'kick start' the economy off its own bat and at its own risk. It was obvious from the beginning that the necessary counterpart to a credit expansion was that the new funds should go to organisations that would be guaranteed to put them to *work* immediately. It is only *public* bodies that can do that, and the second struggle was to establish this complementary principle.

All possible authorities were dragooned into service, all stores of wisdom, from the teachings of the classics to the supposed lessons of the most recent boom, were plundered. To allow municipalities to place orders, from which private firms would profit, was an open invitation to Communism! And there was a plentiful supply of instructive explanations of the benefit of market-oriented, value-creating use of capital, for example in the production of champagne or powder compacts and the like, in contrast to the economically perverse, anti-market, value-destroying uses of capital, for example to build roads, sewers and other similar nonsense.

The result is that this bastion has now fallen as well. Five hundred million marks of additional credit have been diverted to public bodies for accelerated use – and that, according to Herr Gereke,[77] *is only the beginning*. There is justified hope that this first dose, administered quickly and without preparation, will prove to be sufficiently beneficial and harmless to allay all fears regarding a continuation of the treatment and destroy the credibility of all those who for years have blindly and fanatically been fighting on the wrong side, only in the end to go along with the fait accompli that was carried through despite their opposition.

There would be something missing if we failed to mention that these measures are a last farewell to the Schacht era, that era of economic destruction by means of the most stupid policies. The final throes of Schachtism are grotesque enough. We have seen how the long-term foreign loans that he blocked did not cause any problem whatsoever; the short-term loans that he allowed, on the other hand, led to the collapse. We saw the farce he staged of compelling the government to go on its hands and knees to the banks for a mere 300 million marks – the same government that, two years later during the most catastrophic mayhem, was able to conjure up a billion for the banks! And now we see how the very municipalities, whose construction projects he brought to a halt by means of artificial credit crises – in order to reinvigorate the economy! – how these municipalities are now being enabled to resume their construction projects by means of artificial credit creation – again in order to reinvigorate the economy! It is a not entirely unalloyed pleasure, even for the most desensitised nose, to smell the stench given off by the corpse of that era. It is the source of too much misery and, as memory tells us, of too much outrage, too much impotent fury at the way the voice of reason could not make itself heard over all the bluster. But the antitheses have been brought out so sharply, an instructive reality has made sure conclusive lessons about the pros and cons have been drummed into us so pitilessly that the era does perhaps leave us enriched – enriched by insights for which we have had to pay dearly.

Insights at the turning point

First and foremost among the lessons we have learnt is the great discovery that at this stage of development of the capitalist economy, which is characterised by a susceptibility to crisis such as has never been seen, never been suspected before, we will be faced with a series of crises, one following on from the other, *unless we learn to regard the public and private sectors as the scales of a balance, of which the public one must be raised when the private one shows a tendency to sink* – and not the opposite, as Herr Schacht did in his grossly amateurish way. This method of a judicious and flexible interplay between plus and minus in the public and private sectors, of compensating for an incipient depression in industry with increased activity in the public sector, that is in truth the only theory left to a 'Saviour of Capitalism' to protect his system from being increasingly undermined. (A theory which in practice, however, will lead to the progressive extension of the public sector – but that is the preordained destiny of the world, all we can do is take care to keep this machine on its rails, otherwise we will be knocked down and run over by it.) If capitalist mankind has retained just a modicum of sense, this current crisis – which, because it was aggravated by political panic, cut right through to the bone, so to speak – will lead to a new understanding of how crises evolve and of ways of treating them. Herr Gereke, the Commissioner for Job Creation, who *has administered a medicine, at trial strength to start with, which has never consciously been used as a cure for an economic crisis anywhere before*, is only the first of many, and it will become clear that a new epoch in economic theory has started here and now. It will have nothing to do with drivel about self-sufficiency, a return to an agrarian economy and generalised heroic-patriotic whining. It will be based on the cardinal truth that the private sector is driven by profit or loss, that every boom is the sum total of profitable speculations and every crisis the sum total of loss-avoiding manoeuvres; furthermore, that facing it is a public sector for which the driving force of profit and loss does not exist and which therefore has to pause when confidence runs too high in the private sector, and accelerate, without consideration of the chimaera of 'money', when the fear of loss breaks out there. That is the policy which, after years of scribbling our fingers to the bone, it has now been decided to apply for the first time in Germany. If the people who are called upon to play this instrument are just a little circumspect and cautious, and at the same time approach the task with energy – genius is not a requirement! – the prospects for the coming year will not be bad. That is, of course, assuming the politicians – the American politicians aiming to preserve the status quo and the peace treaty, the German politicians aiming for a 'dynamic' line and the abolition of the peace treaty – do not throw a spanner in the works. Although Herr von Papen is unaware of this, even under so-called normal conditions there is no question of 'full bowls of soup' and 'cheerful smiles' for the 'people'. But the Germans will no longer starve. And, however much it may disappoint some people, the counter-revolutionary concentration of the proletaroid petty bourgeoisie and farmers will implode and a new political start, for instance on the basis of 1890, will be possible.[78]

History has its little ironies. A Social Democrat – Friedrich Ebert[79] – was necessary to keep socialism out of Germany; it was during the period when a monarchist – Hindenburg – occupied the presidency that the chance of a restoration of a Hohenzollern monarchy went down the drain; finally, Herr von Schleicher leapt into the saddle with the intention, on the back of a petty bourgeoisie driven mad by economic worries, of setting up a Frederick-the-Great-style empire of patriotic marches and a benevolently strict cane, with a bit of Voltaire, rather more of la Barbarina and an awful lot of 'manufacture', but was immediately forced to deal with the question of how to put an end to the economic worries of those same citizens – and thus also to their madness and to their value as a counter-revolutionary force.

Chancellor Hitler   4 February 1933

I

General von Schleicher spent two months at the head of the government without, during that period, managing to rescue the landowners east of the Elbe from all their distress nor to sort out the problems of the entire rural population of Germany. Even worse, while Herr von Schleicher was willing to fulfil the maximum demands of the Farmers' League's earlier recovery programme, he had certain reservations about implementing the most recent agricultural recovery programmes.

The result was that the Prussian *Junkers* came to regard him as a pest endangering the whole of German agriculture. The industrialists who set the tone in the presidential palace strongly suspected General von Schleicher of having bolshevist, or at least socialist tendencies. In a speech on the radio he had expressed the outrageous view that it was more important at the moment to create work for the six million unemployed than to spend their time arguing about the theories of socialism or capitalism. On top of that, the General had also held talks with, among others, the leaders of the trade unions. And to cap it all, the cabinet had discussed a job creation programme which made no provision for direct subsidies to private industry.

For all these reasons, the camarilla of Prussian *Junkers* and industrial magnates, which enjoys the confidence of Colonel von Hindenburg, could not allow the General to complete two months in office. Herr von Schleicher was so completely finished that even the idea of keeping him in the new cabinet, if only as army minister, was deemed to be utterly out of the question. Falling out of favour with people who are on visiting terms with the son and aide-de-camp of the President does not go unpunished.[80] Because influential circles thought Herr von Schleicher inclined too much to the socialists and not enough to the *Junkers*, he was replaced as chancellor by the leader of a party whose programme demands, amongst other things, the nationalisation of industrial trusts, a profit participation at large conglomerates and the preparation of legislation for the expropriation of land without compensation.

II

That Adolf Hitler has 'conquered power' and 'fought through to victory', as the nationalist myth claims and the National Socialist torchbearers imagine, is a little historical lie. Herr Hitler was already a defeated man when victory was gifted to him. His play for power had already failed when he was offered the opportunity to gain it by the back door. It wasn't a march on Berlin that brought the German Mussolini to power, but a piece of chicanery by the camarilla of Prussian *Junkers* and Westphalian industrialists.

There had been a point at which it was necessary to hand over the reins of power to Adolf Hitler. It was recommended in these pages at the time. The country is paying dearly for the fact that Herr Brüning was allowed to continue in office after the elections of 1930, breaking the rules of the democratic game, instead of letting those who voted National Socialist have the trial with their chosen one they so clearly wanted. It would have been a relatively cheap experiment and could only have ended with the disillusionment of the masses who had put their faith in Hitler. Making Hitler chancellor today is to preserve artificially a movement which, thanks to Schleicher, had lost its most effective slogans, which was threatened with bankruptcy, which was tearing itself apart with factionalism and mutiny and which was bound automatically to revert to being a harmless, petty bourgeois, anti-Semitic party as soon as an upturn in the economy drained off the support which desperation had driven to Hitler. Adolf Hitler's last chance of gaining power has come at the point when the first faint symptoms told us that the economic crisis had passed its climax and we could look forward to a gradual easing of the misery the masses were suffering. They made sure they gave him that chance.

III

In order to get rid of a general who refused to jump to every command of the *Junkers* and industrial tycoons, they have installed as chancellor the leader of a party the most active core of which consists of social revolutionaries. In coalition with Hugenberg and Herr von Papen, Adolf Hitler will not be chancellor for long before he loses that core unit. And perhaps the whip of the new chancellor will awaken and toughen the sleeping forces of German democracy. The arrogance of the class ruling Germany today has given it, as well as Herr Hitler, a chance. The trade union organisations, not to mention the working-class parties, still remain firm and are strong enough to prevent extreme excesses on the part of the new regime. Above all there is still the need of the masses for work and bread, a need which the hordes of Hitler faithful feel just as much as their 'Marxist' counterparts. Whether there is a new Reichstag or not, the masses, whose support still forms a much stronger basis for Hitler's power than the confidence he enjoys in the presidential palace, will flock to whoever shows them a clear route to bread and work. Even today stronger battalions than Adolf Hitler's Storm Troops could be gathered under the banner of an effective job-creation programme.

Fait accompli   11 March 1933

The campaign for the elections which Hitler set for 5 March 1933 two days after coming to power in the hope of gaining an absolute majority in the Reichstag, was marked by a hitherto unknown degree of terror. In Prussia alone around 50,000 members of the SA, the SS and Stahlhelm were appointed as 'auxiliary policemen' to 'keep order'. In addition, the decree issued after the Reichstag fire 'to counter Communist acts of violence endangering the state' was the basis for a state of emergency which lasted until 1945.

Despite an election campaign which was largely conducted from the underground, the Communists maintained their position as the third largest party with 12.3 per cent of the vote; the SPD gained 18.3 per cent. With 43.9 per cent the NSDAP was well short of its goal of an absolute majority. It could only reach a parliamentary majority in coalition with the Kampffront Schwarz-Weiss-Rot (Black-White-and-Red Combat Front). But the result of these last Reichstag elections was merely symbolic – all the Communist deputies who had not already been arrested were banned from taking their seats on the basis of the Reichstag-Fire decree of 8 March. The Enabling Act, which gave the government the power to enact legislation without it being passed by the Reichstag and the Reichsrat and without the president's countersignature, was adopted on 24 March with the 444 votes of the government coalition against 94 of the SPD opposition. The abolition of the Social Democratic and Christian Social unions and their integration in the newly founded Deutsche Arbeitsfront (German Labour Front) was followed on 22 June by the ban of the SPD. Even before the vote in the Reichstag, Frick, the minister of the interior, used paragraph 2 of the Reichstag-Fire Decree to transfer executive power in the federal Länder to the National Socialists. All that was left of Weimar was the constitution – Hitler could not be bothered to repeal or replace it, and it remained in force until the end of the 'Thousand-year Empire'.

Fait accompli   11 March 1933

During the first weeks of March 1933 the struggle for power in the German Reich has proceeded at such a furious pace that these days will presumably figure in future history books as a classic example of a period in which decisive events were compressed into a short period of time. The attacking force has steamrollered its way across two lines in quick succession, leaving next to nothing between it and its destination. One line was crossed with the elections to the Reichstag. Not only has the parliamentary influence of the Catholics been sidelined – they are now only legally required for changes to the constitution – above all the power of the 'South German faction' has been emasculated; almost without exception the police forces of those *Länder* can look forward to a change of supreme commander in the near future. The Prussian monarchists have lost a good deal of their significance too. These events have swept away the most important constraints of the bourgeois centre against the total transfer of power.

But even in the preceding days another line had been crossed through the concerted measures taken following the Reichstag Fire. In part they demonstrated, in part they ensured that the proletarian workers' parties too are no longer a power to be reckoned with in German politics today. That is the clear fact of the matter and no one should try to persuade themselves otherwise. Until Herr Goering launched his attack, it was still possible for there to be differences of opinion about the power of resistance, the physical energy to defend themselves which the SPD and the KPD still had in reserve – as a last resort – for the worst-case scenario of a direct attack on them. The declarations of both parties, especially of the Social Democrats, were full of references to these last reserves and the party members themselves believed those declarations. The intellectuals expended much ink and the workers consumed much beer over discussions of what would happen if the enemy should launch the final, decisive attack. A general strike, the hundreds of thousands of *Reichsbanner* members,[81] the force of millions of workers on the march were the main elements of what they imagined the expression 'unwavering resistance' to mean in concrete terms.

Those who saw the world as it really is had long since suspected that all that was – at best – wishful thinking. They knew that the so-called 'united front' would never materialise. On the one hand the Moscow strategy, which was completely unrealistic, given the situation in Germany, stood in the way, on the other the possibly even more unrealistic belief that anticommunist good behaviour would be rewarded. And as for the two parties themselves, it has long been clear to the dispassionate observer that not only has their physical and economic strength lagged more and more behind that of the opposing side, at least since 20 July 1932 there has been no other word for the quality the military call morale than 'broken'. After that day at the latest, anyone evaluating the true balance of power without deluding themselves was forced to write off the working-class parties. It was only in other camps that forces were still in evidence which were perhaps both able and willing to take an active stand against the total transfer of power. The spinelessness with which the proletarian organisations accepted Captain Goering's brutal attacks revealed *ex post facto* the extent to which they were already devoid of life and spirit; at the same time Goering's *coup* eliminated any remaining spark of resistance. Even if tomorrow the following decree were issued under emergency legislation: 'The Social Democratic Party executive has been dismissed. It has been replaced by Dr Goebbels, Herr Mutschmann[82] and Count Helldorf.[83] All Social Democratic Party officials are to obey their orders.' – even then there would probably be no revolt. Even if a National Socialist Reich commissioner were to be put in charge of the unions – which is perhaps more imminent – and the 'Iron Front' placed under Captain Röhm,[84] even then the most that is likely to happen would be that they would dissolve themselves by their members resigning – provided resignations were not forbidden. All these practical possibilities, which no one can say are particularly far-fetched at the moment, shed a clear light on the fact that Lassalle's[85] creation, the labour organisations, have been eliminated as a physical factor in the political equation. They have been hamstrung, their existence is purely formal.

That leaves: a theoretical system, the memory of seventy years of history, vows and hope still smouldering underground and … . No one can say whether new life will emerge from these remains in the near or more distant future. At the moment, however, what appeared to be the most powerful of the defenders has been eliminated from the final struggle for power in Germany, crushed, impotent, paralysed. The Party, which could have been the sole ruler in and over Germany 14 years go, has issued a clarion call proclaiming its new political goal: 'the noble task of regaining freedom of movement for the workers'. How can one gain freedom of movement without freedom of movement?

The tragedy of such an end is devastating. It is almost incomprehensible to anyone who saw the period of the great advance, of the enthusiastic devotion of millions to the bright hope that was socialism, of the stream of impulses and energy, not only in politics, but in science, culture, art, that flowed from it. It should be a time for mourning, but History is brutally unsentimental and the faster it steams ahead, the less time it allows its creatures to linger. It establishes why a force was extinguished, the reason why a power crumbled, and that is it, until perhaps there is a resurrection. And the witness to a power struggle that has been decided has no other option than this historical attitude. As long as the struggle continued, he could issue warnings, admonitions, but once the scales have tipped, once the final decision is imminent, he must fall silent; once the die is cast, all that is left is to record how it came about. Maintaining the illusion of a force that is no longer there is at least as pernicious in politics as fabricating history is for scholarship and for the psychology of a nation.

The decisive shortcoming in the Social Democratic make-up was its complete lack of understanding of the factor of power. It was not a congenital defect, it did not come from Marx and even less from Engels; the Russia of the Red Army demonstrates that Social Democracy ought to have taken a different lesson from its own theory. As a result of the pre-war economic prosperity and especially under the influence of mediocre, ignorant, unintellectual Party secretaries à la Ebert, Wels[86], Hermann Müller or Noske, awful second-generation nonentities who took over from the founding fathers, the Party's instincts, even its public declarations, reverted to the generalised liberalism, the vaguely progressive outpourings of the old pre-1848 generation, those decent chaps whose heart was in the right place and who are excused because at that time the theory did not exist, nor the experience of the 1848 Revolution. They cannot be reproached for thinking that democracy consists of passing a certain number of laws and having a certain number of seats in parliament. Not for them to know that the democracy they idolised for the radiance of its divine beauty is nothing but a mollusc, a jellyfish, if it has no bones. That they set about creating the most delightful national political organism in 1848, only to forget the skeleton and send it off by itself in a Prussian grenadier's uniform under the command of General Wrangel,[87] quickly put an end to it. It beggars belief that after this lesson, which was part of the historical heritage of the Social Democrats, the 1918 arrangement should have been exactly the same. It is perfectly believable of some vile wretches, who betrayed their comrades with gusto and malice aforethought. What is unbelievable is that the rest of the leadership and the millions of alert supporters were incapable of doing anything about that pathetically botched job, that they could be seriously persuaded that a collection of backsides on a collection of seats meant anything like a new state! They did not understand, did not understand right up to the end, what power is and what powerlessness is, and that is the main reason for the debacle. And to listen to them today, they still think they did everything right!

History is persistent and it imposes itself against all obstacles. The historical significance of the current stage of development, as of the present economic crisis, is that technological progress has reached a point where new, appropriate economic arrangements are imperative. Economic arrangements of the type that no one outlined more clearly than the classic Social Democrat theorists and that no one promised more clamorously than their leaders in 1918, without, however, lifting a finger to realise them. It cannot be stopped; it is inevitable, it is the destiny of the years ahead that this imperative will receive its due, knowingly or unwittingly. Which political group will be the vehicle for this development, we do not yet know. It remains to be seen. It is possible that a ruse of History has taken the mission away from those who were its natural executors, but who proved unworthy and incapable. It is possible that, by the same ruse, History will hand over responsibility for carrying it out to those who have been put into power by the most sworn enemies of any economic change, the most fanatical supporters of the old order. The reality of the National Socialist régime will possibly, intentionally or unintentionally, contain considerably more 'Marxism' than the régime of those apostate disciples which the Founder would not even have given the time of day. One thing is certain: whenever – soon or in the distant future – the call of Destiny once more reaches the forces it has for the moment paralysed and eliminated, it will not, will never reach them with the current ineradicable crop of lilies of the field that adorn the Party list and occupy the Party's seats.

Das Neue Tage-Buch 1933–39

Caught up in the nationalist revolution   1 July 1933

I

Five months have passed since Captain Franz von Papen and Colonel Oskar von Hindenburg, who, shortly before, had seen it as in their own interest to dismiss Hitler's claim to the post of Chancellor with a resounding 'No!', suddenly discovered their interests demanded the opposite. Historians will find it impossible to fathom how it was that on 13 August 1932 the national interest, which is naturally always the sole deciding factor, decreed that the man who insisted on absolute control should be kept out, while on 30 January 1933 it decreed he should be called in.

In the first instance they will simply note that in the interim Herr Franz von Papen had lost the office of chancellor and that he had sworn at all costs to overthrow his overthrower, Schleicher, and to haul himself back up on top.

In the second instance they will simply note that in the meantime Herr Oskar von Hindenburg had become the source of a scandal, which Schleicher had at the very least done nothing to prevent and which was giving off an increasingly foul stench. This scandal – ironically it was General Ludendorff who had taken command of the newspaper campaign – was a regular you-scratch-my-back-and-I'll-scratch-yours scandal involving the neighbouring estates of Herr Hindenburg and Herr Oldenburg-Januschauz[1] in which one back was scratched with millions from a private foundation as well as undeclared taxes, the other with millions intended by the government to support bankrupt East Prussian estates and further undeclared taxes. The whole affair stank to high heaven and the commentaries in the left-wing and Centre Party newspapers grew more and more scathing. Together with other pieces of sharp practice by aristocratic landowners it had been the subject of a question in parliament. An investigation was in progress. A public debate in parliament was imminent.

It was at precisely this point – and that alone is what historians will be able to record – that a new revelation befell Colonel von Hindenburg, namely that the new revelation that had befallen Captain von Papen pointed in the right way and that now the national interest decreed the opposite of what it had decreed in August. Herr Hitler, with his demand for absolute control, with the millstone of his Party's debts round his neck, with the 20 per cent fall in votes at the last election, with Gregor Strasser splitting the Party behind his back and the certain, universally accepted, sharper fall-off of support facing him – this Herr Hitler was summoned to the presidential palace. The new carve-up of posts was agreed by a trio, later a quartet, behind closed doors; and it was further agreed that this *pacte à quatre*, hatched in the dark, under no compulsion whatsoever, contrary to all developments and expectations, by a capricious and despotic clique, should be masked by the glittering firework display of a 'revolution', a 'national revolution'. In the afternoon the nation learnt that since the morning it had been involved in a victorious revolution. In the evening the brown and grey crypto-armies were sent out on a torchlight parade, to make clear to the public, with due pomp and circumstance, the success of the revolution ordained from above, from the very top. Whilst revolutions usually build up pressure, then explode and bring about a change of government through the force of the explosion, in this case the change of government came first and then the non-existent revolution was staged by our new masters, *ex post facto*, so to speak.

When did a nation ever have the opportunity to take part in a 'revolution' that was not led from below against those in power, but led from above against those who had already been overthrown?

When did a nation ever have the opportunity to combine the greatest social ecstasy – revolt – with the greatest social respectability – strict subordination to the legally constituted authorities?

The masquerade worked its magic. The government's call to people to ignore the law, their announcement that savagery and violence were now not just allowed, but actually were the law, their promise that in this way every German would find bread, prosperity and freedom from troublesome competitors, released the raging movement which completely disguised the fact that the whole scene change was nothing more than a backstage fix between three soothsayers with seriously tarnished political or personal reputations.

The 'revolution' broke out and its unleashing really did serve the purpose for which Messrs Papen and Hindenburg II – hardly revolutionary types! – had adopted it as part of their script. In the face of the torrent pouring forth, no one, neither insiders nor outsiders, got round to assessing the individuals and circumstances that had, secretly and treacherously, opened the floodgates. The mere existence of the torrent seemed to prove that it must have forced its own way into history. The tracks of those two noble gentlemen who, for such noble reasons, had picked the lock of the back door to let the current occupiers in and then proclaimed the event from the balcony at the front as the verdict of history were washed away in the deluge of the *ex-post-facto* revolution. A success! The noble gentlemen could congratulate themselves. Five months ago ...

II

The months that have passed since then have presumably taught even those two noble gentlemen that their biggest mistake was to sanction and arrange the unleashing of the masses as the backdrop for their little fix. On 30 January they calculated that it would be they and the forces of their *Junker* class who would actually govern, with Hitler as their figurehead. And their calculation was correct – as long as the result was no more than a change of government and a stricter dictatorial system of government. They had eight ministries against three for the National Socialists. They had the backing of the President. They had control of Prussia. They had the army, business and, in reserve, the paramilitary *Stahlhelm* units. They could be pretty certain of staying in the saddle, provided that while negotiating this awkward hurdle they kept the racehorse – the people – on the tightest possible rein. Instead, they themselves spurred it on, whipped it up into a gallop, lashed it into a frenzy. Their strength lay in precisely those factors by means of which a privileged minority can rule the masses, and can rule them all by itself. As soon as they called on the masses to play an active role, to go out onto the streets, to exercise the authority of the state themselves, they destroyed the foundations on which their privileged position rested. It is impossible to have a 'revolution', that is, to rouse the many to independent action, without at the same time reducing the power of the few by a corresponding amount. One could not foresee that the intelligence and basic instincts of the Hindenburg-Hugenberg clique would be so debilitated that they could not comprehend even these elementary truths. One was justified in assuming that the torchlight processions of 30 January would be the only real concession to the mob. Even the most stupid, we assumed, would not be so stupid as to be taken in by their own slogans to the extent that they would allow the 'uprising' to carry on its merry way until they themselves were swept from power. No one could have imagined that a caste, whose sole asset was its centuries-old tradition, revived between 1918 and 1933, in the exercise of power, would be so intoxicated by patriotic demagoguery, impassioned vows of brotherhood and uniforms marching up and down that they would agree to the drastic measures which prepared their own, later elimination.

It is difficult to cite the precise point at which the 'revolution' had, of its own force, so emasculated its aristocratic partners that they were left defenceless and found themselves transformed from ally into victim. Does it matter? They are *hors de combat*. That most determinedly reactionary of castes, the Prussian *Junkers* and their hangers-on, has paid for its sole revolutionary venture with the end of its rule, at least for the time being and for the duration of the revolution, which seemed such an excellent idea to the talented Hindenburg-Papen duo. This caste, the classic instrument for ruling Germans, seems no more capable of playing any role at all in the phase of German history that will bear the sign and stigma of the swastika, nor even of influencing its course, than all those groups and parties which only yesterday it was helping to subjugate or to vilify.

III

The elimination of the German National Party is particularly striking not merely because it was, of all the groups that were still drifting along in suspended animation, the one with the most solid foundation. It is striking above all because the various stages of the elimination of Hugenberg were quite clearly not the result of a decision from above but of pressure from below. Once the question of power had been decided, it was clear that Mussolini's method of dealing with the party system would also be copied (while the Hungarian fascists, for example, invented different, much more flexible forms). The negative aspect of the one-party programme was settled: not to allow any cell or unit to survive which could become the source of a future attack. But beyond this certainty on the *negative* – namely that the National Socialist Party will not tolerate any political organisation beside its own – there remained uncertainty on the *positive* side – namely how political goals were to be developed within its *own* organisation. And in this area the fall of the German National Party, which is mixed up with all the problems of deciding between a socialist or capitalist, conservative or working-class way forward, provides some important hints.

For it appears that everything that was undertaken in any area against the aristocratic and middle-class right wing, which we can lump together for the sake of convenience, came from *lower* reaches – difficult to specify with any precision – of the Party, and the upper tiers only followed, reluctantly and one step at a time, as far as was unavoidable. Remember the hundreds of attacks on the *Stahlhelm* in the villages, in towns, in whole *Länder* such as Brunswick, which kept being repudiated by the next higher level up the command chain, several times by Hitler himself, only to drag on after every half-hearted compromise.

Remember the hundreds of directives not to do anything to upset industry or any kind of business, the only result of which so far appears to be that works cells, mayors and other Party organisations continue to agitate for change. The clear image is of a Party leadership which naturally wants to consolidate it power all round but does not want to touch the social order because it has made it to the top and because its whole history, its ties and instincts incline it to the upper classes and the aristocracy. Facing them, however, is a hierarchy of many millions, from the second-string of Kerrls,[2] Kubes,[3] Freislers,[4] Leys,[5] right down to the unknown storm trooper, worker, farmer and shopkeeper, who are expecting (or promising) that the real change, the great moment of fulfilment is yet to come; in their revolutionary fervour they are sufficiently uninhibited to continue to push forward, now in one place, now another, on their own initiative. There is a struggle going on between those at the top and those below in which the back-up and support of Hugenberg and his class was of such fundamental importance as a buffer to Herr Hitler, later presumably to Herr Goering as well, that they certainly had no desire to disown and annihilate them during the present phase. It wasn't Hitler – who could now be called a German Nationalist himself; at least one has not heard him use the word 'socialist' for many a long day – it wasn't the 'Führer', with his need for stability, who wanted to give his ally in the fight against his own revolution the *coup de grâce* so soon. And it is symptomatic of the whole process in which Germany has been caught up since the 'revolution' was unleashed that this pressure from below has been strong enough to force the leadership to sacrifice its own accomplice.

One could say that the 'Führer' is in the same position in 1933 as his worthy predecessor, Ebert, was in 1918. Both had to get their revolutionaries quickly back on a tight leash. Ebert's success in shackling the forces of radical change, which laid the foundations of the Third Reich, was both thorough and exemplary. In memory of this achievement, the street leading to the Reichstag in the capital, where all memory of the 'November criminals' and 'Marxists' has been erased, still bears the honourable name *Friedrich-Ebert-Strasse*. For Hitler the task is more difficult. Social Democracy had only made promises to the industrial workers, so they were the only people Ebert had to cheat out of their promised rewards. The promises (the public promises!) made by National Socialism, inflated to extravagant levels, have been showered on the industrial workers and the farmers and the middle class. They are absolutely incompatible, each one directly contradicting the other. Each of the three estates is 'on the move' – to get what they were told was their due. Moreover Hitler's armed force, the SA, is to a large extent identical with the revolutionaries. And they are not peaceable men, nor are they weary of conflict, in fact they have hardly had a proper taste of the intoxication of violence. The outcome of this subterranean struggle can no more be predicted than the outcome of a game of chess that has only just begun.

It is possible that those are right who suspect that all efforts to divert this struggle towards easier targets – and initially such efforts can be expected to come in waves – will only prolong the revolutionary ferment and make matters worse. They may also be right in arguing that under the pressure of the crisis, which no amount of fake statistics can relieve, the revolution will continue to drift along its unpredictably haphazard way, with no guiding idea and no progamme, into confusion, disruption and anarchy. But it is equally possible that eventually the German nation's instinct for obedience will be sufficient – despite years of schooling in ruthlessness, despite the pathological stimulation of every instinct of hatred and envy, despite all the drill and calls for violence and for taking the law into one's own hands, despite the idolisation of emotion and the downgrading of reason, despite the glorification of arbitrary despotism and lawlessness – to restrain and subjugate it, to force it under the yoke of a solid dictatorship, where it will have to suffer in silence whatever joy or misery awaits it. No one can say what the outcome will be. All prophecies, however convincing they sound, however scientific the jargon they are couched in, are pure guesswork. Just one thing is clear: this revolution is not over yet, only now has it reached the stage where it is gradually changing from a matter between the victorious party and its opponents into a process *within* the victorious party.

IV

There is only one patch of dry ground in this murky, seething morass of uncertainty. Whatever happens, one thing is already beyond question today: part of the innate and immutable characteristics of the new era is an unremitting psychological and physical descent into some kind of military conflagration. The field of *war* is the only area in which National Socialist theory and practice are completely clear and in harmony, the only area in which from day one a consistent line has been pursued. What can be said about that is clearly set out not only in Hitler's Holy Writ (of which, at the same time as they take offence at people 'still' quoting from it 'even today', they are pouring thousands and thousands of free copies into schools, universities, associations and factories); it is also set out in all the speeches for home consumption; and it is most clearly set out in the measures taken by the government. The Commissioner for Sport – when addressing the home audience – has made no secret of the fact that he sees his task as fulfilling a 'military' objective; and the Commissioner for the Labour Service – when addressing the home audience – has made no secret of the fact hat he sees his mission in military terms. No one on God's earth can or will deny that the ideals which are instilled in the Hitler Youth, the SA, the SS, the Stahlhelm and whatever else are military, entirely military. Nor will anyone need to rack their brains about what mysterious psychological purpose is served by the patriotic ceremonies and solemn commemorations which have come so thick and fast. And it is a fact that even in the area where the new era is still stumbling around in the dark, in economic policy, the only firm steps that have been taken are those securing Germany's supply of war materials; it was this consideration that was expressly given, in the official communiqué, as the reason for the Law on Fats of April – the sole substantial piece of economic legislation that has so far been enacted.

Bearing all that in mind, it means little that occasionally – for foreign consumption – a peaceful tone is adopted. And it means nothing at all when they protest, 'But we have no military equipment!' – a claim which, despite Goering, Rheinmetall[6] and BMW, may still be partly true today but will, at some point or other, be completely untrue, if only because the current equipment for land warfare is becoming obsolete at a galloping pace and even today is not much more than scrap metal, compared to equipment for the air force. It is not the armaments that are the priority at the moment, but the nation's psychology, whose pressure gauge is constantly kept at the level of an army camp about to march off to war. No, there is no war planned, there is no desire for war at the moment. Nothing concrete, nothing immediate. But there is that terrible gospel according to Herr Hitler and the banalities of his patriotic outpourings on our 'great Fatherland'. Behind them is a very literal interpretation of the word 'great': it is understood in terms of square metres. At Versailles Germany lost some provinces; since then it has lived in poverty and shame. Honour and wealth can only be restored if the film can be run backwards: if those same square metres can be reconquered or at least some others, at best even more, simply conquered.

The gospel according to Hitler appears in a thousand forms. It speaks in the demand for treaty revision. It lies behind the call for colonies. It is the driving force behind the claim to Austria. Messrs Hugenberg and Schacht embrace it when they write and submit memoranda demanding nothing less than a few bordering states and Russian provinces. Territory, territory, territory! Territory that was lost or territory that was never in our possession, it doesn't matter which! Only rulers who win territory earn fame and glory, and Hitler is not averse to glory. Only the honour and good fortune of expanding the reduced country once more can redeem us from the shame and destitution which the 'plundering' of German territory brought upon the country; and Germany does not want shame and destitution. It is a waste of breath to point out that no Swiss or Dutchman feels shamed or destitute because his country is only small and not 'ethnically whole'. Any attempt to make people understand that size has nothing to do with prosperity, defeat nothing to do with honour, the acquisition of land nothing to do with 'vitality', gets nowhere. It is axiomatic, it is part of the creed.

The objectives – concrete and abstract, personal and collective – merge; the desire for glory, concepts of national honour and economic madness all come together in one point: the acquisition of territory. It is the most profound, perhaps the only genuine religion of both the Führer and the faithful, and relates his gospel to the Sibylline Books of traditional Prussian wisdom.[7] The purpose of the systematic militarisation of society is to serve this religion, as is the best possible preparation for the day on which, wherever, the opportunity will present itself to satisfy the dictates of 'territorial dynamics' – whether by threat or by more, whether on old or new frontiers. And there is no escaping this religion. It informs every fibre, especially Hitler's.

But things look different from the perspective of those who are possible victims of these dynamics; among them are all our neighbours, without exception. Making all one's neighbours nervous for a short time, or one neighbour nervous all the time, is one thing. But making all one's neighbours nervous all the time is bound to end in tears. Even to ponder why, when and how the panic, which is inevitable, given such a ceaseless strain on everyone's nerves, will break out would be to play fate. Only one thing is more or less inconceivable: that a country can methodically, noisily, recklessly cultivate in its population a fanatical belligerence such as has never been seen before without one day finding itself in the classic situation of having to take the consequences of its actions, or having them taken for it by others.

Severing rules in Europe   3 February 1934

In March 1933, shortly after Hitler's seizure of power, parliamentary government in Austria collapsed and the chancellor, Engelbert Dollfuss, established an 'Austro-fascist' corporate state with the support of Mussolini. From the very beginning Hitler naturally had one eye on his home country, which he wanted to bring 'home to the Reich' at all costs, if possible without arousing the kind of protests from the Allies that the Brüning/Curtius plan for a customs union had provoked in 1931. Hitler's approaches did not find favour with the catholic Dollfuss, however, who on 19 June 1933 had the Austrian National Socialist Party, which was part of the German NSDAP, banned in Austria. That set off a furious propaganda campaign against the Austrian government, which Hitler sought to give economic weight by selective sanctions against Austria, including a ban on German tourists travelling there. Austria complained to the Western powers, upon which Britain and France delivered a protest note (the démarche amicale referred to by Schwarzschild) to Berlin on 7 August 1933; its effectiveness was, however, seriously impaired by the absence of Italy. Through direct contact with Hitler Mussolini had already received assurances that Germany's subversive activities in Austria would be reduced. During the next few months, as the situation did in fact calm down, the Allies set about reformulating their position on Austria. These deliberations culminated on 17 February 1934 in a joint declaration by the three major powers of Western Europe directed against Germany and supporting Austria. However, by this time Austria was a more or less fascist dictatorship, which meant that the extent of the declaration of support was immediately and justifiably called into question. One week previously Dollfuss, with the help of the Austrian Heimwehr, the Christian Social militia, had successfully put down an uprising by the socialist Republikanischer Schutzbund. Despite the weakness of the Social Democratic Party, which called for but could not bring about a general strike, it did result in heavy fighting in Linz and Vienna. The Austrian Civil War was to remain the sole armed resistance to the fascist rape of European democracy before 1939. The uprising was followed by a ban on the Social Democratic Party, the unions, all Social Democratic workers' associations and the municipal and Land councils run by the Social Democrats. But the National Socialists were more difficult to control, even though Dollfuss imposed ever more draconian punishments against nefarious activities. In July 1934 he was killed in the course of an attempted putsch by a Viennese SS unit which was quickly put down.

In the autumn of 1933 the Austrian project appeared to have been put on ice for a while. In the meantime Hitler set about extricating himself from the tangle of multilateral relationships, which in his eyes worked entirely to Germany's disadvantage, weakening her and preventing her from exercising her legitimate rights. On 14 October 1933 he announced Germany's withdrawal from the League of Nations, provoking consternation among the international community, but no countermeasures, since it was, after all, Germany's sovereign right to free herself from such associations. The second step towards the bilateralisation of Germany's external relationships was the non-aggression pact with Poland which Germany concluded in January 1934, to the great amazement of the Western powers. With this pact Hitler relaxed the atmosphere on Germany's eastern frontier, where the unpredictable Marshal Pilsudski was in charge on the other side, and at the same time prevented a rapprochement between Poland and Czechoslovakia. The pact was also the first nail in the coffin of the plan promoted by the French prime minister, Barthou, who wanted to tie Germany down in an international treaty system with a comprehensive East European security alliance. The pact with Poland was naturally not binding. As early as October 1933 Hitler told Hermann Rauschnigg, the president of the Danzig senate, 'all agreements with Poland are merely temporary. I have no intention whatsoever of coming to a serious understanding with Poland.'

Thus it was immediately after Hitler's assumption of power that the six years of tit-for-tat of aggressive German actions and passive Allied reactions began. Schwarzschild believed the SPD was partly responsible for the collapse of the Weimar Republic; after 1933 it was the social democratic and, later, the conservative parties of Western Europe that drove him to despair. These were his 'Severings', the people who, despite the victory of fascism in Germany, hoped that the German chancellor would turn into a decent fellow if they only treated him politely for long enough. His contemptuous nickname for them, 'Severing', refers to the Social Democrat Carl Severing (1875–1952) who was minister of the interior in Prussia from 1920 to 1926, German minister of the interior in Hermann Müller's cabinet after 1928 and, in response to the growing political tension, once more minister of the interior in Prussia from 1928 on. Despite his powerful position, he was incapable of putting any effective obstacles in the way of the Nazis' rise to power. Severing submitted without resistance to Franz von Papen's 'Prussian coup' of July 1932, by which the last Social-Democratic regional government was dismissed by emergency decree. Given the widespread unemployment, the SPD considered it pointless to call for a general strike and they also decided armed resistance by the Prussian police force had no prospect of success, given the Army's attitude of approval towards the decree. The Social Democrats and union leaders pinned their hopes – ultimately vain hopes – on the Reichstag elections that were to be held on 31 July 1932, which, however, the NSDAP won convincingly. Despite all this, it is certainly unfair to show Severing solely in this light. During the Hitler putsch of 1923 he had mobilised the Berlin police when General von Seekt told him that the Army units in Berlin would not oppose the putsch.

Severing rules in Europe   3 February 1934

Hitler has celebrated the anniversary of his assumption of office with a speech in which he once more declared that he had saved Germany – at the eleventh hour so to speak – from collapse. The country was approaching collapse, he said, because of democracy and the Treaty of Versailles. This officially sanctioned National Socialist version will take up a lot of pages in the writings of future historians. To put them on the right track, we must continue to point out that in the first place there was no question of collapse, that, on the contrary, Germany had emerged from the damage caused by defeat with a speed one would not have thought possible and made immense progress; further, that it was no worse hit by the crisis that started in the middle of 1929 than most other developed countries; and finally, that the deepening of the crisis in 1931 was a purely political matter and was not a consequence of democracy and the Treaty of Versailles, but of a campaign, that rocked both Germany and the wider world, *against* democracy, *against* the Treaty of Versailles. The specifically German crisis, which eventually brought Hitler to power, was not the result of a particular set of circumstances, but of the undermining of those circumstances by the person who set out to undermine them in order to come to power and did in fact come to power.

But that is just a note for historians. It is of no importance for the present. That Hitler is in power is a fact. However interesting the internal dealings and developments of the regime may and will be, the fact that it is governing and that it is a very strong regime is indisputable. It is founded on the bayonet and systematic terror, an excellent basis, unlike formal democratic principles, for remaining in power for a long time. It is a particularly excellent basis for remaining in power for a long time when at the same time one is adept at using all possible means – presents, favours, the methodical misrepresentation of all important matters, modern advertising and the like – to gain popularity. There is disgruntlement, disappointment, bitterness in many places, among churchgoers, monarchists, the middle classes, the workers, and everywhere with good reason. But to a certain extent these feelings are held in check by the fact that the regime adopts a fairly neutral attitude, that it does not entirely deprive any side of hope. That is what happened in the conflict within the Protestant church, that is what is happening with the monarchists, to whom Hitler has just offered a ray of hope that commits him to nothing when he said in his anniversary speech that 'the final decision on the ultimate constitution of the Reich' had yet to be taken. But they are no more than a kind of negative reserve in case a situation should arise in which the regime might be weakened for some other reason. So far nothing of the sort has been evident. On the contrary, the new law for the unification of the German states[8] shows that its power is still expanding.

And looking at it dispassionately, one has to admit that in the international sphere too, its name shines forth, despite all the talk designed to tarnish it. The German dictatorship is advancing towards dictatorship over the whole of north-west Europe, with almost no resistance. In fact, there is only one concrete barrier left: the little patch of earth over which it is in conflict with the other dictatorship, the Italian one, which would like to maintain some insulation, a kind of security cordon, between itself and its German counterpart. This little buffer zone, the point of contact, of intersection between the two dictatorships, is Austria. It is where one determined force comes up against another, the situation is uncertain, the consequences unforeseeable. The great democracies are offering practically no resistance. When he intimated to Austria that he did not want to see complications between the great powers over such a minor matter, Ramsay Macdonald made absolutely clear what everyone knew anyway: namely that if Austria were to be conquered by Germany it could *not* expect any support from the present government of the British Empire. It is equally clear that that is also true of the present attitude in France. France will go along with anything that London decides. It will be even more willing to endorse anything Italy does (Britain only reluctantly, if at all). It is deluding oneself to imagine that Italy would go it alone, without being assured of the collaboration of the two other great powers. That meant that in his speech all Hitler needed to do was to emphasise the formal point that the Austrian Nazis were, of course, Austrians (which is not even true in formal terms, since the Austrian SA, with its headquarters in Linz, is officially recognised as Group VIII of the German SA) to trigger off tumultuous applause in Britain, thereby virtually neutralising

France. That he went on to say that his fervent hopes were with those Austrians 'whose heartfelt desire is to be united with the 66 million Germans in the Reich' and called the separation of the two countries 'unbearable', that he expressed the hope (not the certainty) 'that fate would allow a peaceful solution to this unbearable situation' went too far beyond mere formalities, went to the heart of the matter, and was therefore of no interest.

The significance of this attitude towards Austria for the overall situation in Europe was described in our issue of 12 August after the famous 'démarche amicale'. And developments continue to be consistent with this. Poland was the first to take the logical step. When in November Germany and Poland announced their intention to sign a non-aggression treaty, the direction could be seen. In these pages we asked, 'Is it a warning signal to Paris, saying: "If things come to a head, you'd better watch out."? Or is it a declaration: "Even though we know that we can only come to terms with Germany by making significant sacrifices, we still prefer that to being destroyed. If you continue to pursue a policy which tells us that, if the worst comes to the worst, we may well be on our own, we have no choice but to save our own skins."' The pact that has now been concluded answers the question. It is not simply a non-aggression pact; it contains the provision that the two signatories intend to resolve *all* questions affecting them by means of *direct, bi-lateral* negotiations. That is the exact opposite of the previous method, that is to abandon the League of Nations' principle of multilateral negotiations. And that is precisely Hitler's goal: to face every single one of his neighbours, of which every single one is much weaker than Germany, on its own and to be free to choose how he deals with each one at any given moment. It is understandable why, in his speech, Hitler placed this success at the beginning of his survey of foreign affairs. It is understandable why he put forward this principle of the nations going into negotiations two by two as the solution for the whole of Europe. He wrapped it up in fervent assurances of peaceful intentions – of course, what else should he do? Admit that he's trying to dupe the whole world?

But anyone who wants to check how genuine all these assurances are should consider the following remarkable sentence: 'When I assumed power on 30 January, I had the impression that relationships between our two countries were far from being satisfactory ... There was the danger of hostility arising which over time could turn into deep-seated hatred ...' He had the impression! There was a danger! That he was the one who had spent the previous 13 years doing his best to fan the flames of hostility, to whip up hatred – in speeches and writings full of fanaticism and hysteria – was clearly a fact that had slipped his memory!

So much on the genuineness of his assurances, but it is pointless to discuss it. Hitler has the good fortune to be facing a world of Macdonaldism, a world consisting of precisely the same types as the Severings who had faced him in Germany: formalistic democrats, abstract pacifists. That is, the kind of politician who has some perfect state of affairs in mind; who imagines how harmoniously everything could be done, if that perfect state of affairs had already been reached, but then goes about things in that way, even though that state of affairs has not been reached by a long way; goes about things in that way *in order* to reach that perfect state of affairs. Acting as if the goal – world peace, democracy – were already there. What is meant to be the result of the action becomes the starting point for their actions, trying to create democracy by behaving as if everyone wanted democracy, as if everyone wanted peace. Yes, it is the same sort of opponent as he was able to crush at home, it is exactly the same Severing that he now faces on the world stage. German democracy looked on apathetically as its mortal enemies at home grew too strong for it, even sharpening their butcher's knives openly in the street, and we have here almost the same apathy towards the same phenomenon abroad. We had the constitution, with the protection of its various sections, here there are treaties, with the protection of their various sections. We had the Supreme Court, to which one could appeal; here there is the League of Nations, to which one can appeal. We had our wise and faithful Hindenburg, who at least always showed ... and whose influence was strong enough to ... and here there is our wise friend Mussolini, who has always showed ... and whose influence is at least strong enough to ... In Germany you hear, 'You're forgetting the army. You're forgetting we have the police, the Reichsbanner, proletarian class consciousness. You're forgetting that Germany isn't Italy.' Here you hear, 'You're forgetting Poland. You're forgetting we have the army, fortresses, antifascist sympathies. You're forgetting that France isn't Germany.'

What profound ignorance of this particular opponent! What distinguishes him is that he has not only avowed himself a true believer in violence in practice, but that in everything he calls theory and science he views violence as the outright, absolute creative force, under all circumstances. It is absurd to apply concepts such as negotiation, compromise, pact, treaty – concepts which come from an entirely different outlook – to an outlook in which all they mean is gaining time, dividing your opponents, concealing your intentions. They are modes and terms which have acquired a specific meaning in transactions between sides that accept the status quo and their traditional meaning is assumed when they are employed by this flagrant freebooter. Politics according to the one-size-fits-all democratic, pacifist conventions collapsed when faced with an opponent who simply ignored those conventions; a few months later, in the course of a search for a better way, they suddenly reappeared as the latest thing, the very thing, that at least had to be tried out. These people have no ability to produce any other formula than one that has been proved wrong a dozen times; no aversion to once more proposing, as a means of steadying the ship of state, a process that has already led to instability ten times over. An image of the pathology of the German Republic is being projected onto the screen of international relations: the hypnotised pilgrimage of German democracy to the guillotine of its subjugator, tragically expanded into a similarly hypnotised pilgrimage of the European democracies to the same guillotine.

And both at home and abroad we see the same, not quite sincere arrogance in the face of warnings, the same very sincere irritation at anything that might disturb the phoney peace; the same tactic of lulling the public into a false sense of security instead of doing everything to rouse them to action. Just as at home, out in the wider world we see the same contrast between energetic recruitment, despatching a hundred thousand well-organised, enthusiastic agents into every last corner, coming up with new ideas all the time, spewing out more and more millions in gold, and, on the other hand, a pale, middle-of-the-road routine of yesteryear, just about managing to keep doing what has always been done, just about managing to keep doing it the way it has always been done, with the set-up of an average stationery shop, with the methods of an average city council, with the funds an average car factory would spend on advertising: nations that are being distracted, willingly allowing themselves to be distracted, from the most burning issues of life and death; on this other side are the nations which do not see and are not shown that they have entered on the acute, decisive phase in an international development in which there is nothing less at stake for them than freedom or serfdom, peace or war – fairly significant differences, I would say. What they see instead, because that is what they are being shown, is that on the one hand the Labour Party would like some ministerial posts, on the other so would the Unionists, that some propose to cover a budget deficit with 40 per cent direct and 60 per cent indirect taxes, while others propose 60 per cent direct and 40 per cent indirect taxes – differences of which common sense, with the best will in the world, could not say what the difference actually is.

That is the world which Hitler, after one year in office, has to reckon with and is reckoning with. He has experience in subjugating a world like that.

The memorandum that was unfortunately never sent

15 September 1934

After Germany's defeat in the First World War, the Treaty of Versailles made the Saarland, with its 800,000 inhabitants, a mandated territory of the League of Nations. German anger at the Treaty was increased by the fact that the chairmanship of the League of Nations commission responsible for the territory was given to France, which also received the rights to the Saar mines as part of German reparations. As provided for in the Treaty of Versailles, a plebiscite was held on 13 January 1935, under the supervision of the League of Nations. The vote had been preceded by years of massive propaganda, above all from the German side. As early as 1933 the centre and right-wing parties in the Saarland had combined in the 'German Front'. In the plebiscite, 90.8 per cent of the electorate of 540,000 voted to return to Germany, only 0.4 per cent for France. Germany's success in the Saar plebiscite increased Hitler's prestige abroad and his popularity at home. On 1 March the newly created Saarland Gau became part of Germany.

Barthou, who had become French prime minister in February 1934 and had taken a much tougher stance towards Germany than his predecessors, had planned to make the Saar plebiscite a defeat for Hitler. He had been prepared to carry out an expensive propaganda campaign, for which he had made a few hundred million francs available. But only eight months after assuming office he was shot in Marseilles together with King Alexander of Yugoslavia. His successor was Pierre Laval, who abandoned the strategy of isolating Germany and with it French influence on the Saar plebiscite.

The memorandum that was unfortunately never sent

15 September 1934

We, the undersigned ambassadors of France, Great Britain and Italy, have been instructed by our governments to issue the following statement to the German government:

I

Several times recently members of the German government, first and foremost the chancellor, have made public declarations regarding their foreign policy objectives. In brief these declarations indicated that,

1. the German government has no desire to obtain *any part of the territory* of any other state; nor is it one of its goals to infringe the *sovereignty* of any other state;
2. the German government is determined never *to go to war* to achieve any of its goals;
3. these points are especially relevant to relations with France, though with the proviso that the Saar problem has yet to be resolved between the two countries.

As far as the last point is concerned, the three governments regret to note that the German government is labouring under a false assumption, which they hope is based solely on a misapprehension. There is, in fact, no Saar problem. As has long been agreed, the population itself will decide on the future of the region in a few months' time. All that remains is to wait for this decision and to accept it. There is no problem for any government here.

Even less is it a question that has to be settled between France and Germany. The question was wisely taken out of the sphere of a head-to-head dispute when all signatories to the Peace Treaty expressly ceded any individual rights, whether moral or legal, to third parties. They transferred the actual decision to the people of the Saarland. They transferred the arrangements for this decision to the League of Nations as collective trustee. Thus all signatories to the peace treaty have relinquished – irrevocably relinquished – any legal or moral justification for taking an active role in the matter of the Saarland. It is, therefore, in no way a matter of dispute between any of the signatories to the treaty, not even between France and Germany. The three governments felt it was essential to make this point clear, given the possible consequences.

II

Apart from the misapprehension about the Saar question, the German declarations summarised above seem very far-reaching and satisfactory. If these declarations genuinely represented an accurate and reliable description of the intentions of the current government, if they were beyond doubt, then it would be no exaggeration to say that they could be the start of a new era.

Unfortunately there are certain facts that make it impossible for responsible governments to take these declarations as seriously as they would like. The three governments believe they have a duty to point out one particularly grave obstacle to this. The fact in question is a matter of general knowledge;

it is a constant subject of public discussion in all countries and is the cause of great unease. One could perhaps therefore expect the German government to feel it necessary to deal with this well-known fact openly of its own accord. It decided the right course was silence. But its silence has only increased concern and if the three governments were to ignore it any longer they would expose themselves to the criticism that in taking no action they had allowed a dangerous untruth to be accepted on the international stage.

They therefore feel duty bound to point out that the declarations quoted above are not the only ones regarding the aims of German foreign policy. There are others that state the precise opposite. They are to be found, to mention but one place, in the definitive book, *Mein Kampf*, the author of which is the current German chancellor. Given the position of sole and absolute responsibility for decision-making granted to the person of the chancellor in accordance with the *Führer*-principle, the irreconcilable contradiction between the government declarations quoted above and the approach expressed in that book undeniably constitute a fact of the greatest importance.

III

Many quotations could be found to demonstrate this contradiction, for the book keeps repeating the same propositions and has nothing but scorn and contempt for those who are willing to entertain others. The three governments will limit themselves to just a few references.[9]

On declaration 1 of the German government
Contrary to the declaration that Germany has no desire to obtain any territory of any other state, nor is it one of its goals to infringe the sovereignty of any other state the book contains among others the following statements:

a) *The incorporation of Austria:* 'German-Austria must return to the great German mother country ... One blood demands one Reich.' (p. 3)
b) *New territory:* 'If the National Socialist movement really wants to be consecrated by history with a great mission for our nation it must ... find the courage to gather our people and their strength for an advance along the road that will lead this people from its present restricted living space to *new land and soil* ...' (p. 590)
   'Yes, from the past we can only learn that, in setting an objective for our political activity, we must proceed in two directions; *Land and soil* as

the goal of our foreign policy, and a new, philosophically established, uniform foundation as the aim of political activity at home.' (p. 593)

'As opposed to this, we National Socialists must hold unflinchingly to our aim in foreign policy, namely to secure for the German people *the land and soil* to which they are entitled on this earth. And this action is the only one which, before God and our German posterity, would make any sacrifice of blood seem justified.' (p. 596)

'If we speak of new soil in Europe today, we can primarily have in mind only Russia and her vassal border states. (p. 598)

c) *To smash any other military power:* 'Regard any attempt to organise a second military power on the German frontiers ... as an attack on Germany, and in it see not only the right, but also the duty to employ all means up to armed force to prevent the rise of such a state, or, if one has already arisen, *to smash it* again.' (p. 607, which contains the so-called 'Political Will')

On declaration 2 of the German government

Contrary to the declaration that the German government does not intend to go to war to achieve any of its goals the book contains the following statements among others:

a) 'to employ all means up to *armed force*' (quoted in c above)
b) 'And this action is the only one which... would make any *sacrifice of blood* seem justified.' (quoted in b above)
c) 'For oppressed territories are led back to the bosom of a common Reich, not by flaming protests, but by a *mighty sword*.' (p. 558)
d) 'Today I am guided by the sober realisation that lost territories are not won back by sharp parliamentary big-mouths and their glibness of tongue, but by a *sharp sword*; in other words, by a *bloody fight*.' (p. 574)
e) 'Just as our ancestors did not receive the soil on which we live today as a gift from Heaven, but had to fight for it at the risk of their lives, in the future no folkish grace will win soil for us and hence life for our people, but only the might of a *victorious sword*.' (p. 597)
f) 'An Alliance whose aim does not embrace a *plan for war* is senseless and worthless.' (p. 603)

On declaration 3 of the German government
Contrary to the declaration that the German government has quite specifically no aspirations, especially not military ones, regarding French

possessions and territory, the book contains the following statements among others:

a)   The above-mentioned '*smashing*' of every military power on Germany's borders.
b)   'The inexorable *mortal enemy* of the German people is and remains France.' (p. 565)
c)   'Only when the vital will of the German nation is no longer allowed to languish in purely passive defence, but is pulled together for a *final active reckoning with France* and thrown into a *last decisive struggle* with the greatest ultimate aims of the German side – only then will we be able to end the eternal and essentially so fruitless struggle between ourselves and France; presupposing, of course, that Germany actually regards the destruction of France as only a means which will afterwards enable her finally to give our people the expansion made possible elsewhere.' (p. 616)
d)   'Today every power is our natural ally, which like us feels French domination on the continent to be intolerable. No path to such a power can be too hard for us, and no renunciation can seem unutterable if only the end result offers the possibility of *downing our grimmest enemy*.' (p. 609)

The three governments stress that these are not quotations taken out of context and contrary to the overall sense, they are simply particularly precise formulations of the overall sense of the book. There would be no point in the German government trying to deny this.

IV

The three governments have tried to assess which of the two contradictory expressions of intent carries more weight, the older book or the more recent declarations. In all honesty, they have to say that their conclusions did not come down on the side of the latter. From the outset they had to take into account what history tells us, namely that there is no government which, however aggressive its later actions, did not deny such aims beforehand. Declarations of peaceful intent alone, therefore, cannot be counted as evidence of the true aims of the government. They are only convincing to the extent that they are backed up by other factors. *Mein Kampf* does not back up the German government's declarations.

It is of course possible that the ideas expounded in it do not correspond to the author's present convictions. It is possible that he would reject them today – and not just the excerpts quoted above, but everything else the book has to say on foreign policy, which they accurately reflect. In that case, the recent declarations could be meant as a kind of retraction of the book. However, nothing has emerged which would suggest a retraction. The approach to domestic policy set out in the book has been pursued consistently right up to the present; that the approach to foreign policy no longer applies would be a very shaky assumption. On the contrary, reports in the German press indicate that the book is more widely distributed among the German population than ever before, in part with public funding. The very special position the chancellor occupies means that *Mein Kampf* plays a role no other book plays, whichever masterpiece one considers. It is presented and is expected to be taken as the irrefutable, immutable foundation of a system that, its creator claims, is designed to last for centuries. The ideas behind it are intended to be a binding 'testament' to direct an endless line of future generations, that is long after their author has departed this world and therefore long after any possibility of changes to it has disappeared.

In these circumstances we are forced to conclude that if the approach to foreign policy in *Mein Kampf* really has been superseded by these more recent declarations, it is not enough to spread a new, totally different doctrine alongside the old one, while that remains unchanged in circulation. Given the dangers inherent in the old approach, which can hardly be overestimated, given the provocation it represents to the world at large and the prestige it enjoys in Germany, an express and definitive retraction is necessary, and should be delivered in a form designed to attract and impress itself on the international public. The German government, which has used very effective means to negate the popularity and effectiveness of books they believe to be harmful and dangerous, will surely find the appropriate form.

The three governments hope to have shown one of the main reasons – although not the only one – why the German government's recent declarations lack the effectiveness they need. They would very much like to be able to base their future actions on these declarations, but that is unfortunately not possible as long as a contrary policy, which enjoys equal, indeed superior esteem, continues to exist. The responsibility for this does not lie with the three governments. Their purpose in issuing this memorandum is to make the responsibility clear to all those to whom the German government's declarations are addressed.

After the announcement   23 March 1935
Days that shook the world   30 March 1935
The crucial role of peace   11 May 1935

Hitler's plans for war made Germany's rearmament a central element of Nazi policy. Secret rearmament, which had begun immediately after the Treaty of Versailles, was speeded up after Hitler's assumption of power; Germany's withdrawal from the League of Nations in October 1933 made it easier for him to conceal this. Finally, on 8 March 1935, in the first of what were later to be called 'Saturday surprises', Hermann Goering, the commissioner for aviation, announced the existence of a German air force, which was forbidden under the Treaty of Versailles. There were few protests from the Western powers, since the fact that Germany was rearming was widely known – five days previously the British government had published a White Paper referring to German rearmament and announcing their own plans to increase military capacity. On 6 March France reintroduced conscription. Given this, Hitler felt justified in finally repudiating, on 16 March 1935, the military requirements of the Treaty of Versailles and introducing conscription. Military service was at first set at one year, then extended to two in August 1936. The aim was to build up the Army to 36 divisions with a total of 580,000 men by 1939.

The Western powers did protest against German rearmament, but the differences within the alliance were too great for this to develop into lasting and united resistance to Germany. Initially Britain, France and Italy combined on 14 April 1935 in the Stresa Front and undertook to take joint action in response to any further treaty violations by Germany. Mussolini felt as threatened as France by German rearmament, and even ordered partial mobilisation. At the opening of the conference on Lago Maggiore he greeted the delegates with: 'All of you who are gathered here know that Germany has the intention of conquering everything as far as Baghdad.' France also reacted by reopening negotiations on a treaty with Moscow, with the result that a treaty of mutual assistance against Germany was signed on 2 May 1935. Two weeks later the Soviet Union and Czechoslovakia concluded a similar agreement, which continued the dismantling of the structures set up by the League of Nations and initiated by Hitler with the Polish non-aggression pact of January 1934. The problem for the Western powers was that Britain remained opposed to a policy of 'encirclement' and was thus determined to prevent such initiatives on the part of France at all cost. Whitehall also wearied of the French refusal to

126

sign an arms treaty with Germany while at the same time looking to Britain for military support. Britain had no sympathy for French scepticism towards Hitler for, as the Times had reported two years previously, if a statesman, who is known for keeping his word, solemnly commits himself not to go to war with France, that gesture ought at least to be sufficient to facilitate better understanding between Germany and Britain. In addition to that, Stanley Baldwin's Conservative government believed it would be possible to include Germany in a European peace alliance, if she were allowed a certain degree of rearmament. In January 1935 the Foreign Office and the Army chiefs of staff had agreed to tolerate the following measures: the reintroduction of conscription, the abolition of the military clauses of the Treaty of Versailles and an air force with a maximum of a thousand military aircraft. The British protest note of 18 March was thus more a matter of form than an expression of genuine concern, and ended rather surprisingly by enquiring whether the German government were not in favour of going ahead after all with the visit of the foreign minister, Lord Simon, which Hitler had only just cancelled. Paul Schmidt, Hitler's interpreter, reports that this enquiry 'caused a real sensation, for the last thing we were expecting was a polite enquiry from the English as to whether they might come to Berlin after all.' From the very beginning, then, the Stresa Front, which had just been set up, was on very shaky foundations. Britain's efforts to come to an arrangement with Hitler on her own resulted in a Naval Agreement which the two countries signed on 18 June 1935, the 120th anniversary of the Battle of Waterloo and which allowed Germany to increase its naval forces substantially. In so doing Britain managed to break no less than seven pacts and agreements, according to which she should not have held bilateral negotiations with Germany. After two months the Stresa Front, and with it France's policy of containment, was in ruins. The lessons from this episode were not lost on other expansionist dictators in Europe. Mussolini was quite right to conclude that independent initiatives in foreign policy would not meet with united resistance and that he did not need to allow treaties, accords or agreements to restrict the scope of his activities. Four months later he exploited this knowledge in Abyssinia, which itself formed an interesting precedent for Hitler as he wondered how he could get the Rhineland back.

After the announcement   23 March 1935

I

Why Hitler should announce the existence of the new German army on 16 March and why he should choose the manner of announcing it that he did would provide material for a nice feature article.

If one sticks to the essentials, however, the question of the timing and the manner disappear far, far into the background. And the essentials are that the new German army was in existence long before the announcement, that the whole world had long known this and had still done nothing to prevent it. This makes it abundantly clear that the 'whole world' had long since accepted the existence of this new army and had decided to do nothing to about it. It also makes it abundantly clear that, as far as this essential fact is concerned, nothing will change. Apparently it does occasionally happen that illegitimate children are murdered after – and because – they have been born. But I assume none has ever had to die because an official birth certificate was issued, least of all because of a birth certificate that was only issued after it came of age.

From the very outset, then, it was certain that even after the announcement nothing would be done to interfere with the project that was closest to Hitler's heart, namely his army. It is true that the latest diplomatic communiqués – including the Franco-British one of 3 February[10] – do contain some toothless mumbo-jumbo about unauthorised one-sided rearmament, but that doesn't even 'save face'. For even as they were writing those words, they knew perfectly well that what they described as 'unauthorised' was going ahead despite that, was going full steam ahead. It was described months ago with figures and other details by members of the French government and parliamentary officials from the platform of the French chamber. It can't get more official than that and the figures given there were even more accurate (and more alarming) than the perfunctory Berlin announcement that 'thirty-six divisions' were going to be formed. Stanley Baldwin, in his November speech in the Commons, gave grossly inaccurate figures on Goering's air force,[11] but even he did officially register the existence of a German air force. And in the meantime all the French material has been made available to the British government, and they confirmed it in their White Paper among other things.[12]

The ritual phrases about the unauthorised nature of something of whose existence they were fully aware were sufficient proof that the governments had accepted it. They accepted it because for several months now there has been only one means of taking steps against the new German military power – the only step that is available against a military power: by going to war. But they do not want to go to war, they are in no position to do so. And there we have the reason why nothing was done earlier and why nothing can be done now. Hitler has nothing to fear – the rumbling that broke out round the world was nothing but noise.

II

There were of course times when war would not have been necessary – times when the murder, pestilence and destruction with which Europe is threatened today could have been avoided with a certain amount of determination and inconvenience. Reminding oneself of that is not just a matter of historical interest.

There was the first period, 1919–1932, during which the infrastructure was created little by little: on the ground, in the air and in the factories – all Hitler had to do was to fill it out. It would be childish to imagine that in less than two years he could conjure up a monster army and a monster air force from scratch, without exhaustive preparations by his predecessors. The preparations were made between 1919 and 1932. Those were the years during which the few of us who saw disaster approaching, disaster for all, especially for Germany itself, screamed for help from the foreign democracies – but not for that sham pacifist help, which was nothing more than credulous submissiveness to all the subtle and crude maneuvres of a pseudo-democracy bent on revenge, but for help which would have had to be tough and ruthless towards the destructive tendencies of rising nationalism. But that was not in fashion in those years. People basked in the pleasant warmth of 'rapprochement' – and the framework for men, models and machines was developed with the blessing of the rest of the world.

Then came a second phase: 1933 roughly up to Hitler's withdrawal from the League of Nations on 23 October. The plump buds of preparation burst, the huge framework of 'civilian' aviation filled up with the military life that was lying waiting, the 'associations' began to amalgamate with the army – but at this transitional stage all this could still have been stifled without resistance. It was the time when the French general staff urgently recommended invasion, which likewise would probably not have cost one drop of blood. The French general staff, however, lacks any influence whatsoever. At the same time the ideology of 'rapprochement' refused to give up. The final ingredient was a genuine horror of anything that looked even vaguely like war and violence. To his own immense astonishment, Hitler came out of it unscathed and unhindered.

Then came the third phase, roughly up to the early winter of 1934. By now Hitler had a military force but it was still bound to be defeated if it came to a war. This was the very last chance to shatter the giant, this rapidly growing army, without war and chaos. In my book, *End to Illusion*, I wrote at the beginning of this third stage:

> A few last months still remain in which to make good the mistakes of fourteen years. During these few months it is a task of overwhelming importance to the whole world to throttle at all costs the continuation of German rearmament … The method is simple. It is based upon the fact that Germany will not for some months to come be in a position to cope with the concentrated military strength of France, let alone with that of a collection of states. During the short intervening period of incomplete armament – and only during the intervening period – she would with absolute certainty suffer annihilation if the canons began to roar. This affords the categorical guarantee that the cannons will not begin to roar. One does not become dictator of Germany in order a year later to be shot to pieces on the throne by the cannons of the world. Rather would one give up the preparations which one was making against the world and remain dictator in one's own country. Nothing was ever more certain than this. A Germany which saw a revolver drawn upon herself, knowing all the while that it really would be fired, would give up her own undrawn revolver before it was necessary to shoot … Confronted with a demand, no matter of what nature, and confronted with the certainty that the refusal of this demand would mean war, defeat, revolution and the loss of the pleasant habit of ruling, they would swallow their pride and refuse nothing … By force and yet without war Europe's rush towards a war of annihilation can yet be arrested. But only by force. And only for a few months more. War need not come immediately after the elapse of those few months; it might be postponed for a considerable time longer, perhaps even for years. But after the lapse of those few months there will be nothing more to prevent.

At that point Hitler's air fleet could still have been seized in that way and Europe once more freed of a nightmare. But that was the very last opportunity – 'just a few more months' – and if anyone did realise that, it was only to reject it with a sigh of resignation. Already too dangerous! Such a drastic course would inevitably give the impression, at least for a short while, that we were only minutes away from war. And they felt that even that impression would be too much for their citizens. The inflexible law that governs all these countries – and without knowing this law it is impossible to understand what is going on in the world! – is: 'We cannot be the aggressor. Under no circumstances, in no way, whatever the goal, whatever the danger! As long as no one over there is shooting at us, we cannot, we must not, we will not call upon our citizens to shoot.' That is the inflexible law of Europe today – the law which, to the enquiring visitor, every Briton, every Frenchman will insist on and which evidently is meant to be taken literally – impressive and at the same time terribly tragic.

III

Tragic, for in the fourth phase, which has just started, this inflexible law means carte blanche for Hitler to make his preparations without interference, such thorough preparations as have never before been made for a fighting force, and to choose the moment to pounce that suits him. The 'few months' are past and gone. Everyone knows that no action at all, either direct or indirect, can be undertaken against the existence of the new German army without unleashing a war on the world. Even a *blockade*, a fearsome weapon, would now probably mean war. For, as Sir John Simon said in the House of Commons as far back as 18 May 1934,

> are we sure that the State upon which this pressure is applied will take it like the schoolboy receiving the chastisement or the reproof of his master? Is it not possible that he may say, 'You may explain to me that it is not an unfriendly act, but that is not my view. My view is that it is.'

Of course, looked at objectively it would probably be cheaper by far to have the war now rather than in one, two or three years' time – at a point the German rulers will choose. But the question is not even asked. 'We cannot be the aggressor.' It is all the more terrible that things have been allowed to come to this.

But that is all water under the bridge. The mistake lies in the past, for it was only in the past that there was freedom to act, only in the past were the governments of those countries free to choose the course that suited them best: to put a stop to German rearmament, which they did not do, or not to put a stop to it, which they did do. The 'secret' build-up of the new German army was not disrupted before 16 March 1935 and its open build-up will be subjected to even less disruption after 16 March 1935.

When, two weeks ago, Goering drew the most unsecret veil of secrecy from by far the worst part of the whole business, the military air force, not a single voice was raised in protest. The announcement about the army did at first cause a considerable, though not very logical outcry and that forced the governments to cry out a bit more vociferously themselves. But at no point did their increased vociferousness address the problem of *whether it was still possible to prevent the establishment of this army*. The establishment of the army was and is an acknowledged fait accompli. The sole question was and is, *how can we still deter this army from launching an attack or defeat it if war should break out?*

IV

As for the conclusions that must be drawn, an old truth has been revealed once more. Each individual country must respond by *rearming* and as many countries as possible must *come together* in a clear, determined alliance in preparation for the day that will come. The first is a matter for each state individually, it is not a subject of international diplomacy. The second, however – we have just been able to observe it again in all its awful clarity – *is quite impossible if and as long as it is left to Britain to take the lead*. A clear and determined concentration of power against the approaching offensive of the new German military power will *never come about* if one looks to Britain to take the initiative, hoping to jump on the bandwagon. The position is and always was that when the day comes Britain will – necessarily and inevitably – be dragged into the military alliance of the western nations; but Britain is not only not putting its weight behind the timely creation of that alliance – which is indispensible for victory as for deterrence! – it is positively obstructing it. The moment London raises the baton, the orchestra dissolves into chaos.

V

Everyone must have sensed that a point had been reached at which it was the duty of the signatories to the Treaty to put on a conspicuous show of solidarity – what we got instead was the sight of the British government insisting, with truly stupendous impetuousness, on going it alone. It was essential to prevent this anarchic step from acquiring the halo of a model for further action – what we got instead was the ministerial visit, which, coming at this point, looks like giving the seal of approval, like openly encouraging a further fait accompli, if not more. At this point it was essential to emphasise more than ever the fundamental difference between the forces of aggression and those of defence

132

of the status quo – what we got instead was the continuation of the formalistic game of pretending that all those who can call themselves governments are the same. At this point it was essential to make it crystal clear that the time when peace was 'secured' by mere façades, hollow gestures and empty words is over – what we got instead was the enquiry, like a scene from a farce, whether Hitler was now prepared to rejoin the League of Nations, a new hollow gesture that set hearts pounding with anticipation.

We could go on. But, as we said, there is no point. What is clear to anyone with eyes to see is that this government is not the right one to be acting for a threatened world in this most serious of periods. It is under the thumb of a public opinion which is still partly immersed in the tradition of *isolationism*, partly in the fallacy of *abstract pacifism* – and it is not only under its thumb, it somehow drifts along with it.

Isolationism: that is the exact opposite of coming together; that is once more taking refuge, to a greater or lesser extent, in the idea that it actually has nothing to do with one at all; that is repeatedly abandoning the alliance, avoiding one's share of the responsibility; that is even more, it is disrupting the solidarity others are developing, it is hindering the formation of alliances in general purely so one can avoid having to become involved in them. Abstract pacifism: that is the opposite of deterrence, defence and victory; that is the horror of taking sides unequivocally, an obstinate refusal to make distinctions between one government and another, between one nation and another; that is burying one's head in the sand whenever something disagreeable looms, covering it over in coloured paper and hollow phrases. It is the rigid principle of rejecting as the *cause* of past and future wars all moral and practical policies which were ever – and might in future once more be – successfully used at least to avoid *defeat* in war.

In this condition, paralysed by her old isolationism and duped by her new pacificism, Britain finds herself facing a continent whose reality is highly non-pacifist and with which she is connected in a way that is highly non-isolationist. It is therefore certain that when 'the day' comes she will find herself in the fray with it, coupled with it for good or ill. But it is equally certain that it is completely out of the question that what must happen in Europe now can happen *through* Britain, or even *with* Britain. It will happen *despite* Britain, or it will not happen at all! As far as the big issues of the time are concerned, Britain is so completely lacking in direction, knowledge and willpower, is so at the mercy of grotesque demagogy at home, that she cannot be entrusted with leadership and authority. Like anyone who has no idea what to do, she will eventually end up where she is being driven by a strong force.

The basic characteristic of the Barthou[13] era was that he simply went ahead without Britain – and that was why it was the most successful period for France, the most successful for many, many years! That is what we need to get back to.

The subjects under discussion at the meetings the two supplicants, Simon and Eden, will hold in the next few days in Berlin are completely irrelevant, just as all the talk, haggling and lies that are still to come about the new German army, the League of Nations and other issues that are definitely still open or definitely closed is irrelevant. What does matter is whether, after this experience, Barthou's successor will be able to liberate himself from the tutelage of London, itself in sore need of a keeper, as successfully as his predecessor did.

Days that shook the world   30 March 1935

We need to go back to the events of last week. For now it is unambiguously clear: the bombshell that shook Europe to its foundations was not so much the bombshell from Berlin as the subsequent bombshell from London. The most alarming event was not Germany's breach of the Treaty on 16 March but what was felt as Britain's breach of its treaty obligations on 18 March. For understandable reasons it has not been put that way in public pronouncements, nowhere has anyone spoken of a British breach. Which country would have an interest in doing so? But outside the public domain it had a deep, devastating, disastrous effect, leaving many embittered. In the House of Commons on 21 March Sir Herbert Samuel was fairly open in acknowledging the shock Britain's action had caused throughout the world. His reason for doing so was certainly to reassure the world that there was no reason for such a response. But he correctly described those feelings when he said:

> I can well understand that this has evoked a feeling elsewhere of annoyance. This country, unhappily, has sometimes a reputation in other lands of unreliability, and occasionally we are accused of perfidy.[14]

Sir Herbert, of course, does not at all believe that Britain deserves her reputation for perfidy – and, we hasten to add, we share his opinion. But that does nothing to change the fact that his words are a reliable guide to the effect of the British bomb 'in other countries', in particular among those in authority in those countries. In order to understand the effect we must remember what actually took place before.

Hitler's announcement of 16 March about the army did not create a new situation, nor was it simply confirmation of the well-known fact that Germany is once more a military power. No, it was more than that. This long-established fact was the cause and the real basis of the most recent diplomatic agreements. The Franco-Italian accord of 7 January and the Anglo-French programme of 3 February came about precisely *because* of the re-establishment of Germany as a military force and with the precise *intention* of putting something in place to resist it. It was as a response to Germany's military rebirth that a kind of Anglo-French-Italian community of interest was formed. Its general purpose – as it says in the documents – is to ensure trust and *cooperation* between the three countries in questions concerning Germany. Moreover the word 'cooperation' was more closely defined in the documents as 'joint consultations in all cases where the circumstances demand it.' The Rome accord of 7 January formulates this as follows:

> The Foreign Minister of the French Republic and the head of the Italian government ... affirm their governments' determination to develop the traditional friendship uniting their two nations and to *cooperate* in a spirit of mutual trust to preserve peace worldwide. *To realise this cooperation they will hold all joint consultations the circumstances demand.*

In its communiqué of 3 February the British government had also given its assent to this agreement:

> With reference to the Franco-Italian agreements recently reached in Rome, the British ministers, on behalf of His Majesty's government in the United Kingdom, welcomed the declaration by which the French and Italian Governments have asserted their intention to further develop the traditional friendship which unites the two nations, and *associated his Majesty's Government with the intention of the French and Italian Governments to collaborate* in a spirit of mutual trust in the maintenance of general peace.

On 3 February, then, the British government associated itself with a treaty. It also committed itself to *work together* with the signatories or, to be more precise, to *hold all joint consultations the circumstances demand.* And on 18 March this commitment, this very recent commitment, was simply disregarded and that under particularly alarming circumstances.

What happened after Hitler's announcement of 16 March? Today the facts are clear. On the seventeenth the French foreign ministry sent the following communication to the Foreign Office through its ambassador, Corbin15: 1. In accordance with the Rome pact and the London Protocol immediate consultations between France, Britain and Italy were necessary. 2. France would approach these consultations from the standpoint that the basis for Simon's visit to Berlin no longer existed and what was needed now was a joint protest from the 'cooperation' powers. 3. There followed a request for information as to the British view.

On 18 March the British cabinet's response to the French note was – no reply. *It ignored the demand – based on the agreement – for consultations*, in fact it ignored the entire communication from Paris. Instead it sent a hastily concocted separate so-called protest note to Berlin, which ended with the statement that 'they wish to be assured that the German Government still desire the visit to take place with the scope and for the purposes previously agreed.' When, within a few hours, Berlin replied 'Yes,' it was announced in London that the visit would take place. Even the sending of the note to Berlin, as well as its content and the German reply, was only communicated to Paris on 19 March, that is, only after it had been reported in the press.

One can say, then, that the methods adopted by the London cabinet on 18 March were nothing short of Hitler's own methods. Springing a 'fait accompli' on the world, 'unilaterally', contrary to existing obligations – is that not what Hitler is accused of doing? But there is this to be said in Hitler's favour: at least he was only withdrawing from a *diktat* imposed by the country's enemies 15 years ago, which he had not signed and even his predecessors had only signed under duress, while the London cabinet was disregarding an agreement it had entered into voluntarily with its friends not six weeks previously. Does such an outrageous *démarche* not compel one to draw extremely far-reaching conclusions? If the British cabinet can ignore even the outward form of its obligations so demonstratively (an obligation to 'consult' is not an obligation to agree!) is one not forced to conclude that it has – suddenly, impetuously – galloped over to the enemy camp, all flags flying, breaking all ties like a runaway horse?

That was the devastating impression it gave. During the last few months we have seen much swaying and wavering in the policies pursued by the British, but it could always be explained by their old characteristics: indecision, an attachment to illusions, a tendency to bury their heads in the sand. Was that a possible explanation in this case? Were Paris and Rome not bound to think – and fear – that Britain was leaving them in the lurch? This pointed repudiation of an only recently defined obligation to show solidarity could not possibly be seen as unconscious or only semi-conscious, on the contrary, it must have been calculated and provocative. Was it not a similar act to the defection of the Saxon troops from Napoleon and going over to the other side during the Battle of Leipzig?

For a few days it looked as if Europe were about to fall apart. As always when the solidarity of the great powers – truly the last resort in maintaining peace – disintegrated or was merely called into question, storm clouds immediately gathered. The most agitated response came from Rome. On 19 March Mussolini telephoned Grandi,[16] his ambassador, to command him to protest in the strongest terms against the British bombshell. On the twenty-first he issued a decree deferring the demobilisation of conscripts born in 1913, who were due to be released at the end of March; on the twenty-third he ordered the mobilisation of those born in 1911. Thus within three days he tripled the strength of his army, from over 200,000 to over 600,000 men.

The reaction in Paris was more moderate – following the principle of leaving to others, as far as possible, the first step in all questions regarding Germany. Nonetheless, on the twentieth they did exactly what England was clearly hoping to avoid at all costs: they invoked the League of Nations against Germany. On the same day they accepted the invitation to Moscow. On the twenty-first they announced a law which would allow the billion francs, which had been approved the previous year for the reorganisation of the air force, to be spent in 1935, instead of over three years as originally intended. On the twenty-second they announced that almost two-thirds of the French army, which up to that point had been garrisoned on the Italian border, would be transferred to the border with Germany.

What was the point of all this? Why the feverish haste? Because Hitler had announced something that had long been known? Because he had dropped a bombshell which merely made a bang, the contents having been scattered over the world long before? Not at all. The reason was the devastating bombshell of Britain abruptly dissociating herself not only from the general spirit of the most recent agreements, but even from the precise wording. A new member seemed to have joined the anarchists' club. And what a member! The moment when the policemen's club could not put off a decision any longer appeared to be imminent. The consequence: *suddenly everything started moving rapidly in the opposite direction to that intended by Britain.* Instead of having made it easier for Germany to return to the League of Nations, as Britain ardently desired, she had, because of the French appeal, made it as good as impossible. Instead of holding back the notorious 'encirclement', she had brought an open continental military alliance against Germany closer than ever. Instead of having served the disarmament she idolised, she had triggered off mobilisations and frantic preparations for war, had created a warlike instead of a peaceful atmosphere. In order to avoid a misunderstanding, I hasten to add that in objective terms the first two consequences – the hindrance to Hitler's return to Geneva and the acceleration of the defensive encirclement of Germany – were not a disaster, indeed they were quite the opposite. But that is not the way Britain sees things. From the British point of view, within a few days their démarche of 18 March brought us perilously close to the total collapse of everything London was striving for, including the preservation of peace. Never have the dire consequences Europe will inevitably face if the Western alliance disintegrates been more clearly demonstrated! Four days after the London bombshell, we were indeed facing the immediate prospect of a European catastrophe – without the general public being aware of it!

Seeing the unexpectedly disastrous effects of going it alone, the British cabinet pulled back. The consultations, to which they had been committed *before* their hasty solo manoeuvre, were held *after* it, on the twenty-third – though not without the carefully prepared joint communiqué once more showing a striking difference between the English and the French versions; in the French, the three governments simply affirmed their *entière solidarité*, their 'complete unity', while the English version only talked of their 'complete unity *of purpose*', leaving scope for all kinds of disunity about the ways to achieve that purpose. At the same time they also took the precaution of arranging a second round of consultations, to be held in Stresa after all the travelling, though not without Sir John Simon telling the House of Commons, on 21 March, 'how glad we should be if Germany would take part in them' – which according to later, official interpretation was merely a slip of the tongue and was not meant to refer to the second conference in Stresa but to any third, fourth or fifth that might be held at some place and some future date yet to be arranged. So in fact even *after* the redress of Britain's disregard for her obligation to consult, *after* Britain's peripatetic foreign policy had been brought back onto the rails of a commitment to appear for instruction before and report after the journey, there still remain some vestiges of uncertainty. But even if the return into line has been beyond reproach, can such an experience quickly be forgotten? Is the state of British psychology as revealed in this episode, is the question of the current value of agreements with Britain, which arose with such frightening effect in this episode, not of necessity a new disruptive factor that will be more than a nine days' wonder? Will not the memory of 18 March remain a burden on European politics for months, even years to come?

* * *

It was with this memory fresh in our minds that we saw the two British ministers arrive at the German chancellery on Wilhelmstrasse. As had been expressly noted and agreed at the tripartite meeting in Paris the previous day, the sole purpose of their journey was to gather information. Despite that, they were followed by those gnawing doubts about the value of any agreements which they had foolishly allowed to grow in a few unfortunate moments of confusion; at the very least they were followed by serious doubts about their judgement and understanding. 'The fear of Germany throwing dust in the eyes of Sir John Simon and Mr Eden,' *The Times* reported on 25 March, 'is perhaps causing even more apprehension than would a bluff declaration of Germany's intention to go her own way.'

In fact the only dust was that which they had long since had in their eyes. British policy has a clear goal – peace, at almost any price, if necessary for Britain alone. This double goal is not perfidious, it is justified. However, the means by which it is pursued have unfortunately for years been such that they achieve the exact opposite of what is intended – they constantly endanger peace! Britain's policy is a paradox in that for a long time now her confused pursuit of peace has made it one of the main forces driving us towards war. That explains 18 March. That explains the nervous apprehension that follows those travelling to Berlin.

In Britain the national outlook is dominated, with the usual shades of difference, by a number of axioms about war and peace. Most are derived from the last war and rest on the following deduction: since a war broke out in 1914, one just has to know what the conditions were then to know what led to the war, and therefore to avoid a war, one just has to create the opposite conditions.

In 1914 there was, supposedly, 'encirclement'; encirclement, therefore, is a cause of war, therefore under no circumstances must there be any more encirclement. In 1914 there were military alliances; military alliances, therefore, are a cause of war, therefore they must be strictly avoided. In 1914 every country armed as much as they liked; arming as much as you like, therefore, is a cause of war, therefore armaments must be regulated. In 1914 every country accused every other country of having aggressive intentions, therefore the claim that a country has aggressive intentions is a cause of war, therefore one cannot accuse a country of having aggressive intentions, every country must be treated equally and in the same way. A few other axioms are simply derived from treating desires as already fulfilled in the hope that in that way they will actually be fulfilled. Among them is the axiom of the League of Nations: because people want it to be of significance, they behave as if it were. Among them is the axiom of 'appeasement'. There are others, but this list is sufficient to indicate the range of attitudes that were open to manipulation by the people in Berlin.

What would be attractive to the British way of thinking?

A return to the League of Nations? If you like! It's useless, as has often been proved, not least because of Germany's withdrawal. Even if it did serve any purpose, in the cases that Hitler himself is interested in it could almost always be rendered impotent because unanimity is almost always required. So why not? Welcome! Unfortunately, people in Britain simply have no idea how pacifist Germany is.

A limitation on armaments? But of course! If there is no longer a separate limitation on German armaments, then clearly a general limitation will only make Germany stronger. The others will observe it, will *have to* observe it, but there is no known means of compelling Hitler to observe it. It is truly a perfect means of making Germany's military superiority even greater. Agreed! *D'accord!* Unfortunately, people in Britain have no idea how alarming all this terrible rearmament is for poor little threatened Germany.

Austria? A Danubian pact? Now things are getting serious. Clearly the axioms of equal treatment and of the appeasement of legitimate demands come into play, as well as a number of others. For it would be to misinterpret 'independent' if the word were to mean just 'independent of Germany' and not independent of everyone else. As you can see, a new cause of war is emerging over the horizon. The peace that we are all striving for can only be assured if we let Austria decide herself – the Austrian people, the Austrian voters. The idea of a plebiscite imposes itself. Let's get the Danubian pact to include just a word about a nice little plebiscite, it's so democratic, so pacifistic – then away we go! Unfortunately, people in Britain have no idea how much Hitler's Germany agrees with them that the tiniest bit of Austrian dependence – which, sadly, is the situation today – endangers the peace of Europe.

An Eastern pact? A real military alliance? With the cruel aim that, in particular situations, several countries would have to shoot at one country? Quite unthinkable! Remember 1914. A military alliance, encirclement –

something like that is bound to lead to an explosion. Bilateral pacts, those are the thing, non-aggression pacts without those nasty sections on banding together in case of war. Military alliances – no, no, no, never again. Unfortunately people in Britain have no idea how determined Hitler's Germany is to join her in making sure an encirclement situation doesn't arise again. As is well known, it always leads to a world war.

The Berlin talks must have gone on along these lines – seasoned with the occasional anti-bolshevist murmurs. Exactly as predicted. There was no information left to gather!

It was with somewhat confused feelings, then, that Sir John and the Lord Privy Seal came to Berlin. The explosive reaction to Britain's disregard for her obligations in the steps she took on 18 March had shown them that there was not much room for maneuver. It had brought Europe to the edge of the abyss. They could not but realise that at present excessive insistence on their pacifist ideology could well conjure up a real war in no time at all. It is to be assumed that they were conscious of that throughout the Berlin talks. Even if they should have managed to retain their optimism when faced with the true Hitler, it will presumably be expressed in more moderate and controlled terms than a week previously. At least we have the comfort of knowing that there is a second line of defence behind them – those to whom they will present the results of their information-gathering trip: Rome and Paris, Moscow and Prague. It keeps being borne in on us that at the moment the cause of peace would be in poor hands if London were its main guardian. Perhaps 18 March was the day that ended Britain's *de facto* decision-making authority. That at least would be a positive consequence.

The crucial role of peace   11 May 1935

I

The second of May 1935 is Europe's best day since 11 November 1918.

Just as the latter brought an appalling bloodbath to an end, the former may have prevented an even more appalling one. That is not certain, life is in constant flow, treaties can weaken. Moreover, all the ramparts that are being raised today will only prevent war if the opponent is at least rational enough to assess his chances in a military conflict accurately. Even that is not certain, no one can say how far the madness over there goes. But the truth remains that the Franco-Russian alliance is the strongest and most exemplary of the means of preventing war that are available to us today.

It is only an alliance with a delayed-action fuse – it only comes into effect if the League of Nations fails. It is a reserve which will only emerge when the putative capital of the League proves to be non-existent. Nonetheless, since the greatest encouragement to attack lay in the probability that the League, by its very existence, would prevent any individual assistance for the victim while not managing to put together any collective assistance, even an alliance against the background of Geneva has immense implications. Until now the League was an institution of which a would-be belligerent could say to himself: in practical terms there is a 10 per cent chance it will set the whole world on me and a 90 per cent chance it will keep it off me. That has changed now. The 10 per cent danger remains, at the very least. But the 90 per cent absence of danger has been replaced by the batteries, battalions and squadrons of the two strongest military powers there are on the threatened side.

Now, despite the complicated legal terms of the alliance, a German general staff considering a war of aggression will have to reckon with a campaign against the coalition of these two strongest military powers at the very least, with a most dangerous war on two fronts as a minimum. We may assume that this in itself will make them have second, third or fourth thoughts about it.

But the rest of Europe must also reckon with the coalition of the two strongest military powers. And that means those countries will finally be able, indeed almost obliged, to set up in the same camp. The French camp had become suspect, it was no longer by any means the colossus into whose lap victory seemed bound to fall. People have reservations about alliances that can lead to defeat! The alliance of the two strongest military powers changes that completely. Once more it exerts the potent attraction of a nucleus around which a reliable majority, superior in strength, can crystallise. The rest of the countries can join this huge block at no great risk, thus completing the majority and making their superior power absolute. Supported by this massive citadel, the 'Gleichschaltung' of the defenders can be completed. In truth, there is no real possibility of any other combinations and the influence of the new Paris-Moscow grouping on all other negotiations about collaboration that are still under discussion, especially those between Italy and the Little Entente,[17] will be so compelling that it seems almost inevitable that a broader alliance will be agreed. It is difficult to see how Poland can keep out of it.

For these reasons we spent almost a whole year full of concern that this entente, with all its great psychological, legal and political difficulties, might not come about. For these reasons we were very conscious during all the varying stages that this process was of crucial importance for Europe, that the way it turned out would probably determine the immediate future of the continent, possibly even its ultimate fate. For this reason we are justified in hoping that 2 May really will prove to be a great turning point in European history. This first contractual arrangement that pits force against force – and that the force of the two greatest military powers – is the first and most important stage in the great awakening that began in Europe between the spring and early summer of 1934, the process by which the continent started to free itself from empty words and formalistic treaties with no one to enforce them. It is not wishful thinking to believe it is possible that this day marks the beginning of the continent's escape from the most deadly danger it was ever threatened with in the course of its long history.

II

These hopes are reinforced by the reaction of furious disappointment emanating from the country thus held in check. The gentlemen over there behave as if they had no idea that the two states that have banded together are precisely those whose military overthrow their lord and saviour, in his compilation of tripe, *Mein Kampf* (thank God we have it!), designated as the most noble task of New Germany. He made no bones about the fact that first of all, France was to be 'destroyed', after which Russia – which 'Fate itself' had put in Germany's hands (*Mein Kampf* p. 598) – must bleed and give up some of its provinces. It is a waste of ink even to wonder how an entente between *these* two nations can be claimed to be aggressive.

And there is another reason why it is a waste of ink. The pact and everything surrounding it sounds the death knell for some of the most seductive claims the Third Reich employed, sometimes successfully. Clearly the claim used in their propaganda of the *military threat* to Germany and the further claim of Germany's *anti-bolshevist mission* are dead, sucked dry, of no further use whatsoever for political purposes. For a long time both of these spurious propaganda claims played a certain role. Events have passed over them, consigning them to the international rubbish tip. At the moment German newspapers are still full of them but no one pays any attention to them in other countries.

As far as the *threat* to Germany is concerned, no one is in any doubt as to the defensive nature of the Franco-Russian treaty. More than that, this theory was recently as good as sent to the block and had its head chopped off.

Ramsay MacDonald wrote that before it had aroused suspicion and fear of itself, Germany had been the most secure nation in the whole of Europe. Even clearer and more important was the speech by Viscount Cranborne, Mr Eden's parliamentary private secretary. He spoke in the House of Commons on 2 May and he can hardly have been speaking without his minister's agreement. His speech concerned just one topic: no one is threatening Germany, not France, not Poland and definitely not Soviet Russia, even though that is 'one of the staple subjects of conversation in Germany at the present time.' He gave reasons for this and continued:

> Therefore, the conclusion to which I personally came, and it is the conclusion to which I believe most independent observers come, is that the German idea of a Russian military peril is an absolute myth and I find the greatest difficulty in believing that the German General Staff really believe it themselves. If Germany's neighbours have great armaments – and some of them have – one cannot help feeling that the reason is not that they are hostile to, or that they want to go to war with, Germany. It is because they are anxious. That is obvious to anyone who goes through Europe now.

As far as I can see, this verdict was not refuted by anyone of importance in Britain and it certainly coincides with the views of France and Russian, of Italy and the countries of the Little Entente. Thus a formula, with which Berlin did good business for a while, came to an ignominious end. It is finished as far as practical politics are concerned.

It is not much different with the *Communist peril*, with the 'Watch on the Vistula' against bolshevism. For a long time many people in many countries were dazzled by this particular pearl of Nazi wisdom. But it too, as we can see, has ended up in the junkyard, the world no longer pays any attention to this forgery. That France, the most bourgeois country on the Continent, has opted for the Communist rather than the fascist regime – that it feels impelled to organise protection against Hitler with the Bolsheviks rather than protection against the Bolsheviks with Hitler – indicates the collapse of that brilliant idea, which was hawked all round the world day after day. Today the Russians are *nos amis russes* in the French press, as they will soon be in the Czech press. They enjoy very polite attestations of friendship in Italy. To the applause of the British parliament and with the approval of the British government, Viscount Cranborne has testified that they have been slandered by Germany. So now these deliberately misleading claims too have been finally laid to rest!

III

Do we have to add that there were equally misleading claims on the other side – from those feeble-minded smart alecks who weren't born yesterday and who always knew damn well that all the capitalists and fascists, every single one of them, were in league with Hitler and were up to all sorts of clever tricks with the sole aim of bringing about a world war against Moscow? What nonsense we had to listen to from these one-track so-called minds who know nothing except that there is a phenomenon called the class war, which they insist – it's so simple, for God's sake! – is the universal driving force of history; who absolutely refuse to accept that historical events derive from many sources, that they are compounds of varying forces, just as white light is a compound of many colours. Oh, they knew and didn't they make a fuss: it was so obvious that those Austrian fascists, Dollfuss[18] and Starhemberg,[19] would come to terms with Hitler within a couple of weeks. They were brazenly arrogant towards those idiots or traitors who believed that with a certain amount of patience and determination it could well be possible to prise fascist Benito away from fascist Adolf. With their infallible vision they had realised that fascist Laval[20] would never be persuaded to come to an accord with the class enemy in Moscow and that only one miracle could save France: the fall of that loathsome crypto-Hitlerite.

May we hope that we will hear no more of these half-baked clichés, now that the world is so clearly moving according to different laws, a world where a capitalist/communist alliance was formed today and where fascist/democratic ones will be formed tomorrow and where – let us hope – there will soon be general ad hoc cooperation, irrespective of political or social systems, to deal with one specific temporary danger?

There are good grounds for having greater confidence than ever in what this further extension of the defensive cordon might bring. It is coming along. The 2 May treaty will be followed by another between Moscow and Prague. The general staffs of the three countries will organise their cooperation. Czechoslovakia will make preparations to act as a 'Russian aircraft carrier'. The French air minister will soon meet his Italian counterpart. The Danube conference in Rome will not fail. We Europeans can be more and more confident that we will not wake up one morning to find ourselves dead from poison gas. Once it had started, this great movement required patience, political know-how, historical awareness and a clear determination. They will continue to be necessary – and not only for those actively involved, also for those looking on, certainly for those, from whom both sides should learn something.

A scrap of paper   14 March 1936

On 7 March 1936 22,000 soldiers of the German Army crossed the bridges over the Rhine and, with the assistance of the local police, started the occupation of the demilitarised Rhineland. In occupying the 50km-wide zone, Germany was breaking both the Treaty of Versailles and the 1925 Locarno pact. Hitler based his justification of the breach of the treaties on Germany's right to self-determination, also pointing to the Franco-Soviet pact of mutual assistance, which he called a breach of the Locarno pact. The development of the war in Abyssinia also encouraged the National Socialist leaders to make further plans for foreign enterprises. 'Just keep fighting,' Goebbels noted in his diary for 6 September 1935, 'and while we do, we'll get rid of our chains.' With the occupation of the Rhineland, Hitler removed an important obstacle to an aggressive foreign policy, since it meant that the French could no longer respond to any hostile measures Germany might take by marching into the unfortified zone. Hitler was playing for high stakes, against the advice of many of his advisers, and it came off: fascist Italy had assured him in advance that she would not take part in any international action; France, that had repeatedly been informed of Hitler's plans without making any preparations to counter them, was in the middle of a hotly contested general election and decided not to invade as she did not have the support of either Britain or her own military. Moreover, at the same time as the German troops marched in, Hitler had presented a seven-point programme to the Allied foreign ministries, a new proposal for collective security in Europe which ostensibly took account of Britain's interests and expectations. The German note was sufficient to disarm the British government, which was hardly surprising since they were based on a suggestion of Lord Londonderry, the former minister for aviation, which he had conveyed to the Führer during a short visit to Berlin a few days previously. On 6 March Anthony Eden stated in the House of Commons that the German action put a strain on the international situation but there was no reason to see it as a threat. In general the Allies contented themselves with the (occasional) harsh verbal criticism and a condemnation of Germany at the council of the League of Nations. In a joint memorandum of 19 March 1936 the remaining Locarno powers proposed to take the argument to the court the The Hague, but that came to nothing. Hitler's declaration to the Western powers that German policy was guided by an 'honest striving for true reconciliation and understanding between the nations on the basis of equal rights and equal duties' achieved its purpose.

The remilitarisation of the Rhineland not only strengthened Germany's international prestige, it revealed the exclusively defensive nature of France's military strategy which had devastating effects on France's allies. At the same time it enabled Hitler to give Germany the impression that the military defeat in the First World War could be reversed without military confrontation, simply by successes in foreign policy.

A scrap of paper   14 March 1936

I. The past

'The open declaration that even the demilitarised zone will no longer be respected,' we wrote in these pages on 18 January, 'will probably plunge us into the most serious of the crises which have so far passed over Europe.' But we added, 'although on its own the matter is much less significant than the fact of rearmament itself.'

At the moment when the most serious of all crises so far really has descended upon us, what immediately comes to mind is this discrepancy, this truly tragic discrepancy between the complete absence of a vigorous response to the formation of an army of 1,000,000 soldiers and the strength of the response when, 11 months later, 50,000 of these soldiers are mobilised in the course of a change of garrison. It is a spectacle that fills one with despair at the lack of proportion in the policies that have been pursued for the last 18 years, policies that have always managed to ignore matters of major importance, only to engage in a much more difficult and hopeless struggle on matters of secondary, minor or even minimal importance. How could this happen, again and again? How could it come about that all the establishment of the army produced was a certain amount of hot air, while the transfer of six to eight brigades to a different garrison could set the whole continent alight?

It is clear that the reason nothing was done about the matter of major importance – rearmament – was because there was no specific obligation on the part of Britain to resist it. It is also clear that the reason steps were taken in the matter of minor importance, the remilitarisation of the Rhineland, was because in that case Britain did have a specific obligation, at least on paper. But the question is, how could it happen that on the occasion of the major event, which could easily have been prevented, there was *no* British guarantee and that one only appeared on the occasion of the minor event, which could only be prevented by a major operation?

What emerges, when this question is raised, is the scandalous and at the same time pathetic chronicle of a long period of deceit and self-delusion. Britain emerges, the Britain that, on the day after victory, returned to the 'balance of power' tradition and from that moment on – to its own detriment, to the detriment of Europe and, above all, to the detriment of Germany – did everything it could to strengthen Germany and weaken France. Whilst Germany was encouraged to resist in the assurance of Britain's support, France was urged to yield if she wanted to retain Britain's support. As early as 1925 this system – which was effective on both sides – had led to the watering-down of the Peace Treaty. The Reparations Commission was replaced by the 'neutral' Anglo-American Parker Gilbert, who had the express task of preparing further relaxation of the Versailles terms. The Allied Military Control Commission was replaced by a League of Nations control body and it was an open secret that its mission was not to control anything. But while the main girders supporting the order set up in 1919 were already melting in the glare of the scandalously misused concept of 'reconciliation' – which concealed nothing but Britain's consistent favouring of German nationalism and French pacifism's constant fear of losing Britain's favour – the French still held one safeguard: they were still ensconced on the Rhine, they still controlled the German industrial provinces – and they were well aware of what that meant. How could they be made to leave, lured away with flattery or inducements? It was Lord d'Abernon, the British ambassador in Berlin, the 'Lord Protector' as the German army called him, who found the means: the treaty that was signed in *Locarno*. What a great moment! This time Britain was not just making demands, she was making an offer! She was offering to make a solemn undertaking to come to France's aid in the case of an attack by Germany, assuming the League of Nations agreed (but if the League of Nations agreed, then she was just as solemnly obliged to do so on the basis of the League's constitution!). And while she now rejected for good any further obligation as far as all the other articles of the treaty, especially the restrictions on the army, were concerned – as good as giving carte blanche to anyone to break them! – she was prepared to guarantee one single, minor stipulation: that no German troops should enter the Rhineland and no fortresses be built there. It is perfectly clear that the former will become completely meaningless the moment there is a German army again: if war should break out it makes no difference whether the troops are stationed 30 miles from the frontier or close to it, they can reach it in one single night, as we saw on 7 March. As for the fortifications in the Rhineland, Germany would be at a disadvantage without them if they were on the defensive, if there were a French attack, which no one in their right mind sees as likely; but if Germany went on the offensive, if she were to attack France, it is more or less irrelevant whether there are fortresses in the Rhineland or not. That is to say, all that is guaranteed by the guarantee for the maintenance of the demilitarised zone is a matter of at most secondary importance. Of all the things that need to be guaranteed, the Treaty of Locarno selected those of the most minor significance. Despite that, it was the lure to entice the French to give up their safeguard. Despite that, the pressure from Britain was so strong that the alarmingly vague and indefinite terms, in which the guarantee was couched, were ignored. And despite all that, the treaty was loudly proclaimed and promoted on all sides as the measure that would genuinely guarantee peace and quiet in Europe. Even in 1934 and 1935, when the peace and quiet it was supposed to secure had long since disappeared, the world was still bowing at the word 'Locarno'.

There was no reason why the Treaty of Locarno should be valued so highly. It was never anything other than one of those hand-to-mouth arrangements of which there were plenty throughout the postwar years, that is, one of those arrangements serving a short-term purpose but which, in order to achieve their short-term purpose, had to be set up and presented as if they were permanent settlements. There were dozens of these hand-to-mouth arrangements, the best-known being the Dawes Plan and the Young Plan, both of which covered up the sacrifice of huge claims by staging it as a supposed long-term settlement; but it was at the very moment when they should have proved their value that every one of these long-term settlements turned out to be worthless. The Treaty of Locarno is that kind of settlement. It served the one-off purpose of persuading the French to give up their hold on the Rhineland. In return for this sacrifice of military advantage she was given other military safeguards. But here, too, these substitute safeguards proved insubstantial at the very moment when safeguards were needed. And if the ineffectiveness of the Locarno substitute safeguards did not become obvious as quickly as all the other hand-to-mouth arrangements, that was simply because they consisted of promises whose worth would only be put to the test in the more distant future. The test only arrived after Hitler became chancellor and immediately its worth proved meagre in the extreme. The Locarno Treaty contained no provision for doing anything about the most momentous of all the events, the re-establishment of a German army. And, as we will see, as far as protection against a possible war of aggression is concerned, Locarno contained not one iota more than the Covenant of the League of Nations. Practically the only thing Locarno has done, between its signing and the present, is to stop France doing anything on its own initiative against German rearmament; by its very existence, it delayed resistance to the militarist policy of the Third Reich, delayed it until the moment when it seemed to guarantee Britain's involvement; its very existence meant that resistance was shifted from the time at which it would have been relatively easy and free of risk, to a time when it was difficult and fraught with risk; it meant that steps taken against an army that was in the process of being formed were watered down into steps taken against the location of certain garrisons of an army that was already fully developed.

That, until now, was the Treaty of Locarno. It was the instrument that cleared the main obstacle out of the way of the nationalist German military renaissance in 1926. But in 1933 it was the main factor preventing the National Socialist German military renaissance from being suppressed at an early stage.

II. The present

What will Locarno be tomorrow? After it has done nothing, nothing at all, to help free us from the real evil, nothing to help check Hitler's preparations for war and, consequently, nothing to help pacify Europe either in mood or in practice – will it now at least fulfil the purpose which, according to the wording of the text, it is supposed to fulfil? Will it at least manage to compel Germany to reverse the remilitarisaton of the Rhineland? Since Hitler has broken it, will its punitive clauses at least be invoked against Hitler? And in so doing will it at least manage to teach him a lesson – which would certainly not be without its value – that force does not necessarily lead to success?

First of all let us look at the legal position. Anyone who has not slept through the last few years will certainly not be tempted to regard the legal position as the sole, or even the main decisive factor. But it does have some influence, if only from the fact that we can expect nothing at all if the legal position is in any way ambiguous.

In this case the legal position is in many ways unusually clear. Firstly: all those involved have never denied, on the contrary they have repeatedly emphasised that the Treaty of Locarno remains in force. For the injured parties, *France* and *Belgium*, that goes without saying. *Hitler*, for his part, has also repeatedly committed himself to it. Thus point 6 of a German note to Britain, dated 16 April 1934, says: 'The German government will continue to recognise the Treaty of Locarno in the future.' This has since been often repeated. As for the guarantors, *Britain* and *Italy*, we have, among other things, the second Stresa declaration of 14 April 1935. It says:

> The Representatives of Italy and the United Kingdom, the Powers which participate in the Treaty of Locarno only in the capacity of guarantors, *formally reaffirm all their obligations under that Treaty, and declare their intention, should the need arise, faithfully to fulfil them.*

The British government has repeated this several times, through Hoare as well as Eden. Thus the validity of the treaty has never even been questioned by any of the five signatories.

To continue: on what grounds does Germany justify her two-fold action in breaking one of the treaty's essential clauses and withdrawing from it without notice? The reason put forward is the claim that the Franco-Russian pact is incompatible with Locarno and that France has therefore rendered the Treaty null and void. 'The Rhine pact of Locarno has thereby practically ceased to exist. Germany, for her part, also no longer sees herself as bound by this pact which has lapsed.' This legal claim put forward by the Germans was not only not accepted by the other signatories, it was expressly rejected. On 2 May 1935, only a few hours after the conclusion of the Franco-Russian pact, Sir John Simon said, in answer to a question in the House of Commons, that the pact was perfectly compatible with Locarno. Belgium and Italy both took the same view. The German 'legal argument' was therefore deemed invalid by all the other signatories. In any case, if that was the German government's view of the Franco-Russian pact, they should have taken the matter to *arbitration*, which was the procedure that was not only allowed but was *stipulated* by the Treaty of Locarno; there would have been plenty of time for that between May 1935 and February 1936. On 25 February the French foreign minister, Flandin,[21] publicly offered in the French chamber to have the matter submitted to arbitration. The 'Führer', who considers it outrageous that a French minister does not immediately come running to him in response to a newspaper interview, did not deign to reply; he never mentioned the question of the arbitration procedure laid down in the Treaty of Locarno at all, neither in his speech nor in his memorandum. It is, therefore, clear that even if there were something to this 'legal argument', all it could justify was recourse to arbitration, not to breaking the Treaty and tearing it up; anyway, all the other signatories expressly rejected the 'legal argument' as non-existent.

But *what* is to happen now? Here we are approaching the murkier depths of this Locarno treaty – which is widely recognised to be a model of imprecision, incompleteness and ambiguity, an instrument of almost calculated ineptitude.

The stipulations are as follows: if Germany infringes the demilitarised zone, the signatories are obliged to '*come to the assistance*' of France and Belgium. A distinction is drawn between a simple infringement and a 'flagrant' one. In the case of a 'flagrant' infringement, France and Belgium only have to appeal to the League of Nations retrospectively, they can act immediately and any support can be given prior to the appeal. The reverse is the case for a simple infringement: the appeal to the League of Nations must come first and the right to act and the duty of support only come into play once the infringement has been confirmed. But although it is difficult to imagine a more 'flagrant' infringement of the demilitarised zone than the one that has just occurred, France and Belgium preferred to choose the procedure for the less serious case. We are, therefore faced with a case dealt with in the two following sections – and only those sections – of Article 4:

1. If one of the High Contracting Parties alleges that a violation of Article 2 of the present treaty (attack, invasion or war) or a breach of Articles 42 or 43 of the Treaty of Versailles (demilitarised zone) has been or is being committed, it shall bring the question at once before the Council of the League of Nations.

2. As soon as the Council of the League of Nations is satisfied that such a violation or breach has been committed, it will notify its finding without delay to the Powers signatory of the present treaty, who severally agree that in such case they will each of them come immediately to the assistance of the Power against whom the act complained is directed.

As we will see, naked military aggression and infringement of the demilitarised zone were put on the same level, indeed, were dealt with in the same words. The conclusion that has always been drawn from that is: in line with the Treaty of Locarno, a breach of the demiliarised zone is *synonymous with a military attack*. That is, in fact, the case – but despite that, it means nothing. From here on everything becomes increasingly obscure. The one point I would like to stress is that the signatories themselves have it in their power to determine: firstly, whether support *should in fact* be given and, secondly, *what* this support should *consist of*. The truth is that when it comes down to it, all the Locarno pact says is: 'Should the situation arise, we will do what we want.' The classic expression of this came in Sir John Simon's speech in the House of Commons on 7 November 1933 in which he defined Britain's obligations under the Treaty of Locarno as follows:

First, if the Council of the League finds that a violation of the undertaking *not to go to war against each other*, contained in Article 2, has been committed by Germany, France or Belgium, we are bound immediately to come to the assistance of the Power against whom the act complained of was directed. I observe that it is the Council of the League which is to make that finding, and in that case, as we are a permanent member of the Council, *our assent is necessary to any finding*. Secondly, if the Council finds that a breach of Articles 42 and 43 of the Treaty of Versailles – relating to the demilitarisation of the Rhineland zone – has been committed, we are bound to come immediately to the assistance of France or Belgium as the case may be. There again, let me state that *our assent is necessary to the finding of the Council.*[22]

These points make the character of this treaty – about which such a fuss was made as if it anchored the earth to the sun – depressingly clear. It commits the guarantors to give support, if they themselves agree that they should give support, that is all. It commits them to give the kind of support they themselves decide to give, that is all. That is the grandiose safeguard they thought up at Locarno!

I cannot see how the Locarno safeguards are supposed to be any stronger – at least in this case – than those of the League. All that the League envisaged until the beginning of this year was sanctions in the case of war. After the announcement of German rearmament on 17 April[23] it decided that *economic and financial* sanctions could be imposed for breaking important treaties. In line with this resolution, in the present case 52 countries could be called on to take economic sanctions – provided the League as a whole desires it, provided not a single member of the Council is against it. Thanks to the Treaty of Locarno, in the present case four countries can be authorised to impose sanctions – certainly no more than the same economic sanctions – with the same proviso that the Council of the League as a whole desires it, that is, that not a single member of the Council votes against it. No one can say what is made stronger by Locarno in all this. As this is being written, there is just one thing that is clear: there are two high-sounding *moral* obligations to do something, one based on the Covenant of the League of Nations, one on Locarno; there is a rather tenuous *legal* obligation based on the League, none at all on Locarno.

III. *The future*

It depends on Britain whether it is the force of the moral obligation or the weakness of the legal one that will be the decisive factor.

The case of Italy, the other doubtful Council member, will probably be straightforward. Italy will demand a price for any active or passive involvement demanded of her; and although the price might be higher or lower, it will always be directed towards the same end: Abyssinia and the sanctions because of Abyssinia. There is little more to be said. The time has come which confirms the all too plain and simple truth with which those few who have retained their clarity of vision and sense of realism have countered the balderdash the peddlers of twopenny-ha'penny pacifism have been hawking round for weeks, with which they have repudiated the pseudo-idealistic ramblings emanating from the same Sunday school which for 16 years has been concocting recipes for the disintegration of Europe – the truth that you cannot grapple with the wolf to save the sheep when the tiger is about to pounce on you. These gentlemen have to decide: either they rectify their muddle-headedness or they descend to pure skullduggery. The have to decide whether ethics and justice and collective security and the sacrosanct nature of treaties is more important to them on the Rhine or on the Takaze, in Strasbourg or in Mekele. If Europe means something to them, if they know where it is, they will have to put off the onset of the golden age in Africa for the time being. The case of Italy – however tangled it is, however odd it is that a country branded as a pact-breaker should be needed to resist the breaking of an even more important pact – is straightforward. It is simply a matter of payment.

What will decide everything, what everything depends on, is Britain, nothing but Britain, Britain alone. It is not yet known what decision her government will come to – a government constantly lurching now to one side, now to the other, a government of minimum clarity and maximum fear in all European questions. But it would be doing readers a disservice to conceal the fact that the first signs are discouraging. All the indications of the prevailing mood that have so far appeared in the press in these first days point to a denial of any obligation, either moral of legal, either under the Treaty of Locarno or the Covenant of the League of Nations. Instead of outrage at the breaking of the Treaty, reactions everywhere have ranged from understanding of to enthusiasm for the substitute pacts Hitler is offering. And that is not just the pirates of British pacifism, even newspapers that call themselves liberal or socialist are happy to present the bloodiest brown shit as the sweetest manna of peace if that helps them get their snouts in the tasty trough of opposition to the defence budget; even more decent and respectable papers were saying much the same, though in a more dignified manner, of course. Eden's speech of 9 March was not much more promising. He did declare that Hitler's action had 'profoundly shaken confidence in any engagement into which the Government of Germany may in future enter', but he had nothing to add except that the new treaties that same government was offering would be looked at 'objectively' as 'no opportunity must be missed which offers any hope of amelioration.' Even more alarming perhaps was a hint that Britain had already accepted Hitler's thesis that Locarno was finished. This came in the statement that, even if war should break out, the British government would only consider itself committed to its obligation under Locarno to come to the aid of France and Belgium 'during the period that will be necessary for the consideration of the new situation which has arisen.' But most alarming of all, perhaps, was the speech of Prime Minister Baldwin, who, forgetting everything he himself and his predecessors had said and even had published in White Papers, presented the whole situation in Europe as the result of some kind of private feud between France and Germany: 'I will aportion neither praise nor blame to anyone'; who claimed he could not see the slightest difference between the one side which, as he very well knows, only wants to be left in peace, and the other side, which all its neighbours, not just the French, regard with fear and trembling; who, finally, said of Germany's breaches of treaties, 'Too often she has acted in that way', adding, 'I do not believe deliberately' – introducing a new category of international law and the art of government: breaches of treaties by accident or while dreaming.

However, all the British chopping and changing, whether done deliberately or not, makes it impossible to regard anything that comes from that direction as final until it is final. A remnant of faith in human intelligence and in the instructive value of cruel disappointments makes it impossible to believe that London will not see, or has not already seen, the truth of what the French Prime Minister Saurrat[24] said in the Chamber on 10 March, namely that this time 'the future of peace in Europe is at stake,' that what was at stake this time was whether treaties, laws, formal arrangements still meant anything, or only force and arms. It is not the treaty Germany has torn up, it is the treaty Britain would tear up if yet again she could not be persuaded to do anything that would mean the collapse of all faith in the rule of law, the end of all deterrence. The prospect of finally having to count Britain as belonging to the 'scrap-of-paper' camp is so horrendous that one hesitates to believe she could burden herself with such a degree of responsibility.

Meanwhile a wave is gathering in crisis-ridden, squabble-torn France which appears to justify all those who trusted in her often proved ability to become an entirely different nation in her darkest hours. Despite the darkness of this hour, her prime minister has seen what usually escapes the official eye, namely that beneath the German tyrants and demagogues there is also a German people. From the platform of the Chamber he appealed, in his capacity as prime minister, to the German people, whose 'unity of purpose' is, in fact, just something journalistic day-trippers drivel on about. 'Chancellor Hitler,' M. Saurat said, 'who gave the impression he felt he needed to speak to the people of France over the heads of the French government – as if it were possible that a government which proceeds from the people's elected representatives and governs without force could represent anything other than the sovereign will of that people – by so doing Chancellor Hitler has opened the way for us to address the German people ourselves. In the name of their culture and their virtues as a race, we call on them to think carefully about the new responsibilities with which certain people want to burden them.' That is a new tone, a new appeal, and everything the French Prime Minister went on to suggest, in beseeching tones, to the German people, indicates a new political resolve. May it prove to be steadfast! It is not true, it is ignorant journalism, to say that people in Germany are 'filled with enthusiasm', that they are 'behind' their Führer. Millions of them are horrified, are the best of allies in the search for order and peace. As has been said repeatedly in these pages, mobilising these allies is as important as all the tasks facing the diplomats and general staffs, perhaps it is even the more crucial task. It is the task and it is achievable. The appeal will perhaps not reach Germany directly from the French Chamber, but it can reach the German people, despite all the walls the dictatorship has erected. This army for peace in Germany will not be mobilised through urgent appeals alone, but it can be mobilised, the means do exist. The day when Europe sets about doing that will deal as severe a blow to war as the day of the Rhineland raid did to peace.

From year to year   26 December 1936

After winning back the Rhineland, Hitler's priority in foreign policy was to build up a system of alliances which would give him a free hand when the time came to implement his plans for expansion to the East. This long-term project was of paramount importance for Hitler, but it required an expansion of the borders allocated to Germany between 1919 and 1921. His demands for the revision of the Treaty of Versailles served as a cover for this, but infringing the sovereignty of other states was in a different league from everything he had done so far, which meant that precise preparation was necessary to avoid an armed conflict at the wrong time.

Initially, Hitler tried to lure Britain onto his side and destroy her fragile relationship with France once and for all. With that in mind, Joachim von Ribbentrop and Hitler invited a man called Tom Jones, a close friend of the British Prime Minister, to Berlin to suggest a summit meeting between the two leaders to discuss questions 'which will determine the fate of generations.' Tom Jones was extremely enthusiastic about the proposal and won over Baldwin, but the intervention of the foreign minister, Eden, put an end to the German attempt at rapprochement. Disappointed, Hitler sent Ribbentrop to London as ambassador, where his tactlessness and aggressiveness had the opposite of the desired effect, with the result that the project had to be abandoned. In contrast to that, Hitler had no difficulty reaching an understanding with Italy. After the reoccupation of the Rhineland Mussolini managed to bring his Abyssinian campaign to a successful conclusion, because the disagreement among the Allies meant the threatened oil sanctions were never imposed. Spurred on by this success, Mussolini now determined to establish Italy as the dominant power in the Mediterranean. The Spanish Civil War, which broke out on 17 July, gave him the opportunity to emphasise his pretensions and it was with satisfaction that he realised Germany, too, was intervening of the side of the rebels. It gave Hitler the opportunity to combat his 'Bolshevist opponent' directly, demonstrate the strength of the German Air Force by bombing civilian targets and thus, he hoped, put France at least, perhaps even Britain, under psychological pressure. The pact with Mussolini, which was signed on 25 October 1936, was also of considerable benefit to the Nazis in that it brought about a gentleman's agreement with Austria, which put an end to the strained relations between them; at the same time, however, Hitler wrung concessions from the Austrian chancellor, Kurt von Schuschnigg, which gave him greater influence over events in his homeland. Once the independence of Austria was no longer a major concern of Mussolini's, Hitler could step into the breach with a conciliatory handshake, which was soon to turn into an iron grip.

After the formation of the Berlin-Rome Axis and the signing of the Anti-Comintern pact with Japan in November 1936, there was a 15-month pause in Hitler's individual forays in foreign affairs. On the fourth anniversary of his assumption of office, Hitler therefore emphasised that, 'the time of the so-called surprises is over, peace is our most prized possession.' But 1937 is generally seen as a turning-point, the year of the transition from the relatively restrained foreign policy before 1936 to the period of open expansion in the form of short, sharp military-cum-diplomatic campaigns. Hitler believed that *in the long run neither international trade nor autarky could meet Germany's economic needs. In a four-hour meeting he informed the regime's leaders – Neurath, Goering, defence minister Blomberg, General Fritsch and Admiral Raeder – of his new foreign-policy objectives (the Hossbach Protocol): the absorption of Austria and Czechoslovakia, followed by expansion to the East. Given the chronic problems with the supply of military and industrial raw materials, Blomberg, Neurath and Fritsch expressed misgivings about military ambitions and were also sceptical as to whether Britain and France would, as Hitler believed, tolerate further German acts of aggression. The only effect of these doubts was to strengthen Hitler's determination to take personal control over the conservative foreign ministry and the Army. And the very same month he had a visit from Lord Halifax, a close friend of Chamberlain, who admitted that certain changes in Eastern Europe, especially in Austria, Czechoslovakia and Danzig 'could probably not be avoided in the long run.' Statements from Paris expressed the same attitude. All this meant that Hitler could feel sanguine about starting preparations for a strike against Austria. Essential for these were Hitler's steps in taking complete control of the foreign ministry and the Army. By February 1938 Goering and Hitler had forced Blomberg and Fritsch to resign following a smear campaign, replaced 60 high-ranking officers and appointed Ribbentrop foreign minister in place of Neurath. Hitler himself took personal control over all the armed forces. The way was clear for the final steps on the road to war.*

From year to year   26 December 1936

1936 has ended better than the three previous years. There is no doubt about it, everyone can feel it. It is clear that there are still grave dangers looming over Europe; it is unfortunately true that the end of this period of adversity is not yet in sight. But that is no reason to ignore the fact that the dangers have become less grave. Nor is it any reason to turn a blind eye to the fact that for the first time a vague glimmer has appeared in the mist surrounding the future, perhaps indicating that the end of this period of adversity is approaching. But that is nothing definite, it is always susceptible to further change. At the moment, however, that is the way things are. The prospects for Europe at the turn of this year are more promising than they have been for a long time.

The primary cause of this change is that the tiger among the European states, the Third Reich, has as good as no chance of getting its claws on the victim it has been stalking – its mortal enemy France – alone, in isolation. Neither France nor Czechoslovakia! Its anti-Bolshevist barrage has most signally failed to destroy the bridges between France and Russia. Recently it has – at last! – been made crystal clear that Britain would stand by France in a life-and-death struggle. It has, furthermore, become absolutely clear that the stranglehold on Poland has slackened and that the attempt to undermine Romania and Yugoslavia has ground to a halt. In addition warnings have come from America which suggest a repeat of 1917 is not out of the question. To sum up: any prospect of overthrowing France in a swift and easy *attaque brusquée* – which anyway would probably not be half as swift and easy as Germany imagines in her arrogance – disappeared towards the end of 1936. There is no longer any chance of a one-on-one war. If the Third Reich starts a war today, whether against France or against Czechoslovakia, it will have to do so in the knowledge that it will turn into a war against many countries.

Against which of the many? Against how many of the many? And with which allies on its side? One can never know for sure at the beginning, but if there are people who can count in Berlin, then they will be able to work out the alliances will be even more unfavourable than in 1914. Of its allies in that war Germany will certainly lose Turkey this time, as well as part of the former Habsburg Empire; and I don't imagine anyone will say that Italy, which would not even have to break a formal treaty of alliance today, will be any more reliable than in 1914. On the opposing side, however, the whole list of 1914 could easily be made up again, with the addition of the remaining part of the Habsburg Empire and strengthened by the undeniable fact that Russia is a considerably more powerful military force than in 1914. What prospects are there, then, of such a second war against the many, a second European or world war, being more successful for Germany than the first? As good as none. The sole plus factor for the Third Reich, compared with the Second, is its greatly increased initial speed of mobilisation. But that is countered by the greater strength of the French ring of fortresses, and it is an advantage that will disappear within a few weeks. For no reasonably cautious planner would regard it as a factor influencing the final outcome in a war against a European or world coalition which definitely cannot be won in a few weeks.

Germany's chances in a great war against a coalition – the one type of war that comes into consideration – have thus become so poor that one cannot believe that normal rational people would take the risk. And it is not only militarily that they have worsened, but also economically. That is the third reason why things look brighter. The country that went to war in 1914 was rich, packed with materials, food and hoards of gold. The country that would go to war in 1937 is already gasping for breath, a country that has lost its political attraction precisely because of its economic problems. (That is the true cause of Hitler's sudden failure in Poland, for example, and the Balkans, which shows that the slogan 'Guns are more important than butter' is wrong even in the context of power politics. Even in power politics butter and other products of that kind are at least as important as guns. Who would tie his country's fate to that of a land which suffers from shortages of everything, even in peacetime?) What prospects can normal rational Germans anticipate for the economic aspects of a war – a long war on several fronts, against several countries? How will they manage for food when already it seems that they cannot even procure enough for a dry-bread diet? And how, with no reserves to speak of, will they get supplies for their industry when, after a few months, imports stop and the exports that bring in foreign currency dry up? And how can they expect soldiers and civilians to keep going, militarily and psychologically, when within a very short time there will be shortages of everything? Goering's four-year plan – a pure delusion, and even if it weren't, it won't happen tomorrow – will do nothing to alter these facts, which have never been more obvious than in the last few weeks. Normal, rational Germans, who have to plan for the future, cannot rely on it in their plans that are heavy with responsibility.

Therefore one can say that, especially in recent months, the Third Reich's prospects in a war have deteriorated to such an extent that there would be no danger of it entering into one at the moment – if we were dealing with rational beings. We are not dealing with rational beings and therefore the relief, which would otherwise have been wonderful, is at best partial. Since monomaniacs and berserkers run the show in Germany, it is possible – because things are so bad and are getting worse at increasing speed – that they will go for broke and embark on the madness of war. It is a risk no one can eliminate, it remains the danger looming over Europe. But even if it should come to that, it is comforting to know, to know for sure, that it will result in a terrible end for them, and that perhaps more quickly and cheaply than was feared only a short time ago. If they commit this wanton act, they will be crushed, and the fact that their decline has accelerated so much beforehand, and that the opposite side has recently made such remarkable progress in gathering its strength, perhaps gives us hope that, even if it should come to that, something of Europe might be left standing.

But apart from the question of war – which remains central— we are entering upon this year of 1937 under a more auspicious star than was in the ascendant until recently. Even leaving the threat of war aside, all of us on this continent, people of all countries, Germans at home and abroad, are, to a greater or lesser extent, exposed to the pressure that comes from this regime, which is ravaging culturally, morally, economically and socially in equal measure. Everything is affected by it; it encourages everything that is repugnant, obstructs everything that is desirable. But it is clear that the situation this regime finds itself in is by no means pleasant. It is becoming clearer every day that the fruit borne of the seeds sown by its own amateurism, its own madness, its own imposture is becoming nastier and nastier and that they lack the means to do anything about it. When and how it will come to an end is beyond prophecy, suffice it to say that they are going downhill; that they are heading predictably and inexorably for even greater difficulties; that their susceptibility to unforeseen events which might lead to explosions and their fear of them is bound to grow; that the glory and seductiveness are declining and are bound to decline even further. It is a process of decline; where it will lead, and when, is beyond anyone's ability to judge. For the moment, however, the mere fact that their hold is weakening is a cause for joy; it is a relief, it relieves the pressure; it hampers the support of everything that is repugnant, removes the obstruction of things that are desirable; it is a glimmer of light at the end of Europe's tunnel of adversity.

To see this process of decline continue unhindered is the best New Year's wish for 1937. Unhindered by the madness of war, but also unhindered by naive or not-so-naive initiatives appearing somewhere or other to divert its course artificially by providing aid. To avoid a threat of 'chaos' for example. Or because the extortion screw has been given one last turn, because Hitler is presenting his ultimatum: either we 'buy him off' – at a high price – or we suffer the consequences: war. Since in his days of glory no one intervened against him, may we be equally spared someone intervening to support him in this period of decline. With that proviso, we can enter on this new year in a spirit of cautious optimism.

The Anschluss	19 & 26 March 1938
Taking stock after Munich	8 October 1938

With the new year of 1938 the first signs of a developing crisis between Austria and Germany appeared. During a raid on the illegal Nazi Party on 25 January, the Austrian police came across material which revealed German involvement in ongoing putsch preparations, in clear violation of the 1936 agreement. Despite that, Chancellor Schuschnigg accepted Hitler's invitation to further discussions on cooperation in foreign policy between the two countries at his retreat on the Obersalzberg in Bavaria. On 12 February Schuschnigg, cowed, allowed Hitler to dictate an agreement which removed the ban on the Austrian National Socialist Party, took them into the government and, with the ministry of the interior, handed control of the police over to them, thus creating the conditions for a Nazi take-over in Austria. To prevent this, Schuschnigg announced, on 9 March 1938, a plebiscite 'For a free and German, independent and social, for a Christian and united Austria', to be held the next Sunday, 13 March. The minimum voting age was set at 24, in order to exclude the mostly pro-Nazi younger generation. An ultimatum backed by the threat of invasion by German troops and demanding the transfer of power to the Nazi Arthur Seyss-Inquart compelled Schuschnigg to resign on that day. When the Austrian President, Wilhelm Miklas, refused to appoint Seyss-Inquart as Schuschnigg's successor, Hitler gave the order for the invasion, which took place on 13 March 1938. Once Schuschnigg had ordered all Austrian troops to withdraw from the border, the Anschluss was carried out without bloodshed. Within a few weeks Heydrich, Kaltenbrunner and Eichmann had set about eliminating political opponents and 'criminal elements'.

On 11 March Neville Chamberlain had already informed Schuschnigg that Britain would not intervene if Austria were to be annexed (which led to the resignation of Anthony Eden and his replacement as foreign minister by Lord Halifax). At the crucial moment, the French government was paralysed by yet another cabinet crisis. A further decisive factor was the support of Mussolini who, because of his problems with the Abyssinian campaign, had abandoned his objections to a German satellite state in Austria as long ago as 1936.

Czechoslovakia, which had over three million Sudeten Germans in its population, was now surrounded by Germany on the north, south and west. Hitler decided to proceed with its destruction as early as March 1938, although the preparations had already been going on for a long time. To this end he appointed the chairman of the Sudetendeutsche Partei (Sudeten German Party, SdP), Kurt Henlein, as his agitator. On 24 April 1938 the SdP, at Hitler's bidding, adopted the Karlsbad programme, in which they demanded full autonomy for the Sudeten German areas, compensation for the 'injustice' suffered by the ethnic German community since 1918, and complete recognition of National Socialist ideology. When the crisis deepened, Hitler demanded the cession of the Sudeten area to Germany. On 20 May Czechoslovakia, on the – false – expectation of a German attack, mobilised and only vigorous intervention on the part of Britain and France prevented the outbreak of war. On 30 May Hitler placed the army on stand-by for 1 October 1938. At the same time a huge propaganda campaign started up using the principle of a nation's right to self-determination to give a legal gloss to the German plans; at the same time they constantly emphasised that the Sudeten area was Germany's last territorial demand.

The further course of the crisis was determined by the attitude of Britain, which once more hoped to preserve peace in Europe by granting further concessions. To achieve this she was prepared to negotiate with Germany about border changes in East and Central Europe, especially since she disapproved of Czechoslovakia's restrictive policies towards her ethnic minorities. After Hitler, at the beginning of September 1938, had publicly threatened to invade Czechoslovakia, Chamberlain went to Bavaria on 15 September to act as mediator through direct talks with him. Together the British and French governments forced the Czechs to agree in principle to his demands. When, on 22 September at the Godesberg Conference, Chamberlain agreed to Hitler's demand that the Sudeten area be ceded to the Reich, Hitler responded with an ultimatum: the German Army was to be allowed to occupy the Sudetenland immediately and a plebiscite on nationality held by 28 September in an area that was not precisely defined. When the Prague government rejected the ultimatum (a new military government had ordered general mobilisation on 23 September), the British government asked Mussolini to mediate. Hitler, Mussolini, Chamberlain and the French Prime Minister Daladier met in Munich on 29 September, where the cession of the Sudetenland to Germany was agreed, leaving a 'Rump Czechoslovakia'. The war, which the whole of Europe had prepared for and Hitler hoped for, was postponed for a further year. 'It's peace for our time,' Chamberlain declared, but only a few months later, when what was left of Czechoslovakia was destroyed (March 1939), he finally had to acknowledge how naive he had been.

The Anschluss   19 & 26 March 1938

I

Our sorrow for Austria would be torment enough. The sight of the victim with the loathsome monster, teeth bared, guzzling, gobbling, slurping, belching over her poor, mangled body would be horror enough. It would be enough to drive one to despair to think of the delicate tracery wrought by the centuries disappearing without trace in the melting pot to be turned into more standardised material for that most adroit of all cannibalistic machines. The mute lament of all the hundreds of thousands, their country sinking beneath their feet, their future vanishing before their very eyes, already gasping for breath in the foetid dungeon air, would be heartbreaking enough. Fare thee well, much loved Austria! May God be with you, all you who were Austria! This moment of parting is a moment of unutterable sadness, our sorrow for Austria alone would be more than enough to bear.

But destiny will not leave it at that. It shrouds the first night in a second. Alongside the drama of Austria is the drama of Europe. At the same time as one's heart bleeds for Austria, it bleeds for a Europe profoundly humiliated. At the crucial moment – foreseeable and foreseen – Europe was in a complete vacuum. When put to the test, the continent – and today that means its two western great powers – looked as if it were totally outdone in strength, totally drained in mind, totally broken in will. Never in all the 20 years of increasingly bad mistakes and weaknesses has it so disgraced itself as this time. And, what is even worse, never has it brought the liberal/democratic system, which has its last stronghold here, into such disrepute as in the last few days. All that is no less disquieting, no less menacing than the case of Austria herself – and looking around one has to admit that nowhere are there people or forces who, bearing no responsibility for what has happened, represent an unused reserve on which one could now pin one's hopes. None of the men who led, and still lead, Europe, none of the nations, parties or classes is without involvement in what has happened. They have all, sometimes separately, sometimes together, made their contribution to the disaster. Everyone, individuals and the public at large, Britons and French, right wing and left, can pride themselves on having, over the last 20 years, done their bit to help speed this development on its way, on having added their own item to the bill – their own portion of ignorance, blindness, thoughtlessness, laziness, cowardice, selfishness, deception and delusion. History will not deal lightly with any one them, neither those who individually bear responsibility nor those who collectively shun responsibility. If there is anything that can make our grief more bitter, can heighten our concern, it is this universality of guilt – and the realisation that there is no hope that new people, new forces might reverse the situation; that can only happen if the old ones change their ideas, change them radically. But sorrow, grief, anger, concern are not political concepts. What has happened? Where are things heading?

II

The first thing to note is that we are now clear about the nature of the events that took place in Berlin at the end of January culminating in the changes in the foreign ministry and the army. They were directly connected with the question of Austria.

In January a house search had been carried out at the headquarters of the Austrian Nazi Party in Vienna and some of its leaders had been arrested. In the course of the search a plan for a putsch was found, a timetable for the seizure of power in Austria – identical in content, as it happens, with what actually took place on 11 March. The whole process of the 'national uprising', including the appeal for German military intervention and details of the public buildings to be occupied, was set out in the plan. To crown it all, the plan was signed 'R. H.' which, given the senior reaches of the Party where it must have originated, could only mean Rudolf Hess. Schuschnigg[25] had this document – together with others – photographed and a copy sent to his supposed protector, Mussolini. He could make other use of them, publicly or through diplomatic channels, at any moment. And there was the prospect of a trial for high treason. It was threatening to spread a nasty stench throughout the world. It was threatening to open the eyes of the world to the way the Third Reich had observed its treaty of 11 July 1936 with Austria – hardly 'dictated' by its enemies – its pledge to respect 'the full sovereignty of the Federal State of Austria' and its pledge not to intervene, 'either directly or indirectly,' in her internal affairs, nor to exert any influence on her, even when it concerned 'matters regarding Austrian National Socialism'. Berlin had to do something to stop this scandal becoming common knowledge throughout the world, to stop this graphic demonstration of the value of the Führer's 'promises' being given to the whole world. In this situation Hitler decided to combine immediate necessity with what had always been his ideal, namely to smother the scandal by swiftly founding the Greater German Reich. His solution demanded military preparations. Thus it became one of the points on which the generals felt they could display their opposition to everything these preparations meant. Clearly it wasn't the only point, everything was at stake during the controversy, but this, if not the main point, was at least the most immediate, and the result was that the outcome of the generals' rebellion also decided the fate of Austria.

We know how events unfolded from then on. We know that immediately after the purge of the general staff Hitler repaired to his idyllic retreat in Berchtesgaden, to which – once again immediately – Herr von Schuschnigg was lured on the pretence that Hitler was furious with his Nazi underlings and wanted to discuss with the Austrian chancellor how to resolve the tensions between them. It is also well known that in the course of the change of military personnel General Reichenau[26] had been transferred from command of the Munich Army Corps to command of Army Group IV, to which the Nuremberg Corps also belonged. Now that it has been officially announced that these two corps form the bulk of the army of occupation in Austria, the transfer of Reichenau can be seen as a logical move in the whole process. The secret mobilisation of these two corps had to be set in motion immediately and to be on the safe side it had to be entrusted to the general closest to the Nazis. It appears that the corps were ready to move even as Schuschnigg was arriving in Berchtesgaden. What happened there and later is too well known and too fresh in the memory to need recapitulating here.

There is much to be learnt from this little prelude. Most important of all must be the fact that the Austrian venture, just like the occupation of the Rhineland, was opposed by officials of the highest rank, whose attempts to sabotage it came close to rebellion – and that Hitler, with his 'It will succeed!' and his raging against the faint-hearted, has been proved right once again. One can well imagine – and it is no comfort – how it will have strengthened his belief in his own infallibility, in the divine right of his mission, how it will drive him on to other such acts without, in future, anyone daring to utter even the most tentative words of warning.

III

The second thing to note – and not for the first time, though it has never been so glaringly obvious as in this case – is that treaties with this kind of regime are of no value whatsoever. Even the overused expression 'a scrap of paper' would be out of place here, would be to do an injustice to the late Bethmann-Hollweg,[27] even to the Prussia of yore. The treaty on Belgium[28] had been respected for decades, the men who made it certainly did not do so with the intention of breaking it in the near future. Those who made the treaty with Austria did intend to break it, it has not been observed for even an hour. The Third Reich has never stopped taking an interest in the Austrian Nazis, it has never stopped keeping them supplied and on an operational footing. It has never stopped using all means – both within Austria and from outside – at its disposal to prepare the way for the elimination of her guaranteed 'sovereignty'. The treaty was nothing but a sham suspension of operations which at the time happened to seem useful for other reasons. It was a means of giving themselves an even freer hand to continue doing the opposite of what it said. But even if that could be disputed, what is absolutely beyond dispute is that the treaty was torn up the moment they had the mind and the means to do so. The signature at the bottom was completely worthless and everything that was paid to buy it was paid in vain. The things that have been going on in Europe for years under the title of '*appeasement*', '*causer*', '*rapprochement*' have been nothing but a desperate quest for such signatures. The result is the same every time: one party agrees to pay a substantive price while the other, which has nothing of substance to pay with, is to sign something in return, a promise of future good behaviour. Basically it is always a deal in which cash is paid on the nail for so much hot air in the future delivery. For anyone with normal common sense it is inconceivable that in future there might still be statesmen who long to do such deals.

It was never conceivable. 'Desire for peace' is not a commodity one can bargain with, it is a character trait; and if good character is to be rewarded at all, then certainly only after its existence has been demonstrated over a length of time. The delusionists took a different view but, after our experiences with the Austrian treaty, even the most confirmed delusionist will realise that this signature is not worth paying anything for. And things will not be any worse in Europe if there are no more such treaties here. We can make treaties with each other on customs tariffs, rail traffic or combatting epidemics, but love is there or it isn't. It comes from the heart, not from a contract.

IV

One factor that was of quite particular importance in the case of Austria, and is certain to continue to be so, is the principle of nationality. The nationality principle has somehow swept across Europe but nowhere has it caused such ravages as in its German version. The claim that both reason and ethics demand that all those with the same nationality – which is often understood as meaning the same language – have to be united in the same state is entirely without foundation. That it is taken seriously anywhere is all the more astonishing, given the existence of prosperous and contented states across the world that provide the most striking proof of the contrary. Great Britain and the United States survive separately, as do France and Belgium. In the case of Germany, however, part of the world – for some unknown reason – regards the premise with approval and sympathy. Even now, after what was the plain conquest of Austria, there are many voices, especially in Britain, which only complain about the method used, while the doctrine that all Germans ought to be together is considered highly plausible.

We have to admit that in this particular case the unfortunate Schuschnigg not only contributed to the confusion, he was – tragically – confused himself. The ominous statement in the July treaty that 'Austria acknowledges herself to be a German state' was not simply diplomatic small change that had been extorted from him; the fascination of 'Germanness' had really taken hold of the man. It pervades his book, *Dreimal Österreich* (*Farewell Austria*) and it was probably not unconnected with the way he allowed himself to be lured into the Berchtesgaden trap. Be that as it may, it is a real disaster that the moment Hitler based a whole strategy of conquest on the nationality principle, the world responded with nothing more than reassurances, concessions, compromises, give-and-take, instead of insisting that the nationality principle has no place in international relations. No, it is not the case that the same nationalities belong in the same political structure. No, it is not the case that any state has to have the least moral or political authority over its relatives in other states. Just as one can argue that the union of all those related by language or race in a homogeneous political structure is a blessing for mankind, by the same token one can equally well argue that the competition, cross-fertilisation and friction between different national groups in a state has an enriching, improving, civilising effect. The truth is that history, custom and tradition have produced a wide variety of polities and that these forms that have evolved through history are infinitely superior in status to the simple nationality principle, a principle for the gutter or some bureaucratic exercise. It is untenable as a proposition even when the much-vaunted 'will of the people' is put forward in support – at least not the kind of will that suddenly manifests itself in some situation, in some psychosis. Fortunately the value of the 'will of the people' as an argument has no relevance to Austria. The fury aroused in Hitler by Schuschnigg's proposed referendum, the frantic determination to prevent it, is the best indication that in Austria the 'will of the people' would not have decided in favour of the nationality principle, of the union within one state. But even if it had, and even if such a will of the people – kindled, stirred, fanned to a blaze – were to appear elsewhere today, it is not the purpose of a referendum, it is not the purpose of democracy to leave decisions, the effect of which might be long-lasting, perhaps even irrevocable, to the flash-fire of popular enthusiasms. It is not without reason that a point came where, alongside the lower houses of parliament – the distillation of the popular mood – the democracies set up senates and upper houses as a kind of barrier against these very fleeting psychoses, a kind of balance between the enthusiasms of the moment and a more considered, long-term judgment. There is much sense in these institutions which put a brake on the 'will of the people' and they have more than proved their worth. But common sense throughout the world, the law of the different states and the tradition of the League of Nations have to perform the same function if suddenly, somewhere, the 'will of the people', in a frenzy of nationalism, wants to see the established order torn apart, stable structures broken up. The case of Austria shows us the danger that lies in not responding to the plebeian simple-mindedness of the nationalist premise with the collective and absolute 'No' it deserves, instead of agreeing to concessions and artificial arrangements, which only add further impetus to the wave.

V

The nationality principle is not tenable in theory, and in practice it works to the advantage of Germany alone in Europe. For, given the ethnographic situation on the continent, Germany is the only country that could become significantly larger according to that principle; all other countries would at best stay roughly the same, a number would even have to be reduced in size. If the nationality principle were applied across the continent, it would mean that a strengthened Germany would be surrounded by countries that had been weakened in relative, or even absolute terms; she would be twice the size of even the largest of her neighbours, ten or 20 times that of all the others and would ipso facto enjoy outright dictatorship, unconditional hegemony in the European system. There is nothing more to the nationality principle as put forward by Germany than there would be to a claim to European hegemony put forward openly, without being dressed up in this ideological garb. Anyone who expresses his approval of the nationality principle as a theory, an ideology, should be clear in his mind that in so doing he is also giving his approval to the practical consequence, that is, German hegemony.

Once this is accepted – and I cannot see how it could be disputed – there is a further lesson to be learnt from the Austrian episode. The lesson is that there is no alternative in the form of what might be called a diluted nationality principle, reduced from the level of the state to an undefined 'völkisch' concept. That was the level on which Germany conducted its manoeuvres in connection with Austria up to the day of the full annexation – and it is the level on which she is manoeuvring at the moment in connection with Czechoslovakia. There is no talk of incorporation in the German state, merely of bonds between the German people and their brothers across the border. An ethnic protectorate over those brothers vis-à-vis the state of which they are citizens is declared, setting up a vague 'völkisch community' which stretches across the political boundaries but still, so it is claimed, respects those boundaries. And the struggles in the other country, which are provoked, unleashed, supported and organised in the name of this 'völkisch community' are not presented as struggles for incorporation in the German national state but as struggles to assert their national rights within the foreign country. In this version there are no leaders promoting and encouraging the undiluted nationality principle, there are only their suffering brothers who, in accordance with the diluted nationality principle, are trying to survive as a 'Volk' in their present country, and there is only one Reich which is willing and duty-bound to help them achieve this survival as a 'Volk' within their present state.

To naive people in many countries the nationality principle appears particularly plausible in this more modest, diluted version, and in the case of Austria this version alone was used until the very last minute. In his speech in Linz on 5 March the new government minister, Seyss-Inquart,[29] was still celebrating Austria's entry into 'the spiritual empire of the German people, that has now become a reality'; at the same time, however, he celebrated the permanent, inviolable existence of the 'historically grounded' 'independence of Austria' within Austria's own political boundaries and in its own character as a state. Five days later the mask was thrown off and the gentleman who had just figured as an advocate of the state of Austria, though sharing 'völkisch' ideals in common with the German people, emerged as an advocate of the German state entrusted by the German state with the task of incorporating Austria in it.

Thus the Austrian episode demonstrates with particular clarity that the diluted version of the nationality principle is deliberately misleading – and doubly dangerous, because it looks so modest, so much more attractive, so much more humane. It has become clear that it was totally absurd ever to see the leaders of the Austrian Nazis as proponents of an Austrian state with a passion for their German ethnicity. They were agents of Germany, that is all, with no other aim than to prepare and carry out the full annexation according to the instructions of the master they served. It is equally absurd to see Herr Henlein[30] and his men as fighters for ethnic German rights within the political framework of Czechoslovakia. They are simply instruments of the German government – officials charged with carrying out the full political annexation by and for the Third Reich. Since that is what they are, those who obey them are *de facto* such instruments as well – and the whole diluted version of the nationality principle is nothing more than a ruse to help them along the road to the undiluted version. There can be no serious argument about that since the test case of Austria, which has demonstrated that the Nazi machine was not an Austrian set-up with a 'völkisch' German soul, but a German set-up located in Austria.

VI

The consequences for Czechoslovakia are patently obvious. From the moment the regiments of the Third Reich began to cross the Austrian frontier, all eyes were focused on Czechoslovakia. Geography was not without influence on the situation. The fact that this little state, which already had an enormously long border of 960 miles with Germany (compared with 150 miles of Germany's border with France), will now have to defend a further 450 miles constitutes a threat that cannot be ignored. But even more than the proximity of the new neighbour, it was the political analogy with Austria that immediately came to mind. Whether Hitler will pounce on Czechoslovakia in the same way is a political question that will have to be dealt with by the whole of Europe. But leaving the question of war and peace aside, the incidents that are being contrived within Czechoslovakia and the direction in which she might be driven are problems created by this fiction of nationality. It is already clear that the Nazis' victory in Austria was a signal for the Nazi fighting unit in Czechoslovakia to intensify its attacks; already they feel strong enough to present ultimatums to the government in Prague. On the other hand, it is also clear that their success and their own determination not to miss the boat have brought those elements of the German population in the country which until now have been against their Nazi brethren round to their side. Already one of the German groups that had so far remained loyal to Czechoslovakia, the German Agrarian Party, has crossed over into the other camp, and the influx of individuals will be no less numerous.

In this situation Czechoslovakia has two alternatives. She is faced with them as a result of her own dilemma and of influence and interference from abroad. Should she behave as if the diluted nationality principle were valid, or should she behave as if it were a sham? Should they once again try making concessions to appease the 'völkisch' claims of a group which they treat as if it were part of the population; or should they refuse to make the activities of a group they look upon as agents of a foreign power even easier by conceding further ground? What those in charge in Czechoslovakia think about all this in their heart of hearts has never been made entirely clear. But today that is no longer of overriding importance, since the decision is no longer in Prague's hands alone. On her own, Czechoslovakia cannot resist a determined German push. It is possible if, and only if, she can expect assistance from abroad. If she does not want simply to submit to Germany – and as long as she refuses simply to submit to Germany – she basically has to follow those on whose support she is counting if the worst should come to the worst. To ensure France's support, she cannot pursue a policy that is against France's advice. But from France the connection extends to Britain. For France to be able to count on Britain she, for her part, has to allow London to be involved in deciding her policy. To simplify matters somewhat, one can say that ultimately the policy of the Czech government vis-à-vis the Sudeten Germans is decided in London.

It would be too soon to regard this decision as already taken. Britain is going through a severe crisis. The rift within public opinion, parliament and even the cabinet over problems of foreign policy is steadily growing wider and more acute; at the moment it is completely uncertain which side will gain the upper hand. But the tendency to accept the diluted nationality principle as the key to the situation in Czechoslovakia has been very noticeable during the last few months. At least there was, on that basis, approval for the idea of 'cantonising' Czechoslovakia on the Swiss model; that is, to grant the German areas the status of a federal state with its own regional government, its own parliament, its own courts of law and its own police. If that were to come about – even today, after the experiences in Austria, indeed, as a consequence of them – it would be difficult for the world and for the Czechoslovaks not to be profoundly disheartened. No one who is capable of clear thinking and learning from experience could have any illusions about the consequences. It would not appease the demands of German ethnicity in Czechoslovakia, all it would do would be to hand over three-quarters of the power in the Sudetenland to the German agents there, and from that point on the final annexation would be perhaps even easier than that of Austria after Berchtesgaden. It would complete the greatest paradox in contemporary affairs: at the precise point at which, in a parallel case, a 'movement' turned out to be nothing more than the agency of a foreign power, it was not curbed in a neighbouring country, as one might expect, but given free rein. It is true that states as well as individuals can sometimes find it necessary to offer up a sacrifice to stupidity. Being dependent on the support of other countries, it is possible that Czechoslovakia cannot avoid having to put on a public show – even of things the blind and boneheaded in those other countries approve of. But there are limits. One is the point at which the cost of submission would not be much higher than the price of support – especially when the support remains uncertain nonetheless.

VII

Whether the support will be given – that is the decision that should have been taken years, or at least months ago. Now at least serious debate about it is starting, though there is no telling when it will end. It is a debate that is going on in Britain, but even though her awareness of the danger threatening the moral and material foundations of all Europeans states, including her own, has become more acute, there are two other facts that appear not to have penetrated very deeply into her consciousness. Firstly: the corps of European states which can still be assembled to counter the danger is getting so small that we cannot afford to lose a single one – each one is a more or less irreplaceable part of the total armed force, and each territory a part of the overall battlefield. Secondly: the days are past when it was possible for Britain to have client countries fight for its interests in shaping the balance of power in Europe; 1914 will not be the last time the island had to fight itself, by mistake, so to speak, from now on that will probably always be the case. Perhaps the day has not yet come when these two gaps in her consciousness will be filled, as many have been already, but only on that day will her repeated attempts to avoid her obligations come to an end.

But it would be over-optimistic for anyone to be sure that we will reach that day in time – and 'in time' means while the British obligation still has a *deterrent* effect. It is all very well – and certainly correct – to say that if France becomes involved in a war, Britain will have no choice but to join in, whatever the cause of the conflict. That is so true and such common knowledge that it is gradually beginning to appear in all newspaper articles in Britain – although there are different opinions about the point at which the intervention should come. Some reports I have read suggest this point should only come once defeats have proved that France cannot continue alone. But even if there are no serious doubts about a *de facto* Franco-British alliance, the constant refusal to accept any *de jure* obligation, if the cause of war should be the defence of Czechoslovakia, could have serious consequences. Not only could it encourage a surprise attack, it could also lead to such a disheartened mood as to arouse thoughts of resignation and surrender in Czechoslovakia (and even in France). After seeing what happened to Austria, the way she simply vanished, it will perhaps not be long before things start to move in that direction. The deterrent effect of a British obligation may well depend on

Europe not having to wait much longer for it. And if the recent episode of Austria has brought about a greater need than ever for things to speed up, so far it has not brought about the speeding-up itself.

We are waiting for it, powerless to do anything to expedite it. For the balance is still such that a serious joint decision to defend Czechoslovakia would prevent the decision to attack her. The case of Austria was not even an example of the success of aggressive risk-taking, it was the success of an enterprise with no risk at all. For weeks, months, years it had been made clear in every way imaginable that if Mussolini did not take up arms, no western country would either. The situation is completely different if it involves the ultimate risk, that is, if the other side also accepts the risk without which no person and no state can hold their own. It is still the case that anyone who wants to prevent the use of arms must demonstrate convincingly that he is resolved to use his own arms if need be. That would have saved Vienna. That will save Prague. Without it nothing can be saved anymore.

Taking stock after Munich   8 October 1938

The Munich Agreement, in which the four powers decided the fate of Czechoslovakia on 29 September and with which Prague had to comply within 12 hours, differs from Hitler's Godesberg ultimatum in the following points:

1. Instead of a lightning annexation *all at once*, beginning on 1 October, there will be a rapid annexation *in stages* from 1 to 10 October.
2. The *border* of the annexed territory in the Godesberg ultimatum has not been accepted, but has not been replaced by another. The border will be fixed retrospectively, in the period up to 10 October, by a German-British-French-Italian-Czech commission meeting in Berlin with a German in the chair. We will have to wait and see whether the line they decide on is much different from the Godesberg border, indeed, whether a different line can be chosen once the fortresses are in German hands.
3. The Godesberg demarcation lines for the *plebiscite zones and enclaves* have similarly not been accepted but not replaced by others either. These plebiscite areas will also be determined later by the same commission. Here, too, we will see what departures from Hitler's demands are envisaged and whether they can still be enforced.

4. Similarly the demand in the ultimatum that people who have settled in the areas since the war be allowed to take part in the plebiscite has not been accepted but not been replaced by a different arrangement either. *The definition of who has the right to vote in the plebiscite* has also been deferred and handed over to the same commission.

5. While the Godesberg ultimatum did not include the right of individuals to opt out of incorporation in the Reich, the Munich Agreement allows a *right to opt out* in principle. This principle is, however, not spelt out in any detail, in particular it contains no arrangements regarding the right of those who opt out to dispose of or transfer their property. That task and the supervision of its implementation has been assigned to another, German-Czech commission. The influence of the Czech member of the commission will be as great as one would expect in the circumstances.

6. Whereas in Godesberg Hitler was unwilling to grant even the remnant of Czechoslovakia any further assurances, in the Munich Agreement Germany and Italy declared that they were prepared to join in the guarantee which Britain and France had offered the rump state, but which even they have not yet signed and which is not yet in force. The content and modalities of this future *guarantee à quatre*, therefore, remain completely open. Furthermore, the German and Italian participation will only come into effect once the rump of Czechoslovakia has been the subject of further amputations to satisfy Polish and Hungarian demands.

To sum up, these are the changes brought about by the Munich Agreement. Three things have been *added* to the Godesberg ultimatum: the extension of the deadline by a few days, the opt-out principle and the possibility of a German guarantee after further bits of Czech territory have been hacked off. Three things have been *deleted* from it: three demarcation lines and definitions which, instead of being changed have been left blank and are to be filled in by a commission. These additions and interim omissions have, in the view of the French and British governments, turned the unacceptable demands into acceptable ones, ill-will into goodwill, a cause of war into an earnest of peace. These additions and interim omissions are, if one sticks to the facts, clearly the watershed between the terrible necessity of risking the entire existence of the nations and all civilisations and the joyful opportunity to declare, 'It is peace for our time!'

We have to say that we hadn't expected that the watershed would be so thin. We hadn't expected that the ominous decision of great powers to mobilise

175

would only produce such minimal effects. When people heard Chamberlain speak on the radio on 27 September, when, in the House of Commons on the next day, he described the Godesberg proposals as unacceptable, when London turned into an army camp, when the streets of Paris were darkened and offices and factories emptied because men were called up, they naturally got the impression that it was not being done because of minor points of disagreement. This, as readers will remember, was also the opinion of this writer and he is not ashamed to acknowledge his error today. Whilst at the time I was writing last week – the time at which the Four-Power Conference was starting – it was perfectly clear to see that there would be no war over Czechoslovakia, there were on the other hand grounds for taking a relatively optimistic view of the objectives France and Britain had set themselves with their sudden stand, with their 'unacceptable' and their mobilisations – and of their prospects of realising that objective with those means. The objective for which, following Godesberg, they suddenly, after such lengthy hesitation, demonstrated they were even prepared to go to war, must be of some importance, it seemed. We were surely justified in assuming that they were going to at least insist 'that the booty Hitler carries off will really consist of the Sudetenland alone and not the whole of Czechoslovakia. What is crucial,' I went on, 'is that the country continues to exist, with its own traditions, reduced in size but viable and able to defend itself, with international guarantees and a new cordon of mighty fortifications. If that is what happens we can remain optimistic despite everything.'

Today it is difficult to maintain that that is what has happened. The Munich Agreement does allow *a* Czechoslovakia to exist, but the text and the circumstances surrounding it make it clear that as a state she will no longer have any influence on the international stage, nor even an independent existence. She has not been spared the loss of all her fortresses and most of the heavy material installed in them. She has not been spared the prospect – indeed, it has been given implicit approval – of Poland and Hungary tearing off their chunks, their great chunks, as well. (Incidentally, with the Hungarian chunk Czechoslovakia will lose access to the Danube, her last major link with the outside world.) Furthermore, no one can imagine that the borders of the annexed regions, when they are drawn, will spare her the loss of the greater part of her industry, which is substantial, more important than that of Italy; with this loss not only her military but also her economic and cultural potential will sink to that of, for example, Greece. No one can expect she will be spared seeing her country cut into two almost separate parts along the line between Bohemia/Moravia and Slovakia, not even retaining a continuous rail link between the two; indeed it is not even certain that Slovakia itself will not be torn off. Above all, we have Lord Runciman's programme,[31] the programme of a man who has so far proved to have identical views to his prime minister – and, to make no bones about it, it is a programme which allows for what is left of Czechoslovakia to become completely dependent on Germany morally, economically and politically, not merely a dominion, but a vassal state. That is what it says in his published report and if there was any optimism for the development of Czechoslovakia left, this report has destroyed it.

The consequences for the rest of the world resulting from these new facts mean we will need to revise our thinking as well. They are much more serious than at first appeared. We must realise that the whole of Czechoslovakia's strength, not just part of it, has been excised from that of the West – whilst on the other hand at least a large part of it, above all most of her industrial capacity, has been added to that of the Third Reich. This plus on the one side and minus on the other has produced such a substantial double shift in the relative power of land forces that it is impossible to see how France, the land power in the other scale of the balance, can possibly make good the difference from her own resources, given the other calls on them. Even if France should manage to recover fully from this experience, it is impossible to see where she could find the reserves to restore the balance. It is significant that Duff Cooper, in his resignation speech in the House of Commons, emphasised what a matter of urgency it is for Great Britain to build up a land army of continental type and continental strength. Furthermore, it does not need repeating that, with Germany breaking through the barrier of Czechoslovakia, the rest of the Danubian and Balkan states will not be able to put up lengthy or serious resistance to the pressure from the giant that has arrived – geographically and strategically – at their gates surrounded by the aura of irresistibility. An era is about to start in which, apart from, but also through the policy of the 'unification of all Germans in a greater German empire', *a system of racially alien vassal states* is being established. No one down there can see what could stop it now. The consequences will be further shifts in power.

We have reached a point where imagination fails. The blackest prospect of all is a France abandoned by everyone and attacked on three fronts. But the fact is that the exact opposite remains just as much a possibility, namely the prospect, if the worst should come to the worst, of an alliance of all the great powers against an aggressor who is more dangerous than ever. It is futile to indulge in speculation about this; the more we realise – as we just have – that parchments and seals count for nothing in these times, the less point there is in thinking hard about the alliances and treaties of tomorrow or the day after tomorrow. Whatever happens tomorrow to the Franco-Soviet pact or the

Berlin-Rome axis, it says nothing about what the true position of Russia or Italy will be when the chips are down. The one essential fact is that where there is a powerful and focused centre for an aggressor party, there must be an equally powerful and focused centre around which a defensive coalition can crystallise. We must bear in mind that, after the fall of Czechoslovakia, the shift in relative power has been too great for France to be able to play that role among the great powers. Only Britain can do that, and here we come to the third change of course. I am absolutely convinced that Britain, seen as a whole, has finally become ready for this task and has by and large already accepted it. That is proceeding, even under the guise of official policy, despite the temporary intoxication of having preserved peace. But a man like Chamberlain, in such a decisive post, can always set out for difficult destinations, on dangerous detours and byways. And a further surprise is that Chamberlain has emerged from this crisis not as a wiser man who has learnt his lesson, but as one who is even more convinced than ever of his delusion. The peace declaration which he made after the disastrous Four-Power Agreement is certainly not a concrete accord nor a commitment, it is simply an expression of his absolute lack of understanding of the nature and role of the man he is dealing with and of his stunning ignorance about the forces operating in the world today and determining its fate. The classic expression of this deficiency was his announcement that 'It is peace for our time' – and such a relapse into delusion was not to be expected after his talk on the radio. Here too, then, we have to lower our sights again, we have to anticipate that Chamberlain is on course to undertake further useless and even harmful ventures. But since there is no great mistake left to be made between the Rhine and the Russian border, because the great mistakes have already been made and matters there have already been decided, we are left with the dubious comfort that even a surprisingly inventive deluded mind cannot find much more to sacrifice. In the meantime the country is drifting along on the current of its experiences and every new week shows that it is being carried out beyond the fictions of its prime minister.

On the record   29 October 1938

I Saying and meaning

Sir Samuel Hoare, one of the four of the British 'inner cabinet', has once more (20 October) publicly declared that 'I believe that Herr Hitler means what he says'. He did however add, anticipating objections, 'I know that those who do not share my opinion point to cases when Hitler, after having vowed not to use violence, did do so. I admit that these cases must unavoidably be a cause for concern to us.' Despite that, he insisted he believed Hitler meant what he said.

Diplomacy can be a confusing business. An interpretation for which there is much to be said would be: when Hoare or Chamberlain or Simon declare that Hitler means what he says, they themselves do not at all mean what they say; they may have meant it in the past, but not any longer. And there are some arguments to back up this interpretation. At times it is simply impossible for governments to explain publicly the reasons behind their policies, not even to hint at them; instead they are at times forced to give reasons which they, better than anyone else, recognise as untenable. It is conceivable that this interpretation is wholly, or at least partly correct. It is conceivable that in a few years time it will become clear what the British cabinet – or at least parts of the British cabinet – hoped to achieve, in the terrible situation of 1938, by pretending to believe things it did not believe at all. But if that is conceivable, it does not mean it is certain. Moreover, the 'cause for concern', of which Sir Samuel spoke, does not consist solely of the fact that several times 'Hitler, after having vowed not to use violence, did do so.' It is not only the *method* of pursuing foreign policy, namely the method of using violence that is at issue. In foreign policy as in everything else, even more important than the method is the *matter* – the aims that are declared and those that are actually pursued; the conditions that it claims to be trying to bring about and those it actually does bring about. At a moment when the European and wider foreign policy not only of Britain but of half the world stands at the most decisive crossroads of all, it will be useful to have a survey of the hard evidence available on the subject of 'saying and meaning'. Let us examine a few events of prime importance in foreign affairs and see what Hitler said and what he meant.

II The case of the Rhineland

On 21 May 1935 the Army Law – German rearmament – was announced. On the same day Hitler made a speech to the gathering that goes by the name of the Reichstag in which he calmed fears by saying that from now on there would be no more horrors. In particular he said:

Hitler in the Reichstag, 21 May 1935

> Thirdly: the German government intends not to sign any treaty which it feels cannot be fulfilled. It will, however, *keep to the very last letter* any treaty that was signed *voluntarily*, even if it was drawn up *before* it took office and came into power. In particular it will *therefore observe and fulfil all obligations stemming from the Locarno Pact* as long as the other signatories for their part are prepared to stand by the Pact.'

The Treaty of Locarno was torn up on 7 March 1936 by the occupation of the Rhineland. So Hitler meant what he said in the Reichstag for nine months at most. However, he had added a rider: 'I will observe our Locarno obligations *for as long* as others do so.' This rider is of interest, because such qualifying clauses are not infrequent with him; they have to be looked at very closely if one really wants to know what he means. He referred to this rider nine months later. When he marched into the Rhineland, he said the other side had violated Locarno by the conclusion of the Franco-Soviet pact. But the Franco-Soviet pact had been concluded on 2 May 1935, that is, three weeks before Hitler said he would observe all obligations stemming from Locarno.

III *The acquisition of territory, borders, equal rights, coexistence*

The speeches Hitler made, first of all after the announcement of rearmament, then after the occupation of the Rhineland, calmed fears about further horrors in several other respects.

Hitler in the Reichstag, 21 May 1935

> Following the non-fulfilment by the other states of the obligation to disarm, the German government for its part has renounced *those* Articles [of the Treaty of Versailles] which, as a result of the now one-sided burden on Germany contrary to the Treaty, represent discrimination against the German nation for an unlimited period of time. However, it hereby makes a *most solemn* declaration that this measure refers exclusively to those points *which have been announced* and which discriminate against the German people in both moral and material terms. Therefore the German government will *unreservedly respect the other Articles* [of the Treaty of Versailles] *concerning the coexistence of the nations, including the territorial arrangements ...*

Hitler in the Reichstag, 7 March 1936

> After three years I believe I can today regard Germany's struggle for equal rights as finished ... *We have no territorial demands to make in Europe.*

Thus he said that equal rights for Germany had been conclusively achieved; he would now unreservedly respect the Versailles rules for the coexistence of the nations. He went on to say – adding 'most solemnly' – that the territorial arrangements of Versailles would be respected by him without reservation – he wanted no more territory in Europe at all. Extensive research and calculations would be necessary to determine for how long he meant what he said about the first two points. As for the last two, it can be shown that he meant it at most until the beginning of 1938, that is, until the preparations to overturn the territorial arrangements of Versailles and to acquire European territory in Austria and Czechoslovakia. After this had happened in Austria, and immediately before it was about to happen in Czechoslovakia, he repeated in the Sportpalast on 26 September, using the same formulation, what he had said to Chamberlain in Godesberg on 22 September, 'This is my last territorial demand in Europe.' How long he will mean this is a matter for debate.

IV The case of Austria

Countless times Hitler said that he had no intentions regarding Austria and would take no steps against her – that he would not meddle in her domestic politics nor attack and annex her. He even put that in a formal treaty. A few – by no means all – quotations:

Hitler in the Reichstag, 30 January 1934

> The claim that the German Reich intends to *rape* the Austrian state is absurd, there is no evidence to support it nor proof of it ... I most emphatically reject the Austrian government's further claim that an attack directed against the Austrian state is in preparation or even being planned.

Hitler in the Reichstag, 21 May 1935

> Germany has neither the intention nor the desire to *interfere* in Austria's internal arrangements, to *annex or attach her.*

Hitler, interview with Ward Price, 9 March 1936

Question: 'Does the Führer's offer of a non-aggression pact to every eastern neighbour of Germany also apply to Austria?'

Answer: 'My proposal for the conclusion of non-aggression pacts both to the East and West of Germany was of a general nature, i.e. there were no exclusions. Hence this applies to ... *Austria.*'

Hitler on National Labour Day, 1 May 1936

... What do we find? At the same moment in which we, without consideration of the past or the present, express our readiness to hold out our hand to all nations, to conclude treaties with them, at that same moment a new campaign of hatred breaks out. Once more lies are being spread abroad, that tomorrow Germany is going *to invade Austria.* Do I need to ask who these individuals are, who are constantly stirring up hatred, sowing the seeds of distrust? (A tumult of cries from thousands: '*The Jews!*')

The Austro-German Treaty of 11 July 1936

1. In accord with the declarations of 21 May 1935 by the Führer and Chancellor of the Reich, the German government recognises the *full sovereignty* of the Federal State of Austria.
2. Each of the two governments regards the organisation of domestic political matters, including the question of Austrian National Socialism, as the internal business of the other country on which they *will not try to bring any influence to bear either directly or indirectly.*

What Hitler said there he meant, as far as the non-interference was concerned, at most until the Berchtesgaden meeting with Schuschnigg on 12 February 1938, that is for roughly 18 months. As far as the 'rape' or the 'invasion' is concerned, he meant it at most until 11 March 1938, when he sent his troops into Austria. As far as the 'annexation' is concerned, he meant it at most until 13 March 1938, on which he enacted the law 'Austria is a *Land* of the German Reich.'

V *The case of Czechoslovakia*

Hitler first discovered the sufferings of the 'Sudeten Germans' – and with them a cause for conflict with Czechoslovakia – on 20 February 1938. His speech in the Reichstag on that date contained his very first mention of the topic which had never previously aroused his interest and now suddenly aroused his fury. Consequently it is somewhat surprising that he had ever said anything about Czechoslovakia prior to that, but he had:

Hitler in the Reichstag, 21 May 1935

Thirdly, the German government . . . will *therefore observe and fulfil all obligations stemming from the Locarno pact* as long as the other signatories for their part are prepared to stand by the pact.

Hitler in the Reichstag, 7 March 1936

France has not concluded this pact [with Soviet Russia] with just any European power. Even before the Rhine pact, France had treaties of mutual assistance with both *Czechoslovakia* and Poland. Germany made no objection to *these*, not only because these pacts – in contrast to the Franco-Soviet pact – were subject to decisions of the League of Nations, but also because *Czechoslovakia* and, especially, Poland will primarily always pursue a policy of representing the national interests of these countries. *Germany has no desire to attack these countries.* Sixthly, the German government repeats its offer to conclude *non-aggression pacts* with the states on Germany's eastern border, as it has with Poland ...

Hitler, interview with Ward Price, 11 March 1936

Question: '... Does he consider Czechoslovakia as a state neighbouring Germany in the East, too?'

Answer: 'My proposal for the conclusion of non-aggression pacts both to the East and West of Germany was of a general nature, i.e. there were no exclusions. Hence this applies to ... Czechoslovakia'.

Chamberlain in the House of Commons, 14 March 1938

I am informed that Field-Marshal Goering on 11 March gave a general assurance to the Czech Minister in Berlin – an assurance which he expressly renewed later on behalf of Hitler – that it would be the earnest endeavour of the German government to improve Czech-German relations. In particular, on 12 March, Field-Marshal Goering informed the Czech Minister that German troops marching into Austria had received the strictest orders to keep at least 15 kilometres from the Czech frontier. On the same day the Czechoslovak Minister in Berlin was assured by Baron von Neurath[32] that Germany considered herself bound by the German-Czechoslovak Arbitration Convention of October, 1925 [part of the Locarno Treaty].

Hitler and his representative said that the obligation contained in Locarno to call upon and accept the verdict of a court of arbitration defined in the pact in the case of any disagreement with Czechoslovakia remained in full force. As can be shown, that was meant at most until the moment at which a disagreement was provoked but, despite Prague's request, the court was not called on. Hitler said he would not attack Czechoslovakia. As can be shown, he meant it at most until the moment when – in Berchtesgaden and Bad Godesberg – he informed Chamberlain of the forthcoming attack. (Not to mention 21 May 1938.)[33]

VI The exception: the Naval Agreement

It is almost never possible to determine precisely what a person means while they are saying it. But it is possible to determine precisely how they behave afterwards. In all the top priority areas of Hitler's foreign policy so far he has not behaved as he said he would, but has behaved in the opposite way. If one assumes he always meant what he said when he said it, then it was his misfortune always to come very quickly to the opposite opinion precisely on matters of top priority.

There is, though, one area of foreign policy, presumably also a top priority, in which what was said appears to have remained identical with what was meant for over three years now. That is the Anglo-German Naval Agreement of June 1935. Consequently Sir Samuel Hoare mentioned it – as Chamberlain has done several times already – as a particularly encouraging sign. Hitler, Sir Samuel said, 'has kept precisely to the Naval Agreement both according to the letter and the spirit.' This, he went on, gave hope that he means what he says. However, while it may be true that the Naval Agreement has not been renounced and the tonnage ratio has not been exceeded – which would hardly be possible, given the immense amount of shipbuilding taking place in Britain at the moment – it cannot be denied that what was said in 1935 and what is meant today are by no means still identical in several important details. Compare what Hitler said at the time with what he said recently:

Hitler in the Reichstag, 21 May 1935 (three and a half weeks before signing the Naval Agreement)

> The limitation of the German navy to 35 per cent of the British ... leaves it below the total tonnage of the French fleet. Since the opinion has been expressed in various newspapers that this demand was only a beginning and would be raised, especially with the acquisition of colonies, the German government makes the following *binding* declaration: for Germany this demand is *final* and *binding*. Germany has neither the intention, *nor the need*, nor the ability to enter into any naval rivalry.

Hitler in the Sportpalast, 26 September 1938 (three and a quarter years after signing the Naval Agreement)

> I voluntarily refrained from entering into any naval rivalry ever again ... I did not do this because I would not *be able* to build ships – *let there be no illusion about that* – but solely in order to ensure lasting peace between our two nations. There is, however, one condition. It cannot be tolerated for one party to say, 'I never want to make war again and to that end I offer a voluntary limitation of my armaments to 35 per cent' – and for the other to say, 'If it suits me I will make war again from time to time. *That definitely cannot be allowed.*

Not only has the previously emphasised German 'inability' to enter into naval rivalry now turned into the opposite, namely 'we are well able to do so, let there be no doubt about that', the '*final and binding*' commitment has become a commitment, the continuation of which depends on a '*condition*' – a condition imposed on Britain. Already the pact has become conditional. Precisely the same kind of qualifying clause has been added as was added to the statement about the validity of Locarno on 21 May 1935.[34] This added qualification makes what is meant today different from what was said at the time – and that, as experience shows, is no small difference. At a period during which armament will probably become an urgent problem, this difference looks likely to become the springboard for even more substantial discrepancies between what was said previously and what is meant subsequently.

A model   19 & 26 November 1938

On 9 November 1938 Ernst von Rath, a junior official at the German embassy in Paris, was shot by a 17-year-old Jew, Herschel Grynszpan, who carried out the murder to avenge the forced deportation, on the order of Heydrich, of his parents to Poland, where they had originally come from. His original aim had been to shoot the German ambassador, and in killing Rath instead he chose a victim who was not even definitely a Nazi – the Gestapo had had their suspicions about Rath for some time. Nevertheless Goebbels seized the opportunity to unleash an unprecedented pogrom, which had long been prepared, against the Jews in Germany. During the night of 9 November 1938 more than 250 synagogues were set on fire, around 7,000 Jewish shops destroyed and countless homes ransacked. The SS and Gestapo organised the transfer of 26,000 male Jews to the Buchenwald, Dachau and Sachsenhausen concentration camps. Most of those imprisoned were only released when they signed declarations of their intent to emigrate. Before they were allowed to emigrate they had to pay compensation for the damage (while the state pocketed the insurance payments) and accept a 'fine of atonement' of a billion Reichsmarks. The rights of the Jews were subsequently restricted in almost all areas. On 24 January 1939 Goering gave Heydrich the task of solving the 'Jewish question' by either 'emigration or expulsion', a project in which Hjalmar Schacht was also involved. The pogrom aroused protests from all around the world which, although without effect on the Nazis, did at least contribute to the end of the British policy of appeasement.

A model   19 & 26 November 1938

I

If people were capable of understanding even just the things they have experienced themselves, they would realise that what has happened to the German Jews is a precise model of every one of Hitler's operations, both previous and future ones. As in everything else, the matter of the Jews starts –

stage one – with the openly and bluntly barbaric gospel of annihilation of the pre-government period: passages from *Mein Kampf*; the Party programme; the newspaper articles, pamphlets, speeches and practices over many years; the *Boxheim Papers*[35] seized in November 1931. As in everything else, in this matter as well the Party's coming to power was immediately followed – stage two – by the most mollifying interpretations, the warmest reassurances: 'Everything that has previously been planned and announced naturally no longer counts, has naturally never counted. There have been a few excesses, but there's a revolution going on, I'm sure you understand. It's over now, it won't happen again. My word of honour as a German gentleman, nothing will happen. The Jews will be pushed back a few per cent – they are a bit overrepresented here and there, especially the East European Jews – but they'll only be pushed back in the professional and cultural sphere, and even there in moderation, word of honour. And for the rest? We're a civilised nation, sir.' On 25 March 1933 Goering told the assembled representatives of the foreign press that the few over-zealous Party members responsible for harassment of the Jews had already been punished and dismissed:

The government and I myself will *never* tolerate anyone being persecuted simply because he is a Jew. If the government should take measures to counter the *excessive spread* of the Jewish element, then that is its business.

The Goebbels factory started spewing out whole series of products designed to show that it really was just a matter of reducing the 'excessive spread'. On 26 March 1933 the American Secretary of State, Cordell Hull,[36] could give the concerned *American Jewish Committee* absolute reassurance:

You will remember that at the time of your recent call at the Department I informed you that in view of numerous press statements indicating widespread mistreatment of the Jews in Germany I would request the American Embassy at Berlin in consultation with the principal consulates in Germany to investigate the situation and submit a report. A reply has now been received indicating that whereas there was for a short period of time considerable physical mistreatment of Jews this phase may be considered virtually terminated. There was also some picketing of Jewish merchandise stores and instances of professional discrimination. These manifestations are viewed with serious concern by the German Government. Hitler in his capacity as leader of the Nazi Party issued an order calling upon his followers to maintain law and order to avoid molesting foreigners, disrupting trade ...

In a word, good intentions to be taken in good faith. Hitler means what he says. The 'spirit of Munich' *avant la lettre*. None of the earlier propaganda, none of *Mein Kampf*, none of the vows to exterminate count any longer. 'Things will sort themselves out. People who say that they won't sort themselves out, that they'll end in the most bestial savagery, such people are stuck in their ways and if they pretend differently, you can't believe a word they say – such people have closed minds, they have an axe to grind, they're hysterics. You shouldn't let people like that worry you.'

Stage three: as in everything else, in this as well things do not sort themselves out. They head backwards, to their starting point, to the pre-government gospel. As these gentlemen become stronger and feel less dependent on their fellow human beings abroad, one mollifying interpretation and warm reassurance after another crumbles. 'Pushing back' gradually turns into eradication, the removal of 'excessive spread' becomes progressive strangulation. In May 1933 the Prussian government could still announce that of the 3,515 'non-Aryan' lawyers in Prussia 2,158 had had their registration renewed. The number would then gradually shrink to a few dozen who, moreover, were only allowed to act for their fellow Jews. The same process occurred in all areas outside the economy, maliciousness exuding from every pore. Then came the inexhaustible process of social and cultural exclusion and humiliation, the benches for Jews, the bans from public baths and parks, all the hundreds of ingenious sadistic ploys, culminating in the great Austrian orgy of shit-scrubbing and apartment-occupation. Then came the torment of legal hair-splitting, wholesale arrests, mass transport to the concentration camps. But still, however far back things go, the banner of hope that there might be some reserves of good intentions was planted on the very edge of the grave. There was still an 'after all', a 'despite everything' – even German Jews said so, never mind others. It was to businesses, to the 'economy' that this 'after all' clung on longest. 'After all', the instruction that in the economy the Jews were to be left untouched remained in force, if frequently ignored, for some considerable time. On 28 February 1935 Mayor Lippert[37] of Berlin could still explain in the American Chamber of Commerce in the city:

We are often accused of destroying the economic existence of the Jews in Germany ... You, gentlemen, who have the opportunity of seeing Germany for yourselves, also have the opportunity to clear this matter up. For every impartial visitor to our Fatherland has the opportunity to convince himself that *in economic terms* nothing has happened to Germany's Jews. *Not one expropriation or destruction of a so-called Jewish enterprise* has taken place. Once a Jew has demonstrated to the state that he is ready to fulfil the duties incumbent upon him, as on every other inhabitant of our Fatherland, he enjoys *the same economic rights.*

Even then, this was far from being true and was to become even less so later on. But as long as the tiniest scrap remained true, it remained a specious refuge for the optimism of all those who – in this as in everything else – could not bear to see a direct conclusion drawn from a series of experiences and facts. 'Yes, things are bad. But at least you have to admit that most of them can still earn something and feed themselves. You can't say everything's hopeless, you shouldn't assume there's ill will at work.' It is the same sad game that is kept up, in all areas without exception, until the second before the bomb goes off. As in all the more important matters since 1933, right up to the most recent, Austria and Czechoslovakia, people's actions and ideas have been governed by the remnants of what is made to look like and is perceived as goodwill. Even now, in 1938, the sole idea the dreary conferences of Évian and London could come up with was to appeal to Berlin's goodwill and to ask whether they could not allow those who had applied to emigrate to take a little more of their money and possessions with them. Why should the gentlemen not be open to argument? After all, one can't assume they simply want to annihilate them.

But one night in November 1938 – stage four – the destructive bombshell went off. As it always was and always will be, the hour came when the last bit of make-up was wiped off and the one truth stood revealed: the pronouncements of violence, annihilation and brutality of the pre-government period. Everything that had seemed too risky, too brutal, indeed too absurd ever to be quite believable – what would the Nazis get out of it? It would be madness even from their own point of view! – suddenly became reality like a bolt from the blue. *Allons enfants de cette patrie, le jour barbare est arrivé.* At two o'clock in the morning the Hitler Youth reported for duty – strictly spontaneously. Spontaneously equipped with hammers, axes and crowbars, and going by spontaneous lists, they destroyed every Jewish shop in the country. More adult Party members spontaneously received paraffin, pitch and bombs, and set light to or blew up almost all the synagogues. Goods, books and correspondence were plundered from more or less all Jewish businesses and workshops. Tens of thousands of so-called 'respectable' Jews, the one class still remaining, were targeted – working from 'spontaneous' lists – and arrested. People were struck down, shot, thrown out of windows. Special refinements were thought up, as in Kassel where the Jews were herded together on the cold winter's night, had the hoses of the fire brigade directed at them for half an hour and were then flung into cellars, dripping wet. Patients were driven out of the tuberculosis clinics, the elderly out of the old people's homes, children out of the orphanages and the doors closed for good. The grocery stores, cafés and inns were not allowed to give the starving thousands anything to eat. There were no doctors left in the hospitals. The officially decreed savagery from below was followed by that from above: prohibited from even going to the cinema, prohibited from owning or managing businesses of any kind. With a stroke of the pen, the larger part of all remaining Jewish income and half of all remaining Jewish property was wiped out. The other half – definitely not less than half! – was liquidated 'legally': a billion under the heading of 'fines', a further billion under the heading of 'repairs' – repairs to be paid for by those who suffered the damage – and no 'further measures' were needed to draw a line underneath the whole business. It is finished! Within a few hours the German mind, German heroism and the nobility of soul of the Nordic wonder-race have transformed 500,000 human beings into beggars, corpses, filth. The gospel of the pre-government days, the gospel of brutality, the gospel of annihilation, is accomplished – just as it has been accomplished everywhere and in all things, at the pace and to the extent it was possible.

That is the model: through stage two and stage three to the explosive, triumphal end, then back – or forward – to stage one. We have seen it in every case, right up to Austria and Czechoslovakia; and every time we have also seen the eternally unsuspecting men of few words standing there at the moment the bomb goes off, their faces as empty as and pathetic as their heads usually are. How many more times must the model be rehearsed before they at least understand it, if nothing else? The series is not finished. There are many more chapters to the gospel of brutality and annihilation from the days before the Nazis came into office and there are still several stage-three cases that are visibly approaching their conclusion. It is a safe bet, for instance, that the day of reckoning for the Catholic Church is not far off; the wall still separating it from the vowed execution and annihilation, is already not much stronger than the one behind which the Jews were recently eking out an existence. And their other sworn enemies? The other annihilations announced in their authentic Bible? The model shows that they, too, are at stage three. Anyone who opens their eyes, indeed, anyone with eyes which they are capable of opening, can see Europe filled with more people who are treated in the same way as the Jews and who suffer the same fate as the Jews than is dreamt of in their philosophy – or stupidity.

II

There was only one very short break in the course of the treatment of the German Jews, which was paradigmatic for their procedure in all areas. It was the attempt of 1 April 1933 to get it all done at one stroke. The boycott of Jewish businesses that was decreed on that day represented nothing more than a premature attempt to bring about, with no intermediary stages, the same economic murder of the Jews, which has only now, in 1938, been completed. In the case of Austria as well, for example, two premature attempts were made, in 1933 and 1934, to reach the goal at one stroke without the delay of proceeding step-by-step. There too, as in the case of the Jews, the lightning recourse to denials, protestations and pledges, when the premature attempts had to be broken off, was no proof that the ultimate goals had been reduced at all. Nonetheless, it is interesting to recall that wholesale attempt, which had to be broken off after a single day because of the effective protest of several foreign governments.

For the operation of November 1938 was an almost identical copy of its predecessor of April 1933. Goebbels – who was in charge then (the decision was made during Goebbels' visit to Hitler in Berchtesgaden, 27 March 1933) and whom one has every reason to assume was in charge this time – Goebbels simply took the template they had worked out in 1933 out of the drawer and used it again. Then as now all Jewish businesses in all branches were to be destroyed for good. Then as now a 'moral' pretext was sought – the ultimate and usual tribute paid by bestiality to morality. Then just as now the economic murder of the Jews *in Germany* was dressed up as atonement or punishment or reprisal for (alleged) events *abroad*. This time it was a murder abroad, then it was the 'smear campaign' abroad. The first announcement of a total boycott imposed on all Jewish businesses (including doctors and lawyers) from 1 April appeared in the *Völkischer Beobachter* on 29 March 1933. After a description of the 'international smear campaign' and calling for a boycott against Germany, it went on:

> The *guilty ones* are *among us*; they live among us and daily abuse the hospitality the German people have granted them ... Those responsible for these lies and slanders are the Jews among us. The power to reject the liars in the rest of the world lies in their hands. Since they refuse to do that, we will see to it that this campaign of hatred and lies against Germany is not directed at the innocent German people, but at those responsible for the smear campaign.

The same claim was contained in an appeal issued on the eve of the great day by the 'Central Committee for Defence against the Jewish Smear and Boycott Campaign' which – spontaneously appearing from nowhere! – was responsible for carrying out the operation:

> Fellow Germans! Those guilty of this reckless crime, of this mindless smear and boycott campaign are the Jews *in Germany*. They have called on their fellow Jews abroad to fight against the German people. *They* have reported the lies and slanders abroad. Therefore ...

One can see the extent to which the whole 'outburst' this time is nothing but a drab copy of the 1933 prototype. There is a further point in which it is a copy: just as today, in 1933 the operation did not come from the government. Certainly not! But the government, just as today, saw no reason to curb such a noble, morally justified movement. On 27 March the (at the time official) *Telegraphen-Union* announced:

> Two Berlin evening papers have spoken of '*government measures*' in connection with the defensive measures planned by the National Socialists against the foreign smear campaign. This construction is, as has been made clear in previous publications, *incorrect*. What is correct is that the government will *tolerate* such measures ...

Similarly today no order has been given, certainly not, only there was naturally no reason to prevent it. The model that has simply been taken out of the drawer only stops at the point where, in 1933, a hurried retreat had to be made, which was not necessary this time. The 1933 retreat was announced by Goebbels to representatives of the foreign press in the following terms:

> It is with satisfaction that the government has noticed that the smear campaign abroad is on the wane. The government sees this fact as confirmation of the success of the announcement of a boycott by the National Socialist Party. Beyond that, the government can also see that the united Jewish community in Germany has the opportunity to restrict and halt this smear campaign for good. It is convinced that the smear campaign has passed its peak.[38]

This was followed by an official announcement:

It is with satisfaction that the German government has noted that the defensive boycott against the anti-German smear campaign has not been without effect abroad. Apart from minor remnants, this smear campaign has been *completely discontinued*. The German government takes the view that there is no point in continuing the boycott against these remnants ...

Naturally what was referred to as a 'smear campaign' was never more vigorous than on the day on which the spectacle of the boycott unfolded across Germany. Naturally it was never more vigorous than at the precise point at which the worthy gentlemen in Berlin announced that it had been 'discontinued'. If we can talk of this as a model, then only in their determination to lie away, as brazen as can be, and in this there was no innovation in 1938. The notable article he published in the *Völkischer Beobachter* of 12 November 1938, and which the whole of the German press had to take, is not the worst example of Dr Josef Goebbels' efforts in this genre:

One of the most striking features of the operations against the Jews that have taken place over the last few days is the fact that, although buildings were demolished, there was *never any plundering*.

There is no correspondent in Berlin who did not see and describe the plundering.

Where was Grünspan during the last three months? Who was looking after him? Until today he has remained silent about where he was staying until the day he carried out the murder.

From the day he arrived he reported where he was staying to the police and the police checked it.

He was in possession of a forged passport. Who arranged the forged passport for him?

He was in possession of a genuine passport, issued by the Polish Consulate.

There can be no doubt that he was hidden by a Jewish organisation and systematically prepared for the cynical murder.

There can be no doubt that he was hidden by his uncle and not 'prepared' by anyone. One could go down the whole column, checking the evil gnome's handiwork sentence by sentence. But we would learn nothing new. If there is anything that doesn't need telling to anyone anywhere in the world, even in Germany, it is the fact that this creature – who must be human, since he walks on two legs – is monstrously lacking in even the rudiments of a normal, human sense of decency!

That lying is his standard method is well known to the children in the street from Kiel to the Cape. The fact that in 1938 he could think of nothing better than to copy the model of 1933 exactly is more interesting. It shows how far yesterday's words and actions of these one-track minds always provide a model for and prior notice of tomorrow's events. The matter of the Jews is, then, a model for Nazi methods as a whole and for the way the early stages prefigure the later ones.

People have never understood the extent to which the method the Third Reich employed in the matter of the Jews was symptomatic of the method it employs in general, in all matters. A whole host of mistakes in foreign policy could have been avoided if people had been capable of relating the Nazis' procedure in the matter of the Jews to their procedures in general. It was no less of an intellectual failure that no one realised the disruption the Nazis' policy towards the Jews would bring to Europe as a whole. The abject failure of political thinking and intellectual foresight in this specific area was a reflection of the same failure in even more important areas.

Their failure to take action, to show the energy needed to take action, was no less abject. No one can pretend that transferring 600,000 people to new homelands over about six years would not have been a straightforward task – and that even more so given that at the beginning a good number of them had their own capital. The American continent, Russia and the European democracies alone have 600 million inhabitants between them. Distributed among these, only 160 persons would have had to be absorbed annually per million inhabitants – and a good number of those were still children and adolescents whom it would be no problem integrating into any country, any culture or any profession. But even the ratio of 160 per million could have been reduced to a half or a third if further sensible relocations to the three other continents had been arranged, those huge continents the population of which has largely come from immigration and which still need immigrants – Australia, Africa and Asia. Let no one be fooled into thinking that would not have been a simple task and that, within the framework of a precise global plan, promoted and organised by world powers, every country would not have accepted its precisely defined quota without difficulty or complications. It would have been child's play. Instead, they wasted time and goodwill; confined themselves to conferences at which there was no plan and no determination; made themselves ridiculous with their futile pilgrimages on bended knees to Berlin; basically left everything to chance; and finally watched as the open doors closed one after the other. Who could deny that the inability to make plans and implement them, which has become evident in this specific area, is a model of the same inability in many other, wider areas? And who could maintain that, after the latest shake-up, there is the prospect that things might finally resolve themselves? Does the minor easing of the immigration requirements in Tanganyika, British Guiana and Kenya, and any more there might be, come anywhere near compensating for the deterioration of the general situation? Today, after six almost wasted years, does the long-term nature of these projects reflect the raw urgency of a situation in which those in need are close to being ground into the dust? Is it even certain today that the Nazi Reich, with its shortage of manpower, will be willing to let these people leave? Are their plans not heading in another direction, towards using them as slave labour, perhaps even, occasionally, as shooting targets? Is it not a matter of too little too late again? Be that as it may, the abject failure to do anything material in the matter of the Jews is undeniable and seems likely to continue; nor, unfortunately, can it be denied that it fits the picture in many other areas.

But even more bleak and pessimistic is what one can call the moral symbolism. It is true that in some countries we have seen huge surges of moral indignation, but it is presumably no coincidence that those are countries where religion is still very powerful: Britain, the United States, Holland. There not only public opinion rose in protest, but the governments with it; and they did so not simply out of pure humanity but from a feeling that the few fundamental principles of justice, morality and human rights are the basis of everything about mankind that is worth fighting for and that these basic principles are so interconnected that it is impossible for a single one to be broken without all the rest collapsing. But in other nations and governments one can sense a weary apathy towards such feelings; and one can say that this is the most worrying light that the German destruction of the Jews casts on other, wider problems. For the life, endurance and power of survival of nations are determined above all by morality. Nothing that is purely material is worth fighting for, only moral assets, and those only to the extent to which we value and honour them highly as a sacred trust. In countries where the state that is exterminating 500,000 people is simply regarded as the enemy of those people, not as a threat to moral values which are part of the essence of that country's own existence, in places where it is only the fate of the victims themselves which is regarded as being at stake and not the fate of those values on which that country's own society is founded, where that is the case, moral rot has set in which can only weaken their determination to preserve their integrity in other areas as well. The fact that in significant parts of Europe the reaction to the crime committed in Germany is one of such ethical weariness is, since we are talking of models, the least promising of all.

The Ides of March   25 March 1939

Although Britain and France had issued guarantees for what remained of Czechoslovakia, the Munich Agreement did not provide a lasting solution to the Sudeten question, since Hitler regarded 'Rump Czechoslovakia' as a strategic danger on the southern border of the Reich. On 21 October Hitler ordered the Army to prepare for invasion, which then took place in March 1939.

By exploiting differences between the Czechs and Slovaks, and by using direct threats against the latter, Hitler got the Slovak regional parliament to declare Slovak independence on 14 March 1939 and request the protection of Germany. On the evening of the same day Hitler summoned the President of Czechoslovakia, Emil Hacha, and the Foreign Minister, Frantisek Chvalkovsky, to Berlin. Faced with the alternative of having 'Bohemia' occupied by the German army and Prague bombed or 'confidently placing the fate of the Czech people and country in the hands of the Führer of the German Reich', they were compelled to sign a treaty establishing a 'Protectorate'. The German army entered Czechoslovakia in the early hours of 16 March. A few hours later Hitler was in Hradcany Castle in Prague to announce the establishment of the German Protectorate of Bohemia and Moravia under the 'Protector', Baron Konstantin von Neurath. At the same time Hitler took on the 'protection' of Slovakia, now a satellite state of Germany.

The Ides of March   25 March 1939

I

We've finally got there. After six years we've finally got there. It's come from the film of rape and pillage that was these Ides of March. It needed a state that was a shining light and therefore had to be beaten and crippled to breathe its last. It needed a decent, hard-working, unsuspecting nation to pay for it by being thrown into a dark dungeon. It needed hundreds of thousands of people just like other people, no less valuable and with no more faults, to be plunged into despair. But we've finally got there. Now they understand what they're up against. Now they realise who they're dealing with. Now they know what awaits them. Now it can be clearly seen, recognised, made plain. There will be no more attempts to quibble, to explain away, to equivocate, to indulge in fantasies. Finally it is obvious to everyone, everyone is now aware that these people want to subjugate everyone and everything. To subjugate everything, to have power over everything – that is their sole, their simple, undivided goal, like a beast on heat they will be satisfied with nothing less.

For six long years we tried to make people understand. For six long years most did not understand, or they resisted the realisation that was gradually dawning on them. We told them when the Moloch was still weak or when it was just gathering its strength. 'Watch out before it's too late!' we said. 'Night and day it is scheming and plotting how to crush you, all of you without exception, and enslave you.' 'Huh!' they said. 'What's that to do with us? What's its scheming and plotting to do with us? If it touches us, we'll send it home with a bloody nose. We're man enough for that, it doesn't frighten us. We're not going to let it stop us enjoying ourselves.'

We told them the same when the Moloch was already strong. 'Watch out,' we said, 'night and day it's scheming and plotting how to crush you – yes you, the lot of you, all of you, without exception – and enslave you.' – 'What do you mean?' they said. 'What makes you say that? It's absurd, improbable, unproved and unprovable. It's your own prejudices talking. We absolutely refuse to believe something so unusual, so inhuman, and such an awful nuisance into the bargain. Look at what it said? There you are, then.' There was an action, a suspicious action. 'All the same,' they said, 'it's clear enough that it's just an exception, though it really was a little unfair, a bit hard to bear.' – 'All the same,' they said the next time, 'it's clear enough that it's only limited; the Treaty of Versailles went too far, it couldn't last.' – 'All the same,' they said the next time, 'it's clear enough that it's just the one obsession; it just wants to gather all those of German blood together.' – 'All the same,' they said at the next stage, 'it's clear enough that they're just acts of desperation, because of its terrible plight; it just wants enough to eat, poor thing, and raw materials.' All the same, all the same, all the same, all the same. All it needed was a tiny hole to appear in any argument for hope to come crawling back out into the open. There was no mirage that wasn't used to cover up the increasingly apparent truth that the sole aim of these people was power and control over all, a pan-European, a pan-global despotism. 'It won't come to that!' and 'It's not aimed at us!' were the words of reassurance, of self-reassurance, employed to the limits of human error and well beyond.

That is over now. For all our scepticism and despite all the scepticism that is the product of what we have experienced over the years, this time we can safely say that now it is completely over and will remain so for many years to come. The sight of the raped and murdered corpse of the Czech state has finally hammered into people's skulls the insight we must call the fundamental insight, Insight no. 1. Gone is the pretext of German blood, of the distressing lack of equal rights, of the injustice of Versailles, of economic difficulties, of Bolshevism, of saving Europe; in this case there was not the slightest 'all the same'. All that is left is violence, the most threadbare lies, the crudest forgeries, and the grossest breaking of half a dozen oaths which are still fresh in everyone's mind as highly controversial, highly emotional contentious issues. The conclusion has been drawn, it is common knowledge, proclaimed by a thousand tongues since the Ides of March and contradicted by none: these people will subjugate anything they can, with nothing to hinder them but physical impossibility and driven by nothing but the straightforward urge to subjugate.

Everything else starts out from Insight no. 1. It is the fundamental truth, unheard and not understood for six years, that Nazism is synonymous with the determination to destroy *every* other existing state and nation, synonymous with the boundless urge to subjugate, boundless in spatial terms as well as in degree. Now this truth, which was scorned for six long years, has broken through. It has become common knowledge, common knowledge that has ripened slowly, laboriously, painfully. It will take as long to disappear as it did to come, certainly among those nations famed for their slow thinking and obstinate attachment to points of view once they have taken root.

We can safely call this the beginning of a new chapter in history. We can safely call it the decisive turning point in the relationship between Hitler and the world. Chamberlain was reflecting both the current mood and the permanent nature of his people when he concluded his speech in Birmingham (17 March) with the ominous words, 'I venture to prophesy that in the end she will bitterly regret what her Government has done.' Hitler has made the big, reckless mistake for which we have been waiting in vain for six years. From now on the relationship between Hitler and the world will be based on Insight no. 1. It is terrible that Czechoslovakia had to die for this insight to come alive. It is ironic that for six whole years the intellectual machinery of great nations – the politicians, spies, parliaments, press, academics – failed to produce the truth which a few exiles, familiar with their own country and equipped with nothing but ink and paper, cried in the wilderness from the very first day. It appears there is no dispensation from the great law of history that people have to see things for themselves, that warnings and deductions have no effect, only direct, personal experience. It needed the event that revealed Hitler as a pure Tamburlaine with no 'all the same'. That has happened. Everything suggests this will turn out to be the break in his career and his era.

II

A strategy must be developed on the basis of Insight no. 1 – the realisation that the plans of these people are aimed at subjugating everything and everyone – a strategy, be it defensive or offensive, to frustrate these plans.

Let us discuss the *defensive* strategy.

The new organisaton of this is the topic which, since the Ides of March, has been pursued in the ministries of that nation which has become the absolute centre of Europe and the world with the tireless obstinacy that is one of the oldest traditions of British diplomacy, a tradition we had given up for lost. From the outset its starting point, Insight no. 1, has overturned all the principles by which British policy was guided until now. Until now it had divided the world up into spheres of vital British interest and spheres of lesser interest. The extent to which they were prepared to commit themselves anywhere, to take on a defensive role, depended on the category in which the sphere was placed. They couldn't help the 'vital' category gradually growing larger. It gradually extended from continental France to the Low Countries, then to the whole of the French colonies, finally to Switzerland. But still commitment was dependent on the nature of the sphere; for example the whole of eastern and south-eastern Europe was persistently excluded from these spheres of considerable interest. Now, from the perspective of Insight no. 1, the problem is the other way round. It is no longer important which special interests obtain in the *sphere* that needs defending, what is important is the general interest not to allow the state that is a *threat* to everyone to increase its power at the expense of *any* sphere of interest. Now every threatened sphere is worth defending; peace, to use an expression that has almost been forgotten, is 'indivisible'. We can see that British policy has done an abrupt U-turn and now stands for the precise opposite of what it stood for a week ago. Now she is urgently working towards the establishment of a defensive alliance which will bring her further commitments to spheres of interest where until now she refused commitments as vigorously as she is now offering them: Poland, Romania, even the rest of the Balkans.

It can be seen, then, that a defensive demarcation line is to be drawn round Germany, a line with a warning notice: 'Thus far and no farther,' a line beyond which some kind of 'collective security' is to be set up among the states bordering it. It is exactly what was done before 1914, and it is what German propaganda at the time and since then, deliberately misinterpreting its defensive purpose as aiming at strangling her, denounced as 'encirclement' – with the result that for 20 years, until last week, all the wise men all over the world faithfully repeated that 'encirclement' must never happen again. They have stopped. Even the word has been rehabilitated, and quite rightly so. On 20 March the *Times* concluded its editorial with the following words: 'This country has always been opposed in principle to the policy of "encircling" Germany; but Germany's own policy, and, above all, her methods, are making encirclement a natural and even an inevitable process.' Neither here, in this remarkable newspaper that had been swaying this way and that for the last six years, nor anywhere else in British public opinion has the slightest sign of weakening appeared. Their diplomacy is clearly continuing to work along those lines. The result of Insight no. 1 is an effort to encircle Germany.

At the present moment, when the lines between the governments are buzzing all the time, when every day brings new situations, there is no point in embarking on speculation about where this demarcation line could eventually run, that is which countries will eventually be part of the area that is to be defended and who will defend whom. But it is clear enough that the only practical difficulties are in the *East*, so it is perhaps a good idea to be clear about the reasons.

In the *South*: there the sole neighbour, Mussolini's Italy, would have to do the encircling. Perhaps there is still the ghost of a chance of pulling him over to the other side. A certain disgruntlement is indicated by the lack of a congratulatory telegram such as arrived promptly from Tokyo, Budapest and Burgos. There is no doubt that a further attempt is being made, but its chances of success are surely not seen as very high. The much greater probability is that in the south there will not be a co-encircler, but a co-attacker. The matter is of secondary importance.

In the *West* the opposite is the case and there things are simple. The demarcation line from the Alps to the sea was drawn long ago and the countries sharing its defence are known. They are those that are located in the region, with America in the background. The sole problem there is the collaboration of *Russia*, which, though distant, is no less important. However, it is precisely the distance between Russia and the West which solves the difficulty of the problem. The difficulty resides in the fact that there are two aspects to Russia: on the one hand it is a state and a military power, on the other a totalitarian and Communist state. This means that most countries are filled with horror at the thought of Russian troops marching into their territory, even if it is to assist them. They will come, so it is feared, embodying the former, but will stay and be active as the latter. However, this has never been an issue in the western demarcation zone. Even when collaborating in the defence of the west, the Russian military force would only operate in regions that are far away. It is, therefore, impossible to understand the obstinacy with which, in their ideological fervour, some sections of the population, especially in France, resisted the inclusion of Russia in the alliance to defend Western Europe. (Just as it has always been impossible to understand why Russia, if she regards Hitler as her mortal enemy, should need an invitation, permission and authorisation to join in his destruction if it should come to war.) It is not clear, then, what difficulties there could be about including Russia among the defenders of the western demarcation line if she is willing and would operate in a quite different geographical area. In periods when a direct German attack on Russia seemed a possibility, one could understand the disinclination of people in the West to mobilise in order to help her – for the same reasons as they were disinclined to mobilise anywhere. But since a direct German attack on Russia is a complete practical impossibility, there are no arguments against wanting to see Russia mobilise to help the West.

There are not even the most far-fetched ideological arguments against it. It is true that, despite taking place at a great distance, the political/military collaboration could lead to some political/ideological contamination at home. Despite the geographical distance, the military alliance – especially it if were very successful – could strengthen Russia's ideological attraction in one's own country; it could amount to propaganda for what we called her second aspect. Therefore, as I have often said in another context, it is correct and unavoidable that at the same time as there is closer collaboration in military and foreign affairs, the liberal/democratic powers and forces must strengthen the ideological contrast at home. The latter is clearly a necessary consequence of the former, however difficult it is for primitive minds to understand and however far the apparent contradiction transcends the comprehension of many of our fellow citizens, who only recognise black and white. But there can be no doubt that this necessary consequence – which will initially be of importance in one country, France, alone, for everywhere else the second aspect of Russia exerts little attraction – there can be no doubt that this necessary consequence will be found, when required, simply and without histrionics. In these circumstances, it is to be assumed that the problem of adding Russia to the encirclement in the West can easily be solved, and has possibly even been solved already. It is unthinkable, it ought to be unthinkable, that a matter of such importance for defence and foreign policy – important whatever the circumstances, that is, whatever the true state of Russian military power – should continue to be hampered by the fanatical inability of some people to distinguish between the two aspects.

We have to admit that, as we can clearly see, the problem as it appears in the *East* is different. Russia's involvement in the eastern encirclement is far more important than in the western. She is the sole significant military power present in the area. A quick glance at the map will show that without Russian assistance the chances of defending Romania will be very slim indeed. Leaving the problem of Russia aside for the moment, the prospects for an eastern encirclement seem more favourable than one would have hardly dared to hope even two weeks ago. The Turks appear to have agreed unconditionally. Romania's determination to defend herself, if there is any possibility of doing so, was even expressed in partial mobilisation. Poland, the second most important factor in that area, has similarly expressed her determination to join (if, that is, apart from general promises of assistance, she can get a more precise guarantee of what that assistance will consist of). The events of the next few days which, following the annexation of Memel,[39] will perhaps also bring Lithuania into line, may strengthen this readiness even more. But the great obstacle in this eastern zone is a fact of which no secret is made: the second Russian aspect! On no account does the Polish government want Soviet troops on its territory, neither as friends nor, as 19 years ago, as enemies. And although Romania appears to be letting Poland take the lead, King Carol[40] is known to have expressed similar views. How to untie this Gordian knot – whether by finding other routes for the Russian troops, or by securing guarantees that satisfy the reluctant countries or by some other as yet unknown means – is the question taking up most of the ceaseless discussions in the ministries in London.

III

Of course one can say here too – and it may be some small comfort – that the event, once it has happened, will turn things upside down. The rule that we have to see everything in the flesh before we act is not only an explanation of things that have happened in the past, but also a guide to the future. When the great event comes, greater even than the Ides of March, everything will be seen in a new light.

For the moment that leaves us with the question of where we are actually heading should the event fail to materialise. The purpose of the present activity on the political front is to shackle the Moloch by fear, by the certainty that it would be crushed the moment it crossed the demarcation line. It will be crushed, if it should take that risk, of that we are certain. But what if the shackles work? What if it should pull back – and there are signs suggesting that – what if it should decide to postpone its plans, to bide its time? What if it should lie in wait for the moment when times will have changed and the situation with it? What should we do in that case? Should we let the country, that has been recognised as a threat to all, continue to train further cohorts undisturbed, apparently accepting its own problems for the moment, all the better to prepare itself for its next pounce? Should Europe continue to ruin herself, constantly staggering from one crisis to the next?

That would be the effect of a purely defensive strategy. It is by no means the entire conclusion to be drawn from Insight no. 1. The entire conclusion would doubtless be *not* to give the Moloch the opportunity to *reculer pour mieux sauter*. For the future, indeed for the present, the entire consequence is *not* the defensive strategy.

President Roosevelt has taken one step beyond the defensive strategy by imposing a 25 per cent customs surcharge on Nazi exports to the USA, thus making them all but impossible. It was Hitler who, on 30 January, proclaimed that the watchword for Germany was, 'Export or die.' A response has now come, loud and clear from across the ocean: 'Die!' It is the one complete conclusion from Insight no. 1. It remains to be seen whether Europe as well – after the immediate crises of the current moment and presuming we should once more escape from them – ought to be heading towards that conclusion.

The priority   1 July 1939

Just a few days ago it was the 25th anniversary of the day a young Bosnian, Gavrilo Princip, shot the heir to the Habsburg throne in Sarajevo. One month later mankind went to war. When the assassination was announced, people had no idea this would be the consequence. Even three weeks later, despite the fact that the fatal decisions had already been taken, the decisive orders issued, they were completely unaware of what was to come. The ultimatum and the blaze it ignited came during a short week at the end of July 1914 that swept over a world which, half uncomprehending and half dazed, was certainly taken by surprise. When the mobilisations were ordered, when the armies marched out, an event had come about, the possibility of which had not even crossed the mind of one in ten thousand a few days before. Even less had one in a hundred thousand had any idea what the event might mean.

In July 1939, a quarter of a century later, mankind is in a different state of mind. At least in those countries where brains can still work normally, where they have not for years been exposed to partly paralyzing, partly intoxicating fumes, even the youngest and simplest of minds have had it drummed into them what the reality behind the word 'war' is. We are all aware of the horrors it threatens us with: death, mutilation, diseases, epidemics; exertion, deprivation, starvation, destruction. Everyone can envisage that – and not a few of us can envisage even more frightening prospects. In the later stages of a modern war situations might arise which are completely beyond our experience, beyond our calculation and control. Central government and unified states might collapse and fragment into a maze of local regimes. Whole branches of culture, whole areas of civilisation might disappear, together with all their institutions and professionals and amateurs, all their treasures, traditions, experiences, their schools and communities. Rights and freedoms might be suppressed by tyrannical overlords swept into power from the wreckage caused by the return to primitive conditions. Societies might break up, elites be crushed, leaving us with nothing but the most unpredictable random fragments, a tangle of makeshift expedients. Today such more remote but very conceivable eventualities are contained in the idea of war and come to mind when people talk about war. Unlike people in the summer of 1914, people in this summer of 1939 have no lack of visions; in fact they have, let us hope, an excess, a surfeit of agonising visions. At least this time people have a vivid idea of what war must mean, of what, with extreme bad luck, it can mean.

And this time they do know that there is a threat of war. No one can be taken by surprise this time, though it is not yet certain there will be a war. Even as the 'border-manoeuvres' game we are so familiar with from last summer, starts again, other possibilities, both good and bad, remain. On the good side is the chance that they will decide not to risk it after all, that the defenders' wall will seem too hard and unpredictable to those who would have to attack. On the bad side is the possibility that as soon as the attacking forces start to advance and the trumpets sound their piercing blast the wall will come tumbling down like that of Jericho. And we must not ignore the fact that the Munich variant, capitulation, remains a further possibility; for example if the negotiations in Moscow, whose momentous significance for our destiny has been taken to panic-stricken extremes, should break down, it could trigger an equally panic-stricken collapse of confidence. Good or bad, war is not certain. But it is regarded as a 70 to 80 per cent probability for this summer and since previously, when no one even considered it a possibility, we were plunged into war within four short July weeks, why should we not be prepared for things to happen within a similar short period today, when everyone looks on it as a possibility? Why should it not be the right time to talk about things which, it is true, depend on an eventuality which is still uncertain but which will perhaps be difficult to talk about once it has occurred? Who knows what it will be possible to print then? 'Repent ye the day before your death', it says in the Bible, the day before the event that can arrive – or not arrive – any day. Let us talk about war the day before it comes.

There is much to say about it. But the most important thing for man, that speck of dust that will be caught up in the sandstorm of the catastrophe, is to examine his conscience. What for? A difficult moral issue! Difficult at a time when, on top of the horror that war is in any case, the weary cliché that war doesn't solve anything can be heard even from the lips of ministers. And it is particularly difficult for those exiled Germans who do not even enjoy the naive source of strength that is the national patriotism of the camp to which fate has consigned them and whose true patriotism has often remained with the side they will be fighting against. And I am not just saying that, I have seen how many of them – Christians, Jews, right-wingers, left-wingers – have tried to work out a private world of their own within the wider world, a private goal within the general one, in the event of the great catastrophe happening. One can read and hear them brooding over feelings that set them apart, differentiate them from those around, for example, 'We wouldn't fight for western imperialism, we'd fight for the liberation of Germany.' It has become clear that these private constructs, inspired by deep, hereditary, perhaps atavistic feelings, have already led to serious moral dilemmas and could lead to even more serious ones. It is inevitable that constructing a distinction between war as such and a war 'for Germany, for the liberation of Germany' is bound to give rise to constant argument, alienation, conflict, bitterness, torment and despair. Have we not elsewhere seen examples – milder ones, it is true – of the sufferings brought about by these divided emotions, of the psychological and physical tragedies they lead to, and can we not see new ones in the offing? Are there not now citizens of belligerent countries who regard the simple patriotic victory of their own country as an inferior goal? And do they not try to replace it with private goals, for example: 'We are not fighting for the victory of our own country, we are fighting for the victory of socialism!' to name but one. Is it not well known that these attempts to set oneself apart cause serious crises of conscience, tormenting clashes with reality and, in general, much pointless suffering, disappointment and inner conflict?

I do not believe there is any point in trying to reserve a special channel for oneself in the general flood-tide of war. Of course, standard French or English patriotism is closed to the foreign exile, inevitably he must find another guide to 'what-we-are-fighting-for'. It may be that even for French or English nationals there is good reason to look beyond '*patrie*', beyond 'my country' for a higher meaning to the suffering, for an even more legitimate 'what-we-are-fighting-for'. But it will bring unhappiness and grief if in practice these substitute or more noble goals do not coincide completely with those of the general course, if they are so far removed from it that rifts threaten to open up, if, indeed, their nature is such that they can come into direct conflict with it. It is clearly unimaginable that such conflicts will not arise once individuals, in a war which is physically directed against Germany, are guided by the personal idea that they for their part are fighting a war *for* Germany. 'Freeing Germany' is all very fine as a goal; in practice, however, the subtle psychology behind it is all too likely to come into conflict with the crude reality of the general conflict, the aim of which is quite simply to conquer Germany. And anyway, why this hierarchy of values? Why should it be necessary or justified in this exceptional situation to postulate, parallel to the English or French patriotism, a suitably adapted German patriotism for the Germans who are on the same side?

In this situation these Germans, just like all the others, also have a fatherland of their own, only it does not have a physical presence, it is a concept, a spirit. This spiritual fatherland, as worthy of patriotism as any other, is the sum of everything which, in our opinion, is at least as essential to our sense of belonging as the geographical factor of land. The object of this patriotism is a system of justice and morality which recognises the living individual as the factor that states, societies and laws exist to serve, protect and aid. The object of this patriotism is any environment, wherever it may be, which, thanks to the presence of these conditions, thanks to the recognition of the fundamental elements of justice, tolerance, and freedom and respect for the individual, is a province of the spiritual fatherland. And should not the defence of what already (or still) belongs to this spiritual fatherland be even more important than conquering new provinces for it, or winning back old ones? The application is clear: keeping freedom that exists in the world today is more urgent than the liberation of Germany. Looked at from any standpoint, that has absolute priority. A free world – our spiritual fatherland – can exist alongside an unliberated Germany. A liberated Germany is completely unthinkable alongside a world which has lost its freedom. In the war, if it should come to war, this huge priority, the priority of preserving existing freedom over establishing the freedom that does not exist – or re-establishing that which no longer exists – will ensure the accord of the two 'what-we-are-fighting-fors': the cause of the various national patriotisms and the cause of the Germans in the same camp. That is what corresponds to their special situation and which nonetheless will not create the possibility of bringing them into conflict with the general will. If the catastrophe comes, turn your eyes and your minds away from the other side. Turn them away from the fiction that, although you have ended up in the other camp, you must still, and above all, fight 'for' Germany. Turn them away from the conception that it is your duty, in contrast to that of the rest, to be guided first and foremost by those things that could help free Germany. On the day before the war, immerse yourselves in the truth that above all and together with all you must think of preserving existing freedoms; of preserving the last of them and in the last place where it still exists. Only after that, when the battle has been fought and won, will the time come to turn your eyes back to the other side and to think of Germany, the Germany that has to be liberated.

Even then no one should be in any doubt that liberating Germany will not be as easy as some people might wish. It is unlikely that liberation could be approached as naively at the end of another armageddon as it was in Wilson's time, simply by swapping a few heads around and changing a few laws. It is unlikely, if that were done, that the world would feel secure once more and could even help with the reconstruction. It is unlikely, I might add, that it would on the other hand be able to fulfil the dreams of those who would see the liberation they are talking about as replacing the tyranny of the brown shirts with that of another colour. All these simple things are unlikely, all this repetition of 1918 or 1917, all those naive things which, to go by a few signs, seem to be the sum total of the ideas of many people today who talk about the liberation of Germany. The omens are much more serious and complex. Here, if anywhere, we can see the truth of the ominous statement that even war – especially war – will not solve the problem. The 'liberation of Germany', on everyone's lips at the end of a great war – a war that will have been won to the extent that minds can turn to this secondary problem – this liberation promises to be anything but a triumphal transformation. Rather it looks as if it is going to be an often frustrating, depressingly bitter process, drawn out in stages over a long period. On the day before the war it will perhaps be advisable to consider as far as possible the disturbing question of 'And afterwards?' But 'Afterwards' and 'Meanwhile' are two different things. If war is to be unleashed upon us, then the absolute top priority is the freedom that is threatened where it still exists, not the freedom that is lost and does not exist anymore.

The day after   15 July 1939

The possibility of conditions in Europe being brought to flash point during the three months that lie ahead justifies a particular kind of discussion – discussions which posit the eventuality of war. We need to think about this war under the assumption that that it will destroy the one who unleashed it on the world. The contrary assumption – which we cannot, indeed must not accept – would anyway render all reflection superfluous. And an outcome which lies somewhere between victory and defeat for both parties is one of those confused situations which it is absolutely impossible to think about in advance. War, as we conceive it, is the victory of those who have been attacked over the aggressor. For us its end will be marked by two almost simultaneous events: the defeat of the Third Reich and the fall of Hitler. At the same time the war will leave us with two gigantic question marks: the terms of peace *for* Germany and the succession *in* Germany; the balancing of Germany's page in the ledger of the world and the opening of a new page in Germany's ledger.

What does that mean, the succession in Germany? What should we understand by it? What may we hope for, what must we strive for? If we disregard the possibility that the Reich will be split up – an idea that is sure to crop up after a war, though its only effect on the problem of succession would be that several successor states would have to be found, instead of one – the only idea that has, to the best of my knowledge, so far emerged is that the government that will have been defeated and overthrown should be replaced by one representing some other German political movement and consisting of some other German politicians. That, in essence, is presumably the generally held view. I have to admit that for some time it was my own. It is only gradually that doubts have arisen, doubts which have increased with time.

What we must ask ourselves is: what state will Germany be in at the point when this question is decided? The only realistic assumption is that, at the moment when the country is defeated and the government overthrown, there will be a complete breakdown of all authority. It seems obvious that everything connected with Nazism will have been smashed and scattered – and that will be a considerable step forward. Since almost the whole apparatus of public life, right down to the most minor underling, consists of exponents of Nazism, it looks as if the collapse of that doctrine will necessarily entail the collapse of almost the entire machinery of state. Presumably in the conditions that will obtain at such a moment more or less everyone who occupied any kind of Nazi post, who represented Nazi power in any form, will have been driven from their lairs. In the main the mechanisms of the body politic will no longer function at all, let alone represent any kind of authority. But the repercussions will probably be even more widespread. The authorities on the periphery of the state and Party apparatus and beyond – the military, the clergy, any kind of social elite – will probably be no less affected. During the long years of the Nazi regime most of them will either have become too deeply implicated in it, or there will be too little public awareness of the distance they put between themselves and the Nazi regime for a significant part of the population to look to them for guidance, for leadership during that first moment, in the midst of the convulsions caused by defeat and the collapse of civil order. I am not saying whether that would be a good thing or not, I am merely presenting the likely facts. On the day we are trying to imagine, the authorities present in Germany up to that point will presumably be unable to contribute to the swift formation of a successor administration.

What other authorities – ones that do not exist at the moment – will there be to help the population find their bearings, to provide leadership, an example for them? Those that were suppressed by Hitler naturally come to mind. But we are probably not mistaken in admitting that our contact with every person and every institution which enjoyed authority *before* Hitler is so minimal as to be non-existent. As it is, our memories of them are not exactly glorious, and by then even more time will have elapsed. Already a six-year cohort has grown up that has 'never heard of Joseph', and it is neither unjust nor malicious to assume that at the critical moment names such as Breitscheid or Brüning will have no power to rouse the mass of Germans nor command authority among them. Almost the same as of the individuals could be said of the institutions they embodied – the former political parties. Memories remain, but even for those who once marched under their banners, they will have lost the magnetic attraction which could swiftly turn the throning millions into serried battalions of believers. It would be wrong to assume that at the critical moment appeals and instructions from that quarter would enjoy prestige among any sizeable groups. Realism demands that we accept that the authorities that were suppressed by Hitler will be scarcely more effective than those that collapsed under his regime. The truth is that, as far as we can see, there is no factor at hand that would carry sufficient weight among the German people at this moment of intense convulsion and confusion to act as a reasonably reliable conduit to direct the question of succession into a predetermined channel. If that collapse should occur, there is in Germany at present no equivalent to the clearly defined will of the Czech nation, which is waiting to seize the moment, and its anointed leader, Tomáš Masaryk.[41] There is not even an equivalent to the body of available public figures and clearly defined, popularised ideas through which the transfer of power was carried out in Germany in 1918. There is a complete absence of suitable individuals, and the ideologies are amorphous longings.

The logical deduction from all this is that the succession will be determined by persons and with slogans as yet unknown to us. We do not have the slightest indication of who that will be and how it will come about, but it is 90 per cent certain it will initially be a matter of pure chance. Whoever is swiftest, loudest – perhaps one who, for God knows what reason, has 100 armed men at his command – might manage to gather together in a couple of hours the 50,000 partisans needed, with luck, to occupy the first key government positions in Berlin. And with these positions once occupied, he could perhaps, in the general ignorance of persons and programmes, in the universal chaos and profound exhaustion, rally to his cause within the next ten hours the two or three millions with which, at such moments, power can be seized. In this way a new regime might be born out of the indeterminate fortuity or happenstance of one single moment. This is what is most likely to emerge from the power vacuum.

If this is how things turn out, if the 'alternative German leadership' that replaces Hitler's leadership comes about in this manner, it will leave open the possibility that 'the people' will change again later in the course of this new development. Only when political life has started up again, when the leaders that emerge have a distinctive profile once more, when political programmes reappear and can be compared in practice, only then can what was set up in the immediate aftermath of the collapse be rectified. But it is precisely this possibility that also means that the successor regime, once it has been established, will be tempted to ensure that it cannot be rectified out of existence. The tendency to cling onto power by force, by dictatorship, will be great. In some cases it will be the result not of temptation, but of intention and conviction. If, that is, the Communists should be the first to arrive. What is certain is that the Communists – who will enjoy the advantage of being able, from the very first moment, to call on support from the coffers, the arsenal and the organisation of a major foreign power – have particularly good prospects in a speed race for power.

The stabilisation of the country by force and terror might be a method used, also out of conviction, by non-Communists, even democrats, who have recently gone from the excesses of formal democracy to excessive enthusiasm for power; the kind of people one occasionally hears talk of an 'educational dictatorship' – as if it were agreed that those who initiated the benevolent dictatorship would also be those who continued it, and as if the experience of almost all dictatorships did not show that they never willingly abolish themselves. But even if convictions are not involved, the catastrophe, which will presumably have engulfed the country, will tempt, if not force people to resort to dictatorship. We must assume that the automatic reflexes that will be triggered by the need for revenge on all the uniformed big-, medium and little wigs will require a firm hand. We must assume that the consequences of the war – and of the peace settlement! – will lead to such extensive problems of impoverishment and rebellion that it will only be possible to maintain even the most basic law and order by force. We must assume that a new cohort of officials, to be created *ex nihilo* (when they came to power the Nazis had 100,000 applicants!), will arouse resentments which it will seem easiest to suppress with brutality. Finally we must assume that, at a time when political parties are only just reappearing, when the population is only gradually becoming familiar with political personalities, when political life is only just starting up again, political changes of direction will be frequent and swift; and that this will be a further reason to restrain the 'sovereignty of the people' with a certain degree of absolutism. It is to be feared that all that will combine to lead the successors to the rule of terror to use terror themselves. Let us not deceive ourselves: the combination of defeat and revolution will create conditions which will threaten to force a German successor government onto the dictatorship track from the very beginning – and the new era will thus be in great danger of carrying on inexorably as it started. All these prospects for the future are haunted by the Biblical threat that the chastisement with whips will be followed by chastisement with scorpions.

But even if all this were not to come about, the nation would still be faced with the disastrous anomalies with which the political life of Germany is cursed: the fact that this nation, which has so many talents, is completely unschooled as far as practical politics is concerned and completely *mis*schooled in political ideology. It is a nation which has been excluded from the centuries of often bitter, but essential processes through which the great democracies were gradually nurtured until they were ready for relatively free self-government; a nation which never acquired the instincts, the traditions, nor even the techniques without which such systems cannot function. Whilst the others gradually acquired all of these, the Germans lived under authoritarian systems in which obedience was the only civic virtue. Temporarily released from them, they could make so little of the opposite system that sooner or later the bungled attempt collapsed. Today they are more removed than ever in their history from an experience of and schooling in what we call free, democratic self-government. Today they are more removed than ever from a familiarity with conditions in which many opinions, many nonconformities can coexist. The ability to allow all this to take place in an atmosphere of toleration, while still finding common ground, is more alien to them than ever. What can be expected when the task of governing themselves in freedom is once more thrust upon them without restriction at the very point when they are absolutely unfamiliar with free self-government and do not have even the most basic training in it? More than that, what will come of it in conditions rendered 20 times more difficult by defeat? Is it possible to feel confident that 'somehow it'll be all right'? Can one contemplate it other than with concern and scepticism?

And that is not the only anomaly that must be taken into account. We mentioned earlier how profoundly '*mis*schooled' the Germans were in political ideology – and here our concern has an international dimension. Whilst during the Ebert and Stresemann period we could perhaps declare and believe – with a clear conscience, if rather less self-awareness – that Germany had been won over to the tradition of 'good-neighbourly relations', must we not admit today that the nation has long since been burdened with a quite different tradition. Old teachings and influences, spread by school, culture and example, are lodged in the heads of the majority. Just as domestically it is not the toleration of differences that has become the political ideal, but their annihilation, so we can see in external relations – and much more pronounced in those – that German minds have never been filled with the idea of getting along with others as well as possible, but of advancing, plundering, mastering them. The belief that the Germans are a chosen people is not the preserve of a few mad philosophers, nor is it restricted to those who take: 'Essence of Germany makes the pills/ To cure the world of all its ills' as Gospel truth. In one variant or another – and perhaps in an even more dangerous one! – it has been drip-fed into the instincts of the great majority, flattering every one of them with the sense that they belong to a kind of aristocracy. Even among the broad mass of the people the ideal of domination is a reality, as is the *plus-ultra* tendency, taking things to extreme excesses, the absence of the famous *sens de la mesure*. All these destructive and self-destructive urges, the product of a long process of education, have never been removed from the average German, nor from German society, neither by events, nor by instruction. We have seen how virulent these urges remain, even under the most unfavourable conditions, perhaps especially under such conditions. For more than a century now we have been able to observe how, again and again, these complexes and traumas have given birth to catastrophes for Germany itself, for the continent and the whole world. And after a further collapse are we once more to leave things to chance? After a period in which all these dangerous characteristics – precisely, exclusively these characteristics! – have been more systematically cultivated than ever before, should we calmly wait and see whether the latest dust-up has expunged them, or perhaps not expunged them at all? Will it be desirable or advisable, immediately after these characteristics have plunged this nation, and with it the whole of Europe, into the most horrendous of catastrophes, to leave it without restriction to its own devices?

At this point thoughts about what is best for Germany and what is best for the world come together. The conclusion imposes itself that it is probably best for everyone if a different way forward from the simultaneous defeat of the country and overthrow of the Nazis can be found other than simply letting Germany go its own way, wherever its own force, its own daemon, its own fortune or fate will take it. The possibility suggests itself that for a very considerable time the victors, with their administration and their troops, will take on the role of mentors and trustees. It would be possible for them to keep the question of a successor regime off the agenda until such time as it would no longer be decided by mere chance. It would be possible for them to oversee a slow and gradual initiation into the art of governing and being governed. It would be possible for them to ensure a systematic and gradual process of drumming out of the Germans all the anomalies, all the destructive and self-destructive characteristics that have been drummed into them in the course of the centuries. The first response of those who are to take over this role of mentors and trustees with their administration and troops is fairly certain to be, 'Why on earth should we? What business is it of ours? Why should we lumber ourselves with all this inconvenience for an indefinite period just to see that the Germans are well looked after?' The answer is that one will never get anywhere without inconvenience – as has been shown! – and that it is very much their business anyway. Whether Germany finally goes through a process of liberal-democratic-tolerant education, which it has missed out on for at least a hundred years, will affect their material and physical security: in future no less than today the order, peace and prosperity of Europe will be irrevocably tied to the condition of a great nation that is there and cannot simply be wiped off the map. Even if the nation were to be torn up into mini-states, no one can tell whether that would last longer than disarmament in 1919; and the inconvenience of maintaining that situation will certainly be no less than the inconvenience – which they shied away from! – of maintaining the disarmament of 1919. Moreover the break-up of Germany into mini-states will be absolutely incompatible with an essential task the victors themselves will be faced with as a matter of utmost urgency at the historical moment in which the world will emerge from the furnace of war red-hot and ready to be forged anew: the task of creating larger units allowing more 'space' in our little Europe. Some kind of Pan-European arrangement is necessary, partly for political reasons, partly as the only means of saving economic liberalism which otherwise – especially after a war! – will be unable to replace the collectivism and its partner, autarky, which in the meantime will have established themselves all the more firmly in the countries affected. This most momentous of all foreseeable post-war necessities can be combined with an 'educational' administration in Germany, but hardly with the dismemberment of Germany. If we were to pursue this line of thought, however, thousands of problems would emerge, problems on both sides. This is not an appropriate point to examine them. All we are attempting here is to show – perhaps prematurely, I agree – a conceivable way out of the feeling of helplessness that envelops almost everyone at the thought of 'the day after'. The rest is nothing more than sub-hypotheses grafted on to the main hypothesis.

Notes

Das Tage-Buch 1929–33

1　Gustav Noske (1868–1946) was a member of the right wing of the SPD who suppressed the Spartacist uprising in January 1919 and the Soviet Republic in Bremen a little later. He was the first army minister of the Weimar Republic, but had to resign in March 1920 following the Kapp putsch.

2　Black, white and red were the colours of the flag of the German Empire after unification in 1871 until 1918. Its colours were reintroduced in 1933.

3　Léon-Michel Gambetta (1838–82) was instrumental in voting in the French Constitutional Laws of 1875, which ushered in the Third Republic.

4　Louis-Adolphe Thiers (1797–1877) was the head of the provisional French government that suppressed the Paris Commune uprising in 1871. He subsequently became the first president of the Third Republic until 1873. Thiers was a political opponent of Gambetta.

5　*Vorwärts* (Forward) was the official newspaper of the Social Democratic Party (SDP). It was launched in 1891, moved to Prague in 1933 and, after 1938, to Paris, where it was shut down for good in the spring of 1940. The Allies allowed it to resume publication in 1948.

6　Walther Rathenau (1867–1922) was chairman of the supervisory board of AEG and foreign minister in the Wirth cabinet in 1922. He was a supporter of the policy of accepting the obligations imposed by the Treaty of Versailles but was assassinated by members of the extreme right-wing 'Consul Organisation' in June 1922.

7　Amerongen was the town in Holland where Kaiser Wilhelm II first went after his abdication, before moving to Doorn in 1920.

8　Hermann Müller (1876–1931) was a member of the executive of the SPD after WWI, foreign minister (1919–20), chancellor in the coalition with the German Democratic Party (DDP) in spring 1920 and chancellor in the grand coalition of SPD, Centre Party, DVP and DDP from June 1928 to March 1930.

9　A reference to the Independent Social Democratic Party of Germany (USPD), which split off the main SPD in 1917 in protest against the SPD's support of the war effort. After early successes in 1918/19 (it won 17.9 per cent of the vote at the general election in June 1920), the USPD became politically irrelevant when most of its delegates joined the Communist Party in October 1920.

10 Rudolf Hilferding (1877–1941) was an Austro-marxist economist and politician, finance minister at the high point of inflation under Stresemann (1923) and a member of the Müller cabinet (1928/29). He resigned in protest against Schacht's monetary policy. Hilferding emigrated to Switzerland in 1933 and went to Paris in 1938. He died in Nazi captivity.

11 Wolfgang Kapp (1858–1922) was, with Walther Freiherr von Lüttwitz, the main figure behind an attempted putsch in March 1920 which collapsed after four days because of insufficient support from the military. Kapp withdrew to Sweden, but returned to Germany to face trial in 1922 and died while remanded in custody.

12 Patrice Mac-Mahon, Duke of Magenta (1808–93) was president of the Third Republic from 1873 to 1879.

13 Jules Ferry (1832–93) was French prime minister 1880–81 and 1883–85.

14 Georges Boulanger (1837–91) was a popular French general and politician who was implicated in a planned coup d'état in 1889 and fled to London.

15 During WWI Schacht served on the staff of General von Lumm, the banking commissioner of occupied Belgium, where he was responsible for organising the financing of Germany's purchases of supplies in that country.

16 Jacob Goldschmidt (1882–1955) was chairman of the Danat Bank, which he set up in 1922 through the merger of the Nationalbank für Deutschland, the Nationalbank in Bremen and the oldest bank in Germany, the Darmstädter Bank. As the most important partner of the industrialist Hugo Stinnes, he was in charge of the liquidation of his huge holdings after his death. The collapse of the Danat Bank on 13 July 1931 triggered the banking crisis of that year. Goldschmidt emigrated to the USA after 1933.

17 Georg Bernhard (1875–1944) was a DDP member of the Reichstag and editor of the *Vossische Zeitung*.

18 Arthur Feiler (1879–1942) was an economist on the staff of the *Frankfurter Zeitung* 1909—13, government adviser after WWI and, after 1933, professor at the New School for Social Research in New York.

19 Dr Felix Pinner (1880–1942), author and economic journalist.

20 Karl Helfferich (1872–1924) was a right-wing politician, member of the German National People's Party (DNVP) and economist. He developed the plan for a new currency backed by rye and other agricultural commodities in 1923. His plan was rejected in favour of the Rentenmark ultimately introduced by Schacht, which incorporated many of his original ideas.

21 The Reichsbank was established as a private institution in 1876 and re-established in 1924 following the introduction of a new currency and the end of hyperinflation. It was run by a president and a *Reichsbank-Direktorium* (management board), a board consisting of the president and six or seven members. The supervisory board was the *Generalrat* with ten members whose chairman was the president; prior to 1924 the supervisory body was the *Reichsbank-Kuratorium*, which had five members. In addition, the shareholders

nominated a 15-member *Zentralausschuss* (central committee), whose chairman was the Reichsbank president. The central committee met monthly to review the financial performance of the Reichsbank.

22 Dr Wilhelm Marx (1863–1946) was in 1923–24 and 1926–28 chancellor in minority centre/right governments. He resigned as chairman of the Centre Party after the election victory of the SPD in May 1928 and retired from politics in 1932.

23 Hans Luther (1879–1962) was finance minister in the Stresemann and Marx cabinets 1923–25, and in 1925 and 1926 chancellor of two coalition governments. In 1930 he succeeded Schacht as president of the Reichsbank, who again took over from him in 1933. Thereafter he was Germany's ambassador to the USA until 1937.

24 Hugo Stinnes (1870–1924) was an industrial magnate and right-wing nationalist member of the Reichstag for the German People's Party (DVP). His most important creation, the Siemens-Rheinelbe-Schuckert Union, only survived his death by two years.

25 Louis Hagen (1855–1932) was a main shareholder of the banking house of A. Levy and, later, the old private bank of Sal. Oppenheim & Co. After WWI he was an influential member of the Centre Party and advocated, without success, for the economic autonomy of the Rhineland.

26 Schacht's currency reform involved the creation of the Rentenmark, which was convertible into bonds backed by land and industrial plant. A total of 2.4 billion Rentenmarks were created, each valued at 1 trillion old paper marks. The Rentenmark was introduced in November 1923 and replaced by a new Reichsmark with a 40 per cent gold backing in August 1924. The Reichsmark was not convertible into gold, but the Reichsbank pledged to support a target exchange rate through intervention in the foreign exchange and gold markets.

27 As part of the currency reform of 1923/4, creditors, including mortgagees, could revalue outstanding debts by 25 per cent if their (devalued) debts had been repaid after 15 June 1922. Debts that were repaid before this cut-off date would not benefit from such revaluation.

28 Dr Walter Simons (1861–1937) was president of the German Supreme Court in 1922–29. Following the death of Friedrich Ebert, he served briefly as temporary president of the Republic from 12 March to 12 May 1925, when Paul von Hindenburg was elected and assumed office.

29 The claim was technically extinguished because Dr Simons had repaid his mortgage before the cut-off date of 15 June 1922.

30 Schacht was one of the founder members of the German Democratic Party (DDP), a liberal republican party established in 1918 whose members included the main authors of the Weimar Constitution, Hugo Preuss, Max Weber, Friedrich Naumann and Conrad Haussmann.

31 The Golddiskontbank (Gold Discount Bank) was a publicly owned bank founded in 1924 to make loans to German industry, assist in the procurement of

raw materials, the payment of reparations and, more generally, safeguard the stability of the Reichsmark. It briefly also had the right to issue currency, but never made use of it. The Reichsbank subscribed for 50 per cent of its ordinary share capital, with a consortium of German banks subscribing for the other half, although it then placed a portion of these 'B shares' with foreign banks. The Reichsbank also subscribed for some B shares in order to retain majority ownership, funding its capital contribution with a loan from the Bank of England. Schacht made sure that from 1927 onwards the Golddiskontbank could also manage public funds. After 1933 it played a central role in the financing of German rearmament.

32   The SDP had supported Germany's entry into WWI and thereby alienated its international brethren.

33   General Erich Ludendorff (1865–1937) was joint head with Paul von Hindenburg of the Supreme Army Command from 1916. He was mainly responsible for the unrestricted U-boat war and thereby the entry of the US into WWI. Ludendorff was a vociferous opponent of the Weimar Republic and an early ally of Hitler with whom, however, he fell out in the late 1920s.

34   Alfred Hugenberg (1865–1951) was an industrialist and right-wing nationalist politician who had a great influence on the right-wing press through the extensive media interests of his conglomerate. He was a member of the DNVP and a member of the Reichstag until 1945. Initially he worked together with the NSDAP, but resigned from the government in June 1933 and subsequently had to sell his conglomerate under pressure from Hitler.

35   Hagen was originally Jewish but converted to Catholicism on his marriage.

36   Oscar Wassermann (1869–1934) was one of the most influential German bankers of his time. He was a member of the board of Deutsche Bank from 1912 to 1933, and its spokesman from 1923 to 1933.

37   In Nordic mythology the Norns are the women who rule the fate of the Nordic people. They do so by spinning the thread of fate at the foot of Yggdrasil, the tree of the world.

38   Bertil Ohlin (1899–1979) was a Swedish economist. He was awarded the Nobel Prize in 1977 (together with James Meade).

39   Adolf Weber (1876–1963) was a German economist, professor at the universities of Cologne, Breslau, Frankfurt/M and Munich. He established himself as a critic of the economic policy of the president of the Reichsbank with his article, 'Is Schacht right?'

40   Parker Gilbert (1892–1963) was from October 1924 to May 1930 the Agent General for Reparations appointed by the Allied Reparations Commission under the Dawes Plan. He returned to New York to join JP Morgan.

41   Admiral Alfred von Tirpitz (1849–1930) was a German admiral, Secretary of State of the Imperial Naval Office until 1916 and a strong proponent of unrestricted U-boat warfare. He fell out with Kaiser Wilhelm II over the extent

of the latter and was forced to resign in 1916. He was a member of the DNVP and sat in the Reichstag from 1924 to 1928.

42   A law of 21 March 1925 introduced a *Beratungsstelle* (advisory service), a part of the Ministry of Finance, whose approval was required before municipalities and regional authorities could raise foreign loans and bonds.

43   The Bank für deutsche Industrie-Obligationen (Bafio – Bank for Industrial Bonds) was established in 1924 to provide long-term real-estate financing to German industry. It is the predecessor of today's IKB Deutsche Industriebank (German Industrial Bank) which finances small and medium-sized enterprises.

44   One of the provisions of the Dawes Plan was to use the German railway company exclusively as a means of paying reparations. Thus in 1924 the Deutsche Reichsbahn-Gesellschaft (DRG) was formed as a nominally private holding company which was fully controlled by the German state. Its aim was to earn profits which would be used to make reparation payments. Between 1924 and 1932 it paid 5 billion gold marks to the Allies (including pension payments) and German industry (as dividends on preference shares). The reparation payments to the Allies accounted for ca. 3.87 billion of this amount.

45   Carl Friedrich von Siemens (1872–1941) was the youngest son of Werner von Siemens, the founder of the firm, and chairman of the supervisory boards of Siemens & Halske AG and Siemens-Schuckertwerke GmbH. He relinquished all public offices after 1933.

46   Paul Silverberg (1876–1959) was a leading Rhenish coal magnate industrialist. As publisher of *Wirtschafts-Informationsdienst Deutsche Führerbriefe* he initially supported the NSDAP, but he emigrated to Switzerland in 1938, where he continued to defend National Socialism even though he was a Jew baptised at birth ('their only mistake was that they persecuted the Jews').

47   Peter Klöckner (1863–1940) was the owner of the Klöckner Werke AG, one of the biggest companies of the interwar years.

48   The Young Plan committee of experts met initially in Paris in February 1929.

49   Albert Vögler (1877–1945) was director general of the mining conglomerate, Rhein-Elbe-Union GmbH. He became a fierce opponent of Stresemann's moderate policies and a supporter of Hitler. In various functions Vögler played a decisive role in the organisation of the German arms industry before and during WWII.

50   On 28 October 1908 *The Daily Telegraph* published an interview with Wilhelm II in which the Kaiser claimed for Germany a 'place in the sun', an allusion to her colonial ambitions. The interview caused consternation and harsh criticism in England, France and Russia and triggered a constitutional crisis in Germany, which led to the curtailment of the Emperor's powers.

51   The second Young Plan conference took place in The Hague on 3–20 January 1930.

52   Jackson E. Reynolds (1873–1958) was president of the First National Bank of New York.

53 Germany entered into a 'liquidation agreement' with Poland on 31 October 1929 to settle all remaining financial claims between the two countries which resulted from WWI and the Versailles peace treaty. A similar agreement was signed with the UK in the same year.

54 In February 1929.

55 André Tardieu (1876–1945) was George Clemenceau's lieutenant during the Paris peace conference and, from 1926 to 1934 prime minister on three occasions (1929–30, 1930, 1932). He argued in favour of a tough approach towards Germany, especially after his resignation as a member of parliament in 1936.

56 J. Mrozowski was the Polish delegate at the Allied Reparation Commission.

57 Wilhelm Cuno (1876–1933) was managing director of the Hamburg-Amerika-Linie (Hapag) before becoming the chancellor of a centre minority government from November 1922 to August 1923. When his government fell, he returned to Hapag. In the reparations debate Cuno believed – erroneously, as it turned out – that he could persuade the USA to mediate in the conflict with France.

58 Dr Rudolf Havenstein (1857–1923) was president of the Reichsbank from 1908 to 1923 and the man in charge of financing the war effort.

59 The Tannenberg League was a right-wing political society founded by Erich Ludendorff and his wife, Mathilde von Kemnitz, in 1925. The League believed that Freemasons, Jews, Communists and Jesuits conspired to suppress Nordic civilisation, and that their beliefs should therefore be abandoned in favour of Thule, the Nordic god. The Nazis banned it in 1933.

60 Valentin Zeileis was an Austrian doctor who used high-frequency rays emanating from a 'mysterious' machine to apparently heal his patients.

61 Otto Braun (1872–1955) was the social-democratic prime minister of Prussia from 1920 to 1932. His government was effectively deposed in Franz von Papen's *Preussenschlag* (Prussian coup) in July 1932. He emigrated to Switzerland in 1933.

62 Ernst Thälmann (1886–1944) was the leader of the German Communist Party during most of the Weimar Republic. He was shot in Buchenwald on Hitler's orders after 11 years in solitary confinement

63 Gottfried Treviranus (1891–1971) was a minister in both of Heinrich Brüning's cabinets, first as minister for occupied territories and then as minister without portfolio and transport.

64 Arthur Hamilton Lee, Viscount Fareham (1868–1947) was a Conservative member of parliament, who in 1917 gifted Chequers to the English nation.

65 J. M. Keynes, 'Gold in 1923', Collected Works, volume XIX.

66 Franz Seldte (1882–1947) was one of the founders in 1918 of the *Stahlhelm* (Steel Helmet), the largest paramilitary organisations in the Weimar Republic. He was also one of the founders of the 'Harzberg Front' in 1931, which brought together all the anti-republican forces in Germany. He became minister of labour in 1933, a position he held until the end of the war, though without exercising any great influence.

67 Hans von Seeckt (1866–1936) was chief of general staff after WWI, in which position he refused to employ his troops to put down the Kapp Putsch of 1920 ('Soldiers don't shoot at soldiers').

68 August von Mackensen (1849–1945) was a leading general and field marshal in WWI who was particularly involved in the most important battles on the Eastern Front. He was a member of the Nazi Party after 1933, but as a member of the 'Confessional Church' he condemned the crimes committed during the invasion of Poland in 1939.

69 The *Binnenmark* was an alternative new currency, restricted for use in domestic transactions only, which Alfred Hugenberg and others proposed in the early 1930s to combat the deflationary aspects of the depression.

70 Schwarzschild is here referring to the children of the *Gründerzeit* generation, the golden age during the reign of Kaiser Wilhelm I and Chancellor Bismarck, when German science, industry and trade made significant progress to establish themselves as leading actors on the world stage.

71 On 15 March 1915 five large German economic associations submitted a memorandum to the Chancellor, Bethmann-Hollweg, in which they recommended Germany should not make peace until the Empire had achieved the extension of its power that was its due, demanding among other things the annexation of the French mining districts of Longwy and Briey.

72 On 12 April 1932 the Prussian parliament adopted a new provision whereby the Prussian minister-president could only be forced out of office if there was a 'positive majority' for a potential successor. An NSDAP appeal to reverse this amendment was rejected by the Prussian Constitutional Court in December 1932. This principle of a 'constructive vote of no-confidence' was ultimately carried over into the Basic Law of the Federal Republic of Germany after WWII.

73 On 13 June 1931 Schwarzschild published a detailed proposal to expand the amount of credit in the Germany banking system by ca. 4.2 billion Reichsmarks (ca. 26 per cent) and mandate a central planning agency to spend the additional resources on domestic goods and services. Schwarzschild's proposal contained many of the theoretical elements that Keynes also discussed at his speeches at the New School of Social Research in New York on 15 & 18 June 1931 and later that month in Chicago.

74 Gregor Strasser (1892–1934) led the social-revolutionary wing of the Nazi Party as head of the Party's national organisation. When Schleicher's attempt to split the party in late 1932 failed, Strasser resigned from all his offices. He was killed during the *Night of the Long Knives* in June 1934.

75 The *Deutscher Herrenklub* was a conservative club founded in 1924 by Heinrich von Gleichen-Russwurm and Hans Bodo Graf von Alvensleben-Neugattersleben. Franz von Papen was a member of the club which by 1932 had ca. 5,000 members.

76 Von Papen introduced emergency legislation on 4 September 1932 at the heart of which was a system of tax credits which companies could use to fund future tax

payments in 1934–39. The value of the scheme was ca. 1.5 billion Reichsmarks, or 21 per cent of total government expenditure.

77 Dr Günther Gereke (1893–1969) was 'Reich Commissioner for Job Creation' in Schleicher's short-lived government of 1932–33.

78 A reference to the greater cooperation between conservatives and Social Democrats which followed Bismarck's dismissal as German chancellor in 1890.

79 Friedrich Ebert (1871–1925) was chairman of the SPD from 1913 and first president of the Weimar Republic until his death.

80 Oskar von Hindenburg (1883–1960) was his father's aide-de-camp and as such exercised considerable influence. He had originally opposed Hitler's appointment as chancellor but was persuaded by von Papen to back him. He supported the Nazis thereafter.

81 The *Reichsbanner* was the main paramilitary force of the Social Democrats, which was one of its co-founders, together with the Centre Party (*Zentrum*) and German Democratic Party, in early 1924.

82 Martin Mutschmann (1879–1947?) was a lace manufacturer and from 1925 to 1945 Gauleiter of Saxony. He was a diehard Nazi until the very end and is thought to have died in Moscow, although Albert Speer reports that he was beaten to death in Dresden.

83 Wolf Heinrich, Count Helldorf (1896–1944) was SA Obergruppenführer and chief of police in Berlin and Potsdam; he was executed after being involved in the attempted assassination of Hitler in July 1944.

84 Ernst Röhm (1887–1934) was chief of staff of the SA. He was murdered on Hitler's instructions in 1934, following a power struggle with the army and the SS. The 'Iron Front' was a republican paramilitary force founded in 1931 by the SPD, the Reichsbanner, and a string of other organisations as a counter-weight to the right-wing Harzburg Front. It was destroyed, together with all German trade unions, on 2 March 1933.

85 Ferdinand Lasalle (1825–64) was the founder, in 1863, of the General German Workers' Association, which later became the SPD.

86 Otto Wels (1873–1939) was, together with Hermann Müller chairman of the SPD after 1919. He was a decisive proponent of a policy of tolerating Brüning's government by presidential decree.

87 Friedrich Graf von Wrangel (1784–1877) was a *Generalfeldmarschall* of the Prussian Army. Nicknamed *Papa Wrangel* he remained involved in Prussian military affairs until the Austro-Prussian war in 1866.

Das Neue Tage-Buch 1933–39

1 Elard von Oldenburg-Januschau (1855–1937) was the owner of a neighbouring estate to Hindenburg's in Prussia and president of the Prussian Herrenhaus

(House of Lords) before 1914. In January 1933 Oldenburg-Januschau was one of those who encouraged Hindenburg to approve a government coalition of Stahlhelm, DNVP and NSDAP with Hitler as chancellor.

2   Hanns Kerrl (1887–1941) was the National Socialist president of the Prussian parliament during Papen's government and Prussian minister of justice under Hitler.

3   Wilhelm Kube (1887–1943) was party leader of the NSDAP in the Prussian parliament, SS *Gruppenführer* (equivalent to lieutenant general), *Gauleiter* of the *Ostmark* (Austria, 1928–33) and the *Kurmark* (part of Brandenburg, 1933–36), as well as commissioner general for White Ruthenia from 1941 until his death.

4   Dr Roland Freisler (1893–1945) was Hitler's secretary of state in the – uninfluential – Ministry of Justice. From 1942 he was president of the *Volksgerichtshof* (People's Court) and was responsible for the show trials of those involved in the 20 July 1944 attempt on Hitler's life.

5   Robert Ley (1890–1945) was from 1933 leader of the *Deutsche Arbeitsfront* (German Labour Front), which he developed with leisure organisations such as *Kraft durch Freude* (KdF, 'Strength through Joy'). He committed suicide in 1945 when imprisoned by the Allies.

6   Rheinmetall was a weapons manufacturer during the Third Reich, particularly of bomb fuses which were particularly difficult to defuse.

7   The Sybilline Books (*libri sybillini*) were a collection of oracular utterances in Greek hexameter originating from a sibyl, or female prophet, and which were consulted during moments of crisis of the Roman republic and empire.

8   The *Gesetz über den Neuaufbau des Reichs* (Law for the Reconstruction of the Reich) was passed as a constitutional amendment on 30 January 1934 and finally abolished the federal structure of Germany. It subordinated all *Länder* under the central authority of the Reich. It enabled Hitler to become president, as well as chancellor, after Hindenburg's death in August 1934.

9   All quotations from Adolf Hitler: *Mein Kampf*, translated by Ralph Mannheim, London, 1969. Schwarzschild used the two-volume edition published by Verlag Franz Eher, Nachfolger in 1933. All italics are Schwarzschild's.

10   On 3 February 1935 the French and British governments suggested to the Reich that it should rejoin the League of Nations and prepare a disarmament conference to replace the armaments articles of the Versailles Treaty.

11   On 28 November 1934 Baldwin responded in the House of Commons to a statement by Winston Churchill that Germany's 'illegal air force is rapidly approaching equality with our own' by stating that '… [h]er real strength is not fifty per cent. of our strength in Europe to-day.' However, a fortnight after the British cabinet learned on 8 May 1935 that the RAF had 370 fewer aircraft than the Luftwaffe Baldwin confessed: 'I was wrong in my estimate of the future. There I was completely wrong.'

12   The British government published its Defence White Paper on 4 March 1935, two days after the Saar was reunited with Germany, detailing its plans for rearmament.

13   Louis Barthou (1862–1934) was briefly French prime minister in the summer of 1913 and foreign minister in Gaston Doumergue's cabinet in 1934. As such he advocated a tough stance towards Germany. He was killed by an assassin together with King Alexander I of Yugoslavia during a visit to Marseille in October 1934.

14   The remainder of this quote illustrates both Britain's honourable, if misplaced intentions and her misguided view of other nations' responses to her policies: '… I think the reason is that the British nation has been trained, by long centuries of experience, to try to look at these great matters from other people's point of view. That quality is a sign of strength and wisdom in a nation, but when we do that, those who have been, and are, and will be acting with us, fail to understand our attitude, and think that we are weakening, or abandoning the standpoint which we have taken in common.'

15   Charles Corbin (1862–1970) served as French ambassador to Britain from 1933 to 1940.

16   Dino Grandi (1895–1988) served as Italian under-secretary of interior affairs, minister of foreign affairs (1929–32) and ambassador to the UK (1932–39). His motion at a meeting of the fascist Grand Council in July 1943 asking King Victor Emmanuel III to assume his constitutional authority led to Mussolini's arrest the following day.

17   An alliance between Czechoslovakia, Yugoslavia and Romania first set up in 1920. The cession of the Sudetenland to Germany in 1938 led to the break-up of the alliance.

18   Engelbert Dollfuss (1892–1934) was an Austrian Christian Social politician and as chancellor from 1932 the leader of an Austro-Fascist dictatorship which led to civil war in February 1934. He was assassinated by Austrian Nazis in July 1934.

19   Count Ernst Rüdiger von Starhemberg (1899–1956) was the leader of the Heimwehr, an Austrian fascist paramilitary organisation, from 1930 to 1936. He was vice-chancellor in the Dollfuss and (after his death) Schuschnigg governments. He resigned from his posts on account of his anti-Nazi views in 1936.

20   Pierre Laval (1883–1945) was French prime minister 1931–32 and 1935–36 and a prominent member of the Vichy regime, which he led from 1942. He was mainly responsible for the deportation of the Jews from French territory. After the Liberation he was arrested and executed for high treason.

21   Pierre-Étienne Flandin (1889–1958) occupied five ministerial posts between 1924 and 1934 and was briefly prime minister in 1934–35. Flandin replaced Laval as foreign minister in the Vichy government in 1940, but was removed after 6 weeks. In 1942 he went to North Africa where he was arrested by the Resistance, but later acquitted.

22   There were two more 'obligations' under the Treaty of Locarno in his statement
     to the House which illustrate Sir John's position very well: 'Thirdly, in the event
     of what is called a flagrant violation of one or other of the above undertakings,
     which would really mean the case of something happening in so much of a hurry
     that you could not call a meeting of the Council of the League, we are bound
     immediately to come to the help of the injured party, if we are satisfied that the
     violation constitutes an unprovoked act of aggression, and that immediate action
     is necessary. *In this case we are the sole judges as to whether our obligation is
     applicable.* Fourthly, and lastly, if either France, Belgium, or Germany refuse to
     submit to a peaceful settlement or to comply with an arbitral or judicial decision,
     we are bound to comply with any proposals which the Council may make as to
     the steps to be taken. In that case our assent is necessary to any and every
     proposal that the Council may make.' (italics added)
23   Schwarzschild refers here to the date – 17 April 1935 – on which the League of
     Nations formally condemned Germany's repudiation of its obligations under the
     Versailles Treaty and its ongoing rearmament.
24   Albert Saurrat (1872–1962) was a socialist French politician who was briefly
     prime minister in 1933 and 1936. After the defeat in 1940 he took over the
     management of his family's newspaper *La Depeche de Tolouse*. He was president of
     the French Union from 1949 to 1958.
25   Kurt von Schuschnigg (1897–1977) was Austrian chancellor from 1934 to 1938.
     He was imprisoned in Sachsenhausen concentration camp 1941–45 and
     emigrated to the USA in 1947. He returned to live in the Tyrol in 1967.
26   Walter von Reichenau (1884–1942) was a *Generalfeldmarschall* and personal
     advisor to Werner von Blomberg and as such responsible for the integration of
     the army into the Nazi apparatus. He commanded the 10th Army during the
     invasion of Poland and the 6th Army during Operation Barbarossa. He was a
     radical anti-Semite and reminded his soldiers of the 'severe but just retribution
     that must be meted out to the subhuman species of Jewry …'.
27   Theodor von Bethmann-Hollweg (1856–1921) was German chancellor from
     1909 to 1917. When Germany invaded neutral Belgium on her way to France at
     the beginning of WWI, Bethmann-Hollweg was surprised when Britain declared
     war on Germany in return: 'Just for a word – 'neutrality', a word which in
     wartime has so often been disregarded, just for a *scrap of paper* – Great Britain is
     going to make war.'
28   Belgian neutrality had been established by the Treaty of London in 1839.
29   Arthur Seyss-Inquart (1892–1946) was made Austrian minister of the interior in
     February 1938 and became governor of the Austrian administration following the
     Anschluss. After the start of WWII he was initally deputy to the infamous
     governor general of the occupied Polish territories, Hans Frank, and from 1940
     commissioner for the Netherlands, where he showed exceptional ruthlessness
     and severity. He was executed in Nuremberg.

30 Konrad Henlein (1898–1945) was the founder of the Sudeten German Party, which enjoyed immense support from the National Socialist Party and had 1.3 million members in 1938. After the annexation of Czechoslovakia Henlein was made *Gauleiter* for the Sudeten area.

31 Walter Runciman, 1st Viscount Runciman of Doxford (1870–1949) tried, without success, to broker an agreement between the Czech government and the Sudeten Germans in July 1938.

32 Konstantin Freiherr von Neurath (1873–1956) was German foreign minister from 1932 to 1938 and *Reichsprotektor* of the Protectorate of Bohemia and Moravia from 1939 to 1941. He was ultimately replaced by Joachim von Ribbentrop and Reinhard Heydrich, respectively, on account of the inadequate radicalism of his policies. He was sentenced to 15 years' imprisonment at the Nuremberg Trials.

33 On that day President Benes ordered a partial mobilisation of the Czech army.

34 On that day Hitler presented a programme to ensure international peace and security in which he promised 'restrictions on the endless build-up of arms', although only on *condition* that Germany were treated equally. This would have necessitated a renegotiation of the Treaty of Locarno.

35 Emergency decrees and regulations drawn up by Werner Best, legal adviser to the Hessen Nazi Party, which were to be issued in the event of the Nazi Party seizing power after the overthrow of a Communist putsch.

36 Cordell Hull (1871–1955) was from 1933 to 1944 American Secretary of State in successive Roosevelt administrations.

37 Julius Lippert (1895–1956) was the publisher of the rabble-rousing Nazi weekly *Der Angriff* (Attack), a member of Berlin City Parliament and 1935–40 mayor and city president. He was imprisoned for seven years after the war.

38 *Völkischer Beobachter*, 1 April 1933.

39 On 22 March 1939 Germany annexed the District of Memel from Lithuania. Memel had been part of East Prussia and was handed over to Lithuania as a result of the Memel Convention in 1924. The annexation was the last hostile action by Germany before the outbreak of WWII.

40 King Carol II (1893–1953) established an absolute dictatorship in 1938, but was deposed in September 1940 in a coup d'état by the fascist General Ion Antonescu (1882–1946), who was supported by Germany. Carol II was succeeded by his son Mihai I, who managed to remove Antonescu from power in 1944.

41 Tomas Masaryk (1850–1937) was the first President of Czechoslovakia (1920–35). The Allies recognised him as the head of a provisional Czechoslovak government when the Austro-Hungarian empire fell in November 1918, i.e. before he was formally elected president in 1920.

Index